Mummified Deer

and Other Plays

Luis Valdez

With an Introduction by Jorge Huerta

Arte Público Press
Houston, Texas

This volume is made possbile through the City of Houston through The Cultural Arts Council of Houston, Harris County.

Recovering the past, creating the future

Arte Público Press
University of Houston
452 Cullen Performance Hall
Houston, TX 77204-2004

Cover illustration "Mummified Deer" by Ken Jacques
Cover design by Mendoza Designs

Valdez, Luis
    Mummified Deer and Other Plays / by Luis Valdez
    p. cm.
    Contents: Mummified Deer—The Shrunken Head of Pancho Villa—
    Mundo Mata.
    ISBN-10: 1-55885-417-7 (alk. paper)
    ISBN-13: 978-1-55885-417-8 (alk. paper)
    1. Mexican American—Drama. I. Title.
    PS3572.A387M86 2005
    812'.54–dc22   2004055418
                                                         CIP

∞ The paper used in the publication meets the minimum requirements of
the merican National Standard for Permanence of Paper for Printed Library
Materials Z39.48-1984

5 6 7 8 9 0 1 2 3 4   10 9 8 7 6 5 4 3 2 1

Contents

*Dedicated to the loving memory of my parents
Armida Montaño Valdez and Francisco Leon Valdez,
my Yaqui Flower and Bloodroot of the Great Sonoran Desert.*

El mundo de Luis Valdez:
Mummified Deer, *Mundo Mata* and
The Shrunken Head of Pancho Villa

El Indio baila.
He dances his way to truth
in a way intellectuals
will never understand.
—*Luis Valdez*

Luis Valdez was born in Delano, California, in 1940 to farm worker parents; this was a humble beginning for a man who was to become
the most discussed Chicano playwright and director of his time. For
some, Valdez needs no introduction; for others, his name may only be
associated with his more extensively seen films, *Zoot Suit* (1981) and *La
Bamba* (1986). But any serious student or observer of the evolution of
Chicano Theatre knows that no other individual has made as important
an impact on Chicano theater as Luis Valdez. As the founder of the
Teatro Campesino (Farm Workers' Theatre) in 1965, Valdez and his
troupe inspired a national movement of *teatros* (theater groups) dedicated to the exposure of socio-economic-political problems within the
Mexican and Chicano communities of the United States. He and his
troupe collectively created what he termed *actos*, short satirical sketches that became the mainstay of all of the teatros that followed in the
Teatro Campesino's wake. The first actos exposed the problems of the
farm worker and urged support for their fledgling union. When the
Teatro Campesino left the United Farm Workers Union in 1967, the
troupe's actos began to reflect other issues, including inadequate teach-
ers and schools, *vendidos* ("sellouts"), the Chicano Movement and the
war in Vietnam.[1]

Even as he was guiding the Teatro members, collectively creating
the actos, Valdez was also working alone, writing what he terms *mitos*

(myths), which were expressions of his vision of the Chicano cosmos. In Valdez's interpretation, the acto is the Chicano through the eyes of man; the mito is the Chicano "through the eyes of God" (Valdez, *The Early Works* 11). His neo-Aztec mito, *Bernabé* (1970), and his anti-war mito, *Dark Root of a Scream* (1971),[2] demonstrate Valdez's early interest in the Chicano's indigenous and Mexican roots, a fascination that continues to this day, as evidenced in this collection.

As the first Chicano to have written a contemporary play about a Chicano family, Valdez has had the longest trajectory of any living Chicana/o playwright. Furthermore, no other Chicana or Chicano playwright or director has generated the amount of critical interest as Valdez. His most successful and controversial play, *Zoot Suit* (1978), exposes the racial discrimination suffered by Chicanos in Los Angeles in the 1940s and remains the first (and only) play written and directed by a Chicano to be produced on Broadway (1979).[3] More importantly, the production of *Zoot Suit* in Los Angeles ran over eleven months, breaking all box office records in that city's history for a legitimate play. Valdez adapted and directed the film version of *Zoot Suit* in 1981 and surprised everyone with his most successful film to date, *La Bamba*, the story of 1950s rocker, Richie Valens, released in 1987.

Valdez's experiences in Hollywood undoubtedly led him to write and direct a satire about Hollywood stereotyping, *I Don't Have to Show You No Stinking Badges!* in 1986 and included in his anthology *Zoot Suit and Other Plays*. Although he certainly kept writing plays, audiences had to wait until the year 2000 to see his next play, when he directed the world premiere of *Mummified Deer* at the San Diego Repertory Theatre in San Diego, California. Two years later, our playwright directed the unpublished *Earthquake Sun* for the same theatre. In 2005, Valdez and his son, Kinan, re-wrote an earlier music/movement piece titled *Corridos*, which had run very successfully in San Francisco in 1983 with subsequent runs in both San Diego and Los Angeles.[4] Re-titled *Corridos Remix*, this piece was premiered at the San Diego Repertory Theatre in 2005, directed by Kinan Valdez.

Hopefully, this very brief synopsis illustrates how Valdez's trajectory is an eclectic mixture of actos, plays, videos, films and essays. He remains the most visible Chicano playwright, director and film maker, a theatre artist who continues to dedicate his works to the experiences of the Chicanos.

Growing up in a migrant farm worker family, Valdez attended a variety of public schools, but unlike so many children of his generation and social class, he managed to do well and enrolled in San Jose State College. In 1964, while still a student at San Jose State, he wrote his first play, *The Shrunken Head of Pancho Villa*. He began work on *Mundo Mata*, under the title *El fin del Mundo*, in 1974 and later revised and re-titled it *Mundo Mata* as published herein.[5] The most recent play in this trilogy, *Mummified Deer*, began to stir in the playwright's imagination in 1984 but did not come to full fruition until the year 2000. Thus, this trilogy is representative of three stages in Valdez's playwriting and directing career: from his first play to one from his middle period to his latest theatrical expressions of the Chicano condition.

These three plays serve as a wonderful overview of Valdez's aesthetic, spiritual and political evolution, demonstrating his continuing dedication to *la familia* in crisis. While these plays differ markedly in style and theme, each one is informed by the playwright's unique vision and eclectic style, a mixture of genres that keeps the reader and especially the production teams on their toes. I speak of the production teams because each of these plays must be read with an understanding that they are to be seen and heard, not visited simply on the pages of a book. Valdez's dramaturgy has always demanded careful attention to the spaces between the lines, the stage directions that, if ignored, may leave the reader confused, if only for a moment. Each of these plays is a designer's dream, or nightmare, depending upon the willingness of the design/director team to think out-of-the-box, if you will. And when I say "box," I literally mean the nineteenth- century box set of three walls intersecting with an invisible "fourth wall," that famous fourth wall that the actors and audience are supposed to ignore in a realistic play.

Of these three plays, only The *Shrunken Head of Pancho Villa* actually calls for a box set, but that set should not be realistic or naturalistic. How can one call for naturalism when the central character is a head without a body and oversized cockroaches crawl the walls with impunity? Valdez states his vision very clearly in his stage directions: "The set, particularly, must be 'real,' for what it represents; but it must also contain a cartoon quality such as that found in the satirical sketches of José Clemente Orozco or the lithographs of José Guadalupe Posada. In short, it must represent the psychological reality of the barrio" (132). That reality is clearly drawn in these three plays but it is a "reality" that transforms through time as the playwright's vision evolves.

If the family is, indeed, central to Valdezian dramaturgy, how is that family affected by time? Time has always fascinated Valdez, as a marker not only of the hours, but of the period in which his plays take place.

All three plays are period pieces, connected by their characters and the action to very specific moments in the Mechicana/o's history. Moments in time. *Shrunken Head* takes place shortly after the Korean "Conflict," the late 1950s; *Mundo Mata* takes place in the summer of 1973; the action of *Mummified Deer* begins in 1969, goes back to the Mexican Revolution and in a very brief moment ends in 1999. Both *Shrunken Head* and *Mundo Mata* have linear plots while *Mummified Deer* takes us through multiple flashbacks that expose one family's history as we enter the subconscious mind of the central character, Mama Chu. The play goes back and forth in time and place, with Mama Chu's hospital bed as the central image. The action moves fluidly through time, a time that is measured not in minutes or hours but in heartbeats.

The passage of time in these three plays takes on an other-worldly level, for Anglo-American ("gabacho") notions of time do not matter to the playwright. "You can afford to be late if you are ahead of your time," Valdez told a group of Latina and Latino theatre artists in 1986.[6] Years before that declaration, Valdez wrote the following in his poem, "Pensamiento Serpentino":

Chicano time por *ejemplo* [for example]
has never been *gabacho* time
because the Chicano exists
in time with the *temporadas* [seasons]
and the movement of the planets
and the stars.

Once we start moving in tune
con las estrellas [with the stars]
the time of the wristwatch
nos cae huango. ["sucks"]

The wristwatch is a game
an arbitrary improvisation
invented in Europe.

Measure your time against
la calaca, LA MUERTE [the skeleton, Death]
Si eres [if you are a] materialist
a solid contemplation
of DEATH will show you

that you haven't got
too much time
to waste. (*Early Works* 185)

Time and Death do not matter to Valdez; both are concepts that per-
meate each of these plays, not as markers of emptiness but as events that
must transpire in the natural order of things. When Valdez states that the
Chicano measures his time by the seasons, he is clearly speaking from
his roots as a *campesino*, following the crops in seasonal labor. In both
Shrunken Head and *Mundo Mata*, the people are campesinos, connected to the land and the heavens as well as to the indignities and hardships
of stoop labor. Although *Mummified Deer* takes place in an urban setting, a modern hospital in San Diego, California, Mama Chu is a Yaqui.
She references the campesinos in the following declaration: "We aren't
yaquis here! We're fish out of water, gasping to breathe, and drowning
in the air . . . maids, farm workers, mano de obra [manual labor]" (36).
Further, the Yaqui are a people whose cosmic ties to the desert are legendary. In a discussion of this play, Valdez told his audience that unlike
the Indio, the Euro-American looks at the desert and sees nothing, no
life, no hope. But the Indio looks at the desert and sees life everywhere.[7]
    All three plays in this collection demonstrate another theme that
underlines most of Valdez's works: the constant struggle of Good and Evil.
In *The Shrunken Head of Pancho Villa*, evil is represented by agribusiness,
to be sure, but also by the U.S. Marines, an institution that has transformed
Domingo into a traitor to his people as a farm labor contractor. Mingo represents both the growers and the military, a lost soul who goes so far as to
change his name to Mr. Sunday, rejecting his very family. We never see the
perpetrators of this unnatural transformation (the Military) although we do
see the (ostensibly Anglo) police who come and take away Joaquín, the
opposite of Domingo. Joaquín is the good brother who has become a
"social bandit," attempting to steal from the rich to give back to the com-
munity, encouraged by his oldest brother, Belarmino, who has no body.
Interestingly, the two brothers in *Mundo Mata*, Mundo and Bullet, are also
diametrically opposed in their objectives. Bullet wants to organize the
campesinos against the growers while Mundo is in league with them.
Mundo is also the barrio drug dealer, a Vietnam veteran whose vision of
the world was forever altered by the war. It is no coincidence that both
Domingo and Mundo are veterans; Valdez was an eloquent campus speak-
er in college and, when the Vietnam War became an issue, his views were
no secret. Chicanos have fought valiantly in every war this nation has

waged, only to return too often to discrimination and lives of hopelessness and despair.

While we do not really see the Anglo powerbrokers in *Shrunken Head*, in *Mundo Mata* Valdez brings Gudunritch and Roddenberry, representatives of the growers, as well as the local sheriff into the action. It must also be noted that Whittaker, the union organizer, is an Anglo, a reflection of the reality that people of all races and creeds have worked selflessly for the farm workers union. Few early actos portrayed Anglos positively, if they appeared in the action at all.

These plays also differ markedly in terms of the settings described by the playwright. While *Shrunken Head* calls for a single set, *Mundo Mata* is set in a packing shed with a burlap background and boxes to represent various sites. The cinematic action must move quickly and efficiently from place to place, interiors and exteriors, as the action moves inexorably toward the final climax. Valdez makes a direct reference to the influences of Bertolt Brecht in his stage directions: "Visuals and slides may or may not reinforce the reality of the piece by the addition of overhanging projection screens, while enhancing the spare Brechtian approach." The use of songs is also a well-known Brechtian device, adding to the theatricality of the play. The playwright's description of the setting for *Mummified Deer* calls for a much more technically equipped theatre with visual and sound effects that the early Teatro Campesino could not have realized. Both *Shrunken Head* and especially *Mundo Mata* can be produced minimally. *Mummified Deer* is more complex both in its staging and in its structure, due to the constant changes in time, place and action.

Valdez first began to think about the play that would become *Mummified Deer* in 1984, when he read a newspaper article about the discovery of a 60-year-old fetus in the womb of an 84-year-old woman. Over the years, as he continued to think about that image, he determined that he would write a play centered on the character of an old Yaqui woman who has been carrying a fetus in her womb for sixty years. While preparing for the opening of this play, he told an interviewer, "I immediately saw her in a hospital bed, surrounded by her family."[8] He told me that he based the central character on his own Yaqui grandmother, although of course she had not carried a mummified fetus in her womb.[9] For Valdez, the mummified fetus becomes a metaphor for the Chicanos' Indio heritage as seen through the lens of his own Yaqui blood.

While the main action of the play is framed by a narrative presented to the audience that takes place in the present, or 1999, Valdez places this play in the year 1969. This was the beginning of the Chicano Movement, a time when Chicanas and Chicanos were questioning the power structure and demanding better conditions in the schools, in the workplace, on the streets and in the courts. The Vietnam War was creating schisms in many families, just as the war in Iraq is doing today. This period was also the era of the Chicanos' deepening interest in their Indio roots. Chicanos knew that they owed their culture to Mexico, but beyond that Mestizo nation they were more interested in what the Native Americans on both sides of the man-made border had to say to them.

As he began to picture the 84-year-old Yaqui woman in her hospital bed, Valdez also imagined a Yaqui deer dancer as her alter-ego, a vibrant reminder of her own past and that of her peoples. The Deer Dancer is named after Cajeme, a legendary Yaqui rebel who fought against the Mexican government in the nineteenth century. Thus Cajeme becomes an integral part of Valdez's play, a symbol of the mummified fetus in the old woman's womb.

The play opened at the San Diego Repertory Theatre in early April, 2000, directed by the playwright and starring Alma Martínez as Mama Chu. Ms. Martínez revived her role for a revised version of the play, also directed by the playwright at El Teatro Campesino's theatre in San Juan Bautista, California. In portraying the central character, who is constantly on stage, perhaps Ms. Martínez knows the play and, certainly, her character better than anyone else. When I asked her what she thought Cajeme represented, she answered: ". . . Cajeme . . . is both my beloved son and the lasting memory of my dead husband. . . . His death is my physical death, and his life is the life of the memory of the Yaqui's way of life as it was."[10]

We see the visions in Mama Chu's mind because Valdez wants to contrast the Yaqui culture with that of the Mestizo. Thus the Mexican Circus clown, Cosme Bravo, appears as counterpoint to Lucas Flores, the resistance fighter, and as adversary to Cajeme. Cosme represents the *torocoyori*, who Mama Chu describes as ". . . a turn-coat Yaqui, who was slaughtering his own people like a rabid dog at the service of his Yori [Mexican] masters" (59). Every culture has its *torocoyori*, the *vendido* character that has his roots in Domingo/Mr. Sunday in *Shrunken Head*, pitted against and contrasted with the young social bandit, Joaquín, as we have seen. Likewise, in *Mundo Mata*, the title character is determined to stop his people's union activities, but eventually finds redemption during the last moments of the play.

When Mama Chu does finally die, Cajeme "dances to a climax at the foot of the bed. With his deer head up in triumph, he collapses, lifeless"

(62). At the end of the play, Mama Chu has died and taken Cajeme with her, or does Cajeme die, taking Mama Chu with him? Most importantly, Cajeme dies dancing, with his head "in triumph." Both Mama Chu and Cajeme have endured beyond endurance and will now pass to the next stage of the cosmic Indio vision. They have served their purposes and the revolution will continue.

The final moments of all three plays demonstrate a triumphant moment: Belarmino waiting for his mother to place his head on Joaquín's body in *Shrunken Head*, the successful campesinos at the end of *Mundo Mata* and the image of the victorious deer dancer at the climax of *Mummified Deer*. None of these endings reveals simple solutions but all require thoughtful action on the part of the audiences, action that will hopefully result in change for the better, change that can only come through knowledge of one's past. There are no easy answers to the situations in any of these plays. What Valdez hopes for is your visceral response to his plays. Recall his declaration quoted at the beginning of this Introduction:

> *El Indio baila.*
> He dances his way to truth
> in a way intellectuals
> will never understand.

Our playwright is not being anti-intellectual with this declaration; his Truth does not come solely from books. Luis Valdez understands the dance, invites us to join in that dance and, hopefully, we can.

Jorge Huerta, Ph.D.
Chancellor's Associate's Professor of Theater

Notes

1. The Teatro Campesino's early *actos* are published in Luis Valdez, *Early Works: Actos, Bernabé and Pensamiento Serpentino* (Houston: Arte Público Press, 1990) pp. 17–133.
2. *Dark Root of a Scream* is published in Lilian Faderman and Omar Salinas, eds. *From the Barrio* (San Francisco: Canfield Press, 1973) pp. 79–98.
3. *Zoot Suit* is published in Luis Valdez, *Zoot Suit and Other Plays* (Arte Público Press, 1992), pp. 21–94. See also, the ground-breaking bilingual (Spanish-English) edition of this play, also published by Arte Público Press, 2005.
4. *Corridos* was produced by PBS, adapted and directed by Valdez in 1987. Re-titled *Corridos: Tales of Passion and Revolution*, the televised version starred Linda Rondstadt.
5. For earlier discussions of the various versions of *El fin del mundo,* see Betty Diamond, *Brown-eyed Children of the Sun: The Cultural Politics of El Teatro Campesino* (Ann Arbor: University Microfilms, 1977), pp. 203–234; and Jorge A. Huerta, *Chicano Theater: Themes and Forms* (Tempe: Bilingual Press, 1982, 1987), pp. 207–213. While earlier versions of this play (1974–75) were modified by the collective, as pointed-out by Diamond, the present version owes more to the 1976 version and to Valdez's own vision.
6. From my personal records of a meeting of the leading Hispanic American artistic and managing directors in 1986.
7. Before the play was premiered in the year 2000, the producers hosted a public reading of *Mummified Deer*, then titled *The Mummified Fetus*, at the Centro Cultural de la Raza, in San Diego, California. I moderated the post-reading discussion, which was when Valdez made this observation.
8. Jennifer de Poyen, "Roots Rockero: Luis Valdez Reaches into His Family History to Create 'Mummified Deer,'" *San Diego Union-Tribune* 26 October 2000, Sec. "Night & Day," p. 4.
9. In a telephone conversation with Luis Valdez, 15 March, 2002.
10. E-mail from Alma Martínez to me dated 18 March 2002. Ms. Martínez is a *veterana* of many of Valdez's plays, beginning with *Zoot Suit* in 1978. Besides being a very busy professional actor, she is also a doctoral candidate in Theatre at Stanford University and is an Assistant Professor of Theatre at the University of California, Santa Cruz.

Mummified Deer

MAIN CHARACTERS

Mama Chu Flores, 84, a Yaqui survivor
Armida Bravo, 24, her granddaughter, a graduate student
Profe, 56, her son, a barber
Oralia Snyder, 49, her daughter, a housewife
Tilly, 18, her granddaughter
Doctor Jory, 40, resident at the hospital
Nurse Blanche, 32, in intensive care

IN THE OTHER REALITY:

Cajeme, 25, a Yaqui deer dancer
Cosme Bravo, 47, a Mexican clown
Don Güero, 40, a Spaniard
Agustina, 27, a singing trapeze artist
Lucas Flores, 38, a Yaqui resistance leader

SETTING

A modern hospital, a theatrical matrix that reveals the psychic interior of a patient. At the core is the stark reality of a bed in a cubicle. Around it are as many levels as a spherical empty space may provide. Four corridors provide passage onstage and off. A secret passageway up center is hidden behind the bed. The action must flow freely from daily reality to the other reality of the subconscious mind.

Metaphorically, the sterility of the hospital must bely a profound fecundity, like the great Sonoran desert. The walls must speak across time and space with ancient petroglyphs, shadows, transparencies, lightening and thunder; at other times, with the miasma of veins and muscles vibrating with every heartbeat. This is a womb of birth and death, full of the memories, fears and dreams of generations.

TIME AND PLACE

The present: San Diego, California. Spring 1969,
The past: Tijuana, Mexico. 1939–1950
Tucson, Arizona. 1917–1929
Sonora/Yucatán, Mexico. 1906–1911

ACT ONE

PROLOGUE

Night. ARMIDA BRAVO, *54, appears downstage, looking up at the the deep sparkling blackness of the Cosmos. Santana's "Black Magic Woman" plays softly under.*

ARMIDA: If it hadn't been for Carlos Castañeda, I never would have known what deep secrets Mama Chu was hiding. In the Spring of 1969, *The Yaqui Way of Knowledge* was a bestseller . . . in Berkeley . . . With tales of indio sorcerors, power spots and peyote hallucinations, Castañeda opened the doors of perception to parallel universes and blew the minds of my hippy generation . . . But for me, *The Yaqui Way* led back home . . . to reality. (*Segue the musical strains of "Sonora Querida." Lights change.*) I was four when my mother died, so I was raised by my grandmother in San Diego. I remember whenever the radio, always tuned to the Mexican station in Tijuana, played "Sonora Querida." Mama Chu would dance to the music as if it was the anthem of her soul. (*An old woman enters gleefully waltzing toward the bed.*) She ran a boarding house for immigrant workers. Her "mojaditos" as she called them. For over thirty years, she kept our large, transient family going—chronically broke and out of gas, always looking for the quick fix, a small loan, "just a couple of bucks 'til payday, compadre," as if poverty was our addiction . . . but it was Mama Chu we were hooked on. . . . (*The woman crawls into the bed.*) Whenever she got angry, she'd say: ¡No hagan que se me suba lo Yaqui! as if getting-her-Yaqui-indian-blood-up was like tempting God. I had to tempt God just go to high school. Years later, when I told her I was going away to graduate school, she said it would break her heart. She left me no choice. . . . (*She exits.*)

Fade to back.

3

SCENE ONE

Spring, 1969. We hear an amplified heartbeat and deep labored breathing. Lights up. Upstage center, MAMA CHU, 84, lies unconscious, elevated on her hospital bed. In the background, we hear bone scrapers and rattles. Chanting voices. Then drums.

Upstage center. A YAQUI indian DEER DANCER bolts in, running half-naked to the waist, deer hooves on his belt, butterfly cocoons on his ankles, and a deer's head on his white turbaned crown. Rattling his gourds, he vigorously circles the bed, bristling with animal power to the music of flute and drum, never dropping his deer persona. He dances, then suddenly freezes sensing danger.

NURSE BLANCHE, 40ish, enters the room, monitoring the patient. She checks her chart, then lifts her patient's closed eyelids.

NURSE: (*A jovial sort.*) How's it goin' in there, Flores? Do you know where you are? Peek a boo, I see you. . . . I need your Social Security number. Are you on Medicare? Do you speak English? You don't hear a word I'm saying do ya, hon? Immigration! Nope . . . you're dead to the world.(*Upstage ARMIDA BRAVO, 24, anxiously appears in the doorway.*)

ARMIDA: Excuse me? (DEER DANCER *leaps into the shadows as the* NURSE *snaps around.*)

NURSE:Yes, may I help you?

ARMIDA: I'm looking for a patient. Her last name's Flores. She was just admitted this morning.

NURSE: You're too late.

ARMIDA: (*Stunned.*) What do you mean I'm too late?

NURSE: Visiting hours are over. Finito.

ARMIDA: Oh, well . . . I'm famiglia, capice. . . . Is that her? (*She skirts around her and goes up to the bed. Antsy.*)

NURSE: Jeezus.

ARMIDA: (*Correcting her Spanish.*) No, Jesús. Her name is Jesús María, but the family calls her Chu . . . Mama Chu.

NURSE: I don't care if you call her the Virgin Mary, Hon. She's sedated. You people've been coming and going in here all day long. Singing, playing guitars. Why don't you just let your sweet momma rest now, hmm?

ARMIDA: (*Bristling.*) You people . . . can you be more specific?

NURSE: This unit is closed.

ARMIDA: (*Used to intimidating the establishment.*) To everybody—or just to Mexicans?

NURSE: Do you know what sedated means?

ARMIDA: (*Flaring.*) Don't patronize me. I know how to speak English! What kind of fucking racist bullshit is this?

NURSE: Keep your voice down! And watch your mouth, honey. This is a county hospital, not the fucking Tijuana jail. Well, I never . . .

ARMIDA: (*Concilatory, holding her temper.*) Look, let's not make a civil rights case out of it. Okay? I've come a long way. She's my grandmother, more like my mother, actually. . . . I was hoping just to have a minute to see her.

NURSE: I don't have a racist bone in my body. I just work here! (NURSE *exits.* ARMIDA *walks around the bed, stunned by the stillness of her grandmother.*)

ARMIDA: (*Suddenly awkward.*) Mama Chu . . . can you hear me? It's me, Armida. Your . . . heartbreaker, remember? Well, I'm back! I've been away a long time, I know, but even if you haven't heard from me lately . . . I swear . . . I've missed you, grandma. Are you still mad at me? I've been doing a lot of thinking. I'm sorry, okay . . . I didn't even know who I was till I left. I've changed, Mama Chu. Please don't give me the silent treatment. (*In the background, we begin to hear scrapers and rattles again.*)

ARMIDA: I know you can hear me, Mama Chu. Go ahead, let her rip. *Get-your-Yaqui-up!* I'm here. Be pissed at me, I don't care. I can take it. We've got too much to talk about. Can you hear me, Mama Chu? You've got to fight this! (*We hear drums.* ARMIDA *stays put, oblivious to chanting voices. Downstage, the* YAQUI DEER DANCER *bolts in, freezes, immediately senses danger, then bolts out.* NURSE *reappears in the doorway.*)

NURSE: Satisfied? She's out for the night.

ARMIDA: What have you done to her?

NURSE: She was in quite a bit of pain when they brought her in. Nausea, vomiting. We gave her something to help her rest.

ARMIDA: What kind of pain?

NURSE: Cramps, distended bowels, swollen colon. All the good stuff. Blood pressure's up. Heart's not in any great shape either. We're keeping an eye on that.

ARMIDA: Is it serious?

NURSE: Ask Doctor Jory . . . our staff oncologist.

ARMIDA: (*Sinking feeling.*) Oncologist . . . Okay. Where can I find him?

NURSE: Tonight? Good luck. He's scheduled her for a biopsy first thing tomorrow morning.

ARMIDA: Biopsy?!

NURSE: Just a little exploratory.

ARMIDA: Surgery?!

NURSE: X-Rays detected a growth in her abdomen. Something the size of a grapefruit. (*The shock hits* ARMIDA *like a wave.*)

ARMIDA: Oh, my god . . . let me get this straight . . . You're telling me there's a possibility she might have . . . Is she going to . . .

NURSE: We'll know tomorrow.

ARMIDA: Mama Chu, you can't . . . die!

NURSE: That's a no no, deary. Never say die. Mañana's another day. Come on now. Let this sweet old Spanish lady rest, hmm?

ARMIDA: (*Passionately.*) She's not Spanish, she's Mexican . . . She's a fighter. Okay? She was in the 1910 Revolution.

NURSE: Mercy. How old *is* she?

ARMIDA: (*Holding back tears.*) I don't know! Nobody in my family knows. She's outlived all but two of her twenty children . . . She'll make it! (ARMIDA *is escorted out by* NURSE.)

NURSE: Sure, she will. Must be tired, poor dear . . . ready for a good long siesta.

Lights down.

SCENE TWO

MAMA CHU's *room in light and shadow. Flutes, drums and voices.* CAJEME, *the* DEER DANCER, *bolts in again. Rattling his gourds, he circles the bed and dances, bristling with animal power.* MAMA CHU *suddenly sits up.* HE *freezes.*

MAMA CHU: ¡Cabrón Cajeme! What do you want from me? Haven't I suffered enough for you? Look, how they have me here, on my culo in the hospital. I need to get back to my own house . . . ¡Yo quiero estar en mi casa! (CAJEME *rattles agitatedly. SHE winces in pain.*) ¡Ay! Stop that, you're hurting me. (CAJEME *rattles again softly.*) I know . . . no es tu culpa. You don't mean to, but it hurts just the same. It all hurts, and there's nothing we can do about it. We are put on this earth to suffer, porque nomás by suffering can we rise to a greater gloria with our blessed señor, Jesus Christ, Aleluya! (CAJEME *rattles furiously. MAMA CHU twists in pain.*) ¡Ayyyy! Demonio, what did I just tell you! I'm ready to rise to La Gloria now, Señor, why don't you take me? (CAJEME *begins a slow sinewy dance. SHE hurts.*) Ay, mi'jito . . . what are you doing? Stop that! Stop that, I tell you! Soy tu madre. STOP, ANIMAL! (CAJEME *freezes beside the bed, looking mystified. MAMA CHU addresses him tenderly, as to an idiot.*) I know, I know, you're not an animal. It's not your fault who you are. . . . What do you know of God and sins of the flesh? The white Yori priests in their black skirts never taught you. The patrones never worked you as a peon. Loose women never touched you. What do you know of salvation? (CAJEME *pulls away, as a deer going to drink at a riverbank.*) For you, there is nothing. For you, there is no sun. For you, there is no night. . . no pain, no heat, no thirst, no hunger, no rain. . . . You are free, like a savage . . . A coyote. A wild deer! (SHE *touches him tenderly. Suddenly startled, the* DEER DANCER *looks up, eyes wide with alarm. The shadow of a* HUNTER *with a bow and arrow appears in the background.*) What is it? (CAJEME *bolts, toppling* MAMA CHU *back onto the bed.*) Animal! You're hurting me again! You're evil. Do you hear me? ¡Malo, malo, malo! The child of the very demonio! (*Simultaneously, the* DEER DANCER *gets up and furiously circles the bed rattling his gourds.*) (*Mortified, in pain.*) Demonio, STOP!

Blackout.

SCENE THREE

The waiting room. ARMIDA *enters to find* PROFE, *56, sitting alone, in a dapper suit and tie, playing his old worn guitar, reeking of sadness.*

ARMIDA: (*Behind him.*) Profe . . . ? (PROFE *stops playing, red-eyed and startled.*)

PROFE: Agustina . . . !

ARMIDA: It's me, Tío. Armida. Your niece. (HE *turns and stands, looking embarrassed.* HE *hugs her.*)

PROFE: ¡Mi'ja! Pos qué va, look at you. . . . More and more like your mother. I swear to God! I thought you were Agustina. You don't know how much you look like her. (ARMIDA *is sensitive about always being compared.*)

ARMIDA: You're right. I have no real memory of her . . .

PROFE: (*Sign of the cross.*) ¡Descanse en paz!

ARMIDA: I remember being scared of her picture though, there in Mama Chu's house . . . with all those dead faces in old wooden frames.

PROFE: Your aunts and uncles. Lucas Flores, your grandfather . . . rest in peace. How could they scare you?

ARMIDA: I don't know, Profe . . . There's a lot about our family I don't understand. We've always been so . . . rascuachi.

PROFE: Who you calling rascuachi?

ARMIDA: It beats fucked up.

PROFE: What's that? University language? I like it better when you call me Tío.

ARMIDA: What are you doing here all alone, Tío?

PROFE: Just passing the time. Your tía Oralia went to eat. We were upstairs, serenading your grandma, but the nurse threw us out. . . . (NURSE *appears upstage, adjusting* MAMA CHU'*s oxygen and bed.*)

ARMIDA: (*Channeling her frustrations.*) I was just up there. Is it me, or is that nurse treating us like crap? They've got Mama Chu all drugged up. She didn't even know I was in the room.

PROFE: She's getting old. . . . Who knows how much longer she'll be with us.

ARMIDA: It's serious, isn't it? I got here as fast as I could.

PROFE: (*With an edge.*) Pos sí. It only took you two years.

ARMIDA: I came as soon as I got tía's phone call . . . She made it sound like Mama Chu was . . . I didn't know what to think. I couldn't get back sooner. Honest. (PROFE *studies her with mixed feelings.* NURSE *exits upstage.*)

PROFE: What are you now, one of those hippies?

ARMIDA: I'm supporting myself through graduate school, Profe. I'm a teaching assistant in the Anthropology Department. Before that I waited tables for a year. Aren't you just a little bit proud of me?

PROFE: I'd rather have you at home . . .

ARMIDA: Where's home?

PROFE: Where the hell do you think it is? With your family! Are we too rascuachi now? Now that you're supporting yourself.

ARMIDA: Don't be mean. It hasn't been easy.

PROFE: (*Emotionally.*) I've lived with Mama Chu all my life. . . . The only time I ever left her was in World War II . . . when I was in the Navy. . . . In the Pacific, I never thought about her. Once I came back home, I realized . . . she was home.

ARMIDA: (*A sudden shiver.*) Profe . . . what are you going to do once Mama Chu's . . . not around anymore?

PROFE: I don't want to talk about that. (ARMIDA *pauses, upset but respecting his feelings.*)

ARMIDA: How's the barber shop?

PROFE: Closed.

ARMIDA: Permanently?

PROFE: Maybe. I dunno . . .

ARMIDA: You're a great barber, Profe. Don't quit. (PROFE *lifts up a trembling hand;* HE *has the shakes.*)

PROFE: See this hand? I'm fifty six. Nobody wants a haircut anymore. They all look like Yaquis brought down from the mountains with drums. Todos greñudos.

ARMIDA: (*Tenderly.*) It's the 60's. You've been like a dad to me, Tío. It's time to think of yourself. It's still not too late to find a wife. How about that widow in San Ysidro? (PROFE *scoffs and looks at* ARMIDA *with suppressed anger.*)

PROFE: I saw you, you know. About a year ago. In Tijuana, on Avenida Revolución. You saw me and walked away.

ARMIDA: (*Taken aback.*) Me? I haven't been to TJ in years . . . I've been in Berkeley. Boycotting grapes.

PROFE: You broke Mama Chu's heart, you know . . . when you left.

ARMIDA: She broke mine. She swore never to speak to me again.

PROFE: She says you told her to go to hell.

ARMIDA: The day I told her I was going away, she refused to give me her blessing. Then she started in on my mother. Cursing me right along with her. God knows, Mama Chu made it a clean break, not me . . . Not that I believe in God.

PROFE: You're Agustina's revenge. Ni modo.

ARMIDA: (*Perturbed.*) Why do I get the feeling I'm paying for my mother's sins, Tío? There's not one picture of my father in grandma's house. She wouldn't even pronounce his name . . .

PROFE: (*Sardonically.*) You mean, Cosme Bravo?

ARMIDA: I know Mama Chu hated him. Even as a kid I could tell she despised him by the way she spit out "tu pinche padre," but she never told me anything about him.

PROFE: Well, now isn't the right time to talk about that pendejo neither.

ARMIDA: Really? When will it be right? Every time I've ever asked about my mother's life I've never gotten a straight answer. Why?

PROFE: Maybe there's none. Just crooked ones.

ARMIDA: What do you mean?

PROFE: (*Evasively.*) She was a beautiful woman, your mother. A flower, a butterfly, a shining star. But stubborn as a mule. Just like you. . . .

ARMIDA: See? You're avoiding the question.

PROFE: Agustina ran away at sixteen . . . to join the fleabitten circus of Cosme Bravo who stole her for himself. . . .

ARMIDA: (*Old stuff.*) I know that story. They were in love . . . The butterfly and the clown.

PROFE: (*Bitterly ironic.*) N'ombre. It was during the Depression. . . . Eating was more important than being in love. . . . We all ended up on the road with the payaso. Tucson, Arizona to El Paso, Tejas to Los Angeles, California . . . all up and down the border . . . the San Joaquin Valley. Fog, rain or shine. If the raza had no money to come to the Circo Azteca, we worked in the fields . . . Cosme always pocketed the money . . . like a pimp.

ARMIDA: And you blame me for staying away for two years! I know you hated my father too. Why is our family so fucked up?

PROFE: Why do you have to talk dirty like that? You sound like a whore!

ARMIDA: Oh, come on, Profe . . . Up until ten hours ago I was in the middle of the Third World Strike for Ethnic Studies at Berkeley . . . I'm a Chicana! Okay? Give me a break!

PROFE: You got it. Watch my lira. I'm going to the "excuse me." (SHE *grabs him and holds him.*)

ARMIDA: No, you don't! Not until you give me at least one uncrooked answer.

PROFE: Armida, mi'ja, I'm not kidding.

ARMIDA: Agustina didn't run away with Cosme. He liberated her.

PROFE: That's not all he did . . .

ARMIDA: Tell me about it, Tío. . . . What's the skeleton in the family closet?

PROFE: Only your mother . . . dying so young. Excuse me, eh? (*PROFE frees himself and hurries out. ARMIDA looks nonplussed.*)

Fade to black.

SCENE FOUR

MAMA CHU'*s room. Drumroll. A travel spot slashes back and forth across the bed.*

COSME: (*O.S.*) ¡Señores, señoras, señoritas y señorito-o-s! El Circo Azteca is proud to present, COSME! ¡El Matador B-R-A-V-O! (*Cymbal. Bullfight music. Enter COSME BRAVO, 47, a CLOWN MATADOR strutting in a ragged suit of lights and cape. CAJEME enters upstage, and COSME gives him the come-on with a red cape.*) Uh-huh, ¡Toro . . . torito! (*CAJEME runs past, behind him, leaving COSME befuddled.*) ¡Órale, baboso! (*Pulls out a donkey's ear.*) ¡Ole! ¡Ole! Check out this burro's ear. What a piece of ass, no? ¡Ole! (*Tosses the ear.*) A pelado was standing on the corner, when his compadre came up to him and said: "Oiga, compa', I don't want to alarm you, but did you know your vieja has a tumor in her you-know-what?" "What do you mean my wife has a tumor in her you-know-what? . . . And how the hell would you know that?" "Bueno," said the compadre, "I really don't know for sure, but it sure feels like a tumor in her you-know-what!" (*COSME executes a bump and grind, ba-da-boom, drumroll.*) ¡Y ahora! The star of El Circo Azteca, the Singing Butterfly of Tijuana, Agustina, La Mariposa fina! (*AGUSTINA, mid 20's, enters, a dark beauty in tutu and tights, wearing gossamer wings. SHE sings a comedic soprano on a swing.*)

AGUSTINA:

    Cuando eschuches este vals

    haz un recuerdo de mí

    piensa en los besos de amor

    que me distes y que te di

    (COSME *pushes her, singing a comedic love duet.*)

AGUSTINA & COSME:

    Si alguien pretende robar

    tu divino corazón

    diles que mi alma es de ti

    y la tuya tengo yo

    (MAMA CHU *sits up in her bed, squinting like a hawk.*)

MAMA CHU: Agustina! . . . are you still running around like a puta?

AGUSTINA: I love you too, mamacita.

MAMA CHU : When are you going to settle down, mujer? Are you still in heat? I'm no dump for your puppy litters!

AGUSTINA: I only came by to say hello . . . or goodbye.

MAMA CHU: Que goodbye ni que la chet. Who's going to take care of that little she-dog you left me, eh? Ungrateful. You never appreciated all that I did for you. You just left me. And for what? A pendejo, a clown!

COSME: Gracias, Doña Chu. El Circo Azteca is here to salute you! Up yours, eh?

MAMA CHU: You shut up! You godammit fool. Thief! You stole my daughter and abandoned her to a life of sin and wickedness. Get out my house!

AGUSTINA: (*Laughing bitterly.*) Ay, Mamá. That was always your problem. Always stuck to the house.

MAMA CHU: Where do you expect me to be? The streets where you ended up? I own my own house, mi propia casa! And so does your sister. Oralia didn't have to run around showing her *nalgas* to the world. She got married!

AGUSTINA: So did I, Mama Chu. So did I.

COSME: Several times.

AGUSTINA: Oralia's got nothing on me.

MAMA CHU: She married a tall, handsome güero from Texas. Their children look like beautiful blue-eyed angels.

AGUSTINA: (*Spreads her butterfly wings.*) Bueno, ya pues, ¿no? That was all over a long time ago. Can't you see? Wings.

MAMA CHU: Have you no shame?! What's to become of your daughter . . . what's her name?

AGUSTINA: Army . . .

MAMA CHU: Armida! I had to raise that ungrateful child on my own. May God forgive you.

AGUSTINA: (*Coldly, bluntly.*) May God forgive you . . . for not forgiving me.

MAMA CHU: (*Suddenly realizing.*) ¡Santo cielo! Agustina . . . You've been dead for twenty years . . . !

AGUSTINA: Gone but not forgotten, Mama Chu. R.I.P. Or, as they say in Spanish, D.E.P.

MAMA CHU: Where am I . . . ? This isn't my house! ¡Qué chingados! What is happening?

COSME: ¡El Circo Azteca! (*Music.* THEY *spin her bed around.* AGUSTINA *resumes her comic duet with* COSME.)

AGUSTINA:
¿Cómo quieres, ángel mío,
que te olvide si eres mi pasión
si en el cielo en la tierra en el mar
en la tumba estaremos los dos?
(COSME *sings with her.*)
¿Cómo quieres, ángel mío,
que te olvide si eres mi ilusión
si mi vida es toda tuya
y tuyo es mi corazón.
(AGUSTINA *and* COSME *exit dancing.*)

MAMA CHU: (*Lying back painfully.*) Agustina . . . !

Fade to black.

SCENE FIVE

The waiting room. ORALIA, *49, enters with her daughter* TILLY, *18, who is hiding her pregnancy, carrying a doggy bag.* THEY *spot* ARMIDA *waiting alone, listening to her transitor radio.*

ORALIA: Pos mira nomás, what the cat dragged in! Our little Army!

When did you get here? (*Gives* ARMIDA *a sloppy hug.*) Where's Profe, in the "excuse me" again? That old pedorro's nothing but a leaky faucet. Back and forth. Back and forth. We've been here all day and night. We went out to dinner. We had shrimp! Are you hungry? Here's my doggy bag.

ARMIDA: No thanks, Tía. But hello.

ORALIA: You're looking stylish. Como la Tina what's her name? (*Out of* TILLY's *mouth.*) Ike and Tina Turner. I wasn't expecting to see you tonight.

ARMIDA: (*Irked.*) After your life and death message? I took the first bus to LA. Then the train. Ten hours . . . nonstop. Thanks, Tía.

ORALIA: I didn't mean to scare you, but I had to make sure the baboso on the phone got the word to you. . . . Who is he? Your loverboy?

ARMIDA: Just a friend.

ORALIA: With a sexy name like Cage?

ARMIDA: Hello, Tilly. (TILLY *is already embarrassed;* SHE *does not want to be there.*)

ORALIA: Say hello to your cousin, ándale. Miss America! Don't just stand like a boba.

TILLY: Hi, Army. How's graduate school?

ARMIDA: Berserkly. How's Lincoln High?

TILLY: (*Evasively.*) I . . . graduated. Last year.

ARMIDA: In three years? Great! Any plans for higher ed?

ORALIA: You know what, now that you mention it, what does that mean, graduate school? If you graduate, you're out of school, how can you be in again? Puras papas. All that higher education . . . for what?

ARMIDA: Career advancement, Tía. I'm working on my Master's.

ORALIA: Masters de qué—Masturbation?!

TILLY: Mom! (ORALIA *laughs uproarously.* TILLY *is mortified.*)

ARMIDA: Cultural Anthropology. In fact, I'm going after a Ph.D.

ORALIA: Uy yu yuy. That's the study of gorillas, ¿qué no? Maybe you can get a job at the Zoo. Peeling their big bananas! (ORALIA *cackles obscenely again.* PROFE *returns.*)

PROFE: Is the city sewer at it again? There's nothing Oralia enjoys more than filth.

ORALIA: ¡Cállate el hocico!

PROFE: I know you love it. So does mi 'amá.

ORALIA: Look, who's talking. Profe, the family dog. Your zipper's open. Did you wash your hands in the escusado? Here's your dinner. Eat it. (SHE *gives him the doggy bag.* THEY *all settle down.*)

ARMIDA: Tell me about Mama Chu . . . when did she start getting stomach pains? (NURSE *re-enters upstage, adjusts* MAMA CHU'*s bed.*)

TILLY: Last Tuesday.

ORALIA: (*Scoffingly.*) Qué last Tuesday ni que nada. She's had these pains off and on for years. They always go away. It's nothing I tell you. Puro pedo. It's only gas. She's got to stop cooking with lard. Es puro fat.

ARMIDA: What about the tumor in her stomach?

ORALIA: What tumor? You got X-ray vision to see what's in her panza? It's undigested food, I tell you. A big bodoque of . . . cuacha!

TILLY: Yuck.

PROFE: (*Putting his food away.*) N'ombre. This is like eating in a toilet. (NURSE *exits upstage.*)

ARMIDA: I think it's a little more serious than that, Tía. We'd better be prepared for the worst.

TILLY: Why, is Mama Chu going to die?

ORALIA: She's not gonna die! ¿Qué traes, tonta?

ARMIDA: (*Incredulously.*) Your own message said to come if I still wanted to see her alive.

ORALIA: That was just to get you here, smarty-pants. We only brought Mama Chu to this hospital for stomach cramps and a little basca. You better watch what you say, eh? Don't wish death on your grandmother.

PROFE: She didn't say that!

ARMIDA: Are you serious?

ORALIA: You want it to be serious.

ARMIDA: (*Getting peeved.*) Why would I want that, Tía?

ORALIA: (*Steamrolling.*) To be done with her! Where the hell have you been for the last two years? No visits, no calls, ni madre. Now you come only because it's some kind of life and death situation? I don't think so, ¿sabes? This is the thanks your grandma gets for raising a . . . smart aleck!

ARMIDA: It was hard on us both. I didn't mean to be away so long. I'm sorry about that . . .

ORALIA: You've always blamed Mama Chu for your madre's . . . you-know-what.

ARMIDA: What?

ORALIA: You know what.

TILLY: Suicide?

PROFE: ¡N'ombre!

TILLY: I mean! Sorry, Army.

ARMIDA: It's no big family secret. . . . In fact, I told you, Tilly. My mom killed herself. Okay? So why did Mama Chu say such terrible things to me when I left for school?

PROFE: What terrible things? No, don't tell me.

ARMIDA: She said my mom was a yori puta . . . and where I was going, I'd turn into one, too . . .

ORALIA: She said that? ¡Ah, qué mi mamá! (SHE *cackles with laughter.* PROFE *is perturbed.*)

PROFE: Bueno, mi 'amá has her own way of saying things. It's not always pretty, but it's not what you think . . . no, sister?

ORALIA: I don't think nothing. Sometimes it's better not to think . . .

TILLY: What's a yori pu-ta?

ARMIDA: A white man's whore. . . . Mama Chu said I inherited her hot Yanqui blood.

TILLY: (*Pleasantly surprised.*) Mama Chu's a Yanqui?

ARMIDA: Freudian slip. Not Yankee. Yaqui, as in tribe. We're second cousins to the Apaches.

ORALIA: (*Chagrined.*) Mira, mira. Speak for yourself. My papá was born in Spain . . . What do you know?

TILLY: I thought Mama Chu was . . . Mexican.

ORALIA: Half French! On your great grandfather's side. Before the Revolution, in Sonora, your grandmother lived in a big house with Indian servants. *La Familia Petit.*

ARMIDA: Are you sure she wasn't one of the servants?

ORALIA: Cállate. Some of us was born'd looking Petit, and some of us wasn't. That's it! I don't want to talk about this no more.

ARMIDA: Of course you don't. Mama Chu's always favored the white chocolate in the family. And you know it, Tía.

TILLY: What the hell do you mean by that?

ARMIDA: Just that she's racist against herself.

ORALIA: Okay, that's it. We don't have to sit here and listen to this! Is this what you're learning at your mierda university?

PROFE: Oralia's right. There are some things in a family it's better not to discuss . . .

ARMIDA: What's wrong with the truth?

ORALIA: Everything! Mama Chu's the only one holding this family together . . . without her . . . ya no hay nada! (ORALIA *exits with* TILLY *in a huff.* TILLY *comes back and pauses before* ARMIDA, *then* SHE *reaches down and grabs the doggy bag.* SHE *rushes out.*)

PROFE: Hey, I was eating that . . . (ARMIDA *looks at* PROFE.)

ARMIDA: Is that what we're afraid of . . . nada?

Fade to black.

SCENE SIX

MAMA CHU*'s room. A rustling of footsteps comes from the dark shadows, with the echo of Yaqui ceremonial music in the background.* MAMA CHU *sits up, her eyes wide open, fully awake.*

MAMA CHU: Cajeme! Cajeme, is that you? I know you're there. Where are you? What are you doing? Don't you know by now you can't hide from me! (CAJEME *playfully runs across upstage, behind* MAMA CHU. *Affectionately, she says.*) I feel your every move . . . every breath, every fear. ¡Soy tu madre! Did you forget how to sleep? There was a time when you couldn't get enough. You slept for years . . . muy mansito, peaceful and quiet. Sleep, *mi'jito,* sleep. (CAJEME *exits up center.* ORALIA *enters alone downstage.*)

ORALIA: (*Sips on a bottle.*) Mama Chu? It's me again, your favorite daughter. I just came to say buenas noches, okay? Don't worry about a thing.

MAMA CHU: (*Eyes closed.*) I'd know that whiskey voice anywhere.

ORALIA: (*Not hearing her.*) Tilly and I will be staying on at your house till we can bring you back home again . . . okay? Maybe longer . . .

MAMA CHU: (*Sighing.*) Oralia. She's drinking again . . . Ave María Purísima . . .

ORALIA: (*Choking up.*) I hate to see you like this, Mama Chu. I know you can't hear me, but—(*Sputters uncontrollably.*) Do you know what my sonavubitching husband Jack did? He ran off with our nineteen-year-old maid! To Tijuana. . . . He's living with her over there.

MAMA CHU: I don't hear a thing.

ORALIA: How could Jack do this to me! If papá was still alive, he'd shoot his ass. What kind of man screws his maid?!

MAMA CHU: H'mmm. . . Don't ask. . .

ORALIA: (*Blubbering.*) I can't even face the neighbors anymore, I'm so ashamed . . . All of Chula Vista knows! On top of that, Tilly's pregnant, too . . . (TILLY *enters and exits.*) ¡Panzona! Six months, that's why she had to drop out of high school . . . Y pa'cabarla de chingar, her boyfriend has been drafted. They're sending him to Vietnam. I'm glad you can't hear this, Mama Chu, because I know it would kill you! I don't know what I'm going to do!

MAMA CHU: Who's going to clean the house? (ORALIA *sobs.* TILLY *re-enters and freaks out.*)

TILLY: The nurse is coming . . . Mom . . . What's wrong? She's not . . . dead, is she?

ORALIA: (*Composing herself.*) No, tonta. Can't you see she's sleeping?

TILLY: She looks dead. Did she say anything?

ORALIA: Nada. Let's go home . . . (TILLY *gasps.*) To Mama Chu's.

TILLY: (*Disappointed.*) When are we going home to Chula Vista?

ORALIA: Maybe never. ¡Vámonos! (*The two women leave.* MAMA CHU *sits up.*)

MAMA CHU: ¡Oye! Who's gonna clean la chingada casa? (MAMA CHU *squints into the shadows. Distant drums start beating backstage.* CAJEME *runs in, trembling in utter fear, like a wide-eyed deer looking for escape.* HE *spins around in a panic.*) Cajeme! So you finally decided to show up. What's the matter with you? (CAJEME *desperately rattles his bones and scrapers.*)¡No, tonto! Nobody's coming to get you. Nobody can touch you . . . as long as I live. You're safe. . . . You're in Paradise and you don't even know it. What more do you want? (*More rattling and scraping.*) You're not an animal. You have a soul. I hear you . . . even without words. Speak to me in the language of God. (CAJEME *tries to speak. A ghostly figure appears in shadows.*)

LUCAS: (*O.S.*) E BETCHI-BO-O-CA-ITA INTO!!!

MAMA CHU: Who's there? You don't scare me, baboso. Show yourself or go away! (LUCAS FLORES, *in his early 30s, enters with a
bow and arrow, wearing overalls and a fedora, but no shirt.) (Mortified.)* ¡Ave María Purísima! Cajeme, hide! (*The* DEER DANCER
bolts out, rattling his gourds. LUCAS *stops.)* Are you from the living or the dead? I haven't seen a flechador with a bow and arrow
since I was a girl. What do you want? Why are you haunting me?

LUCAS: (*Gently.*) Don't you remember me, Chu?

MAMA CHU: ¡Adió! You're not. . . Who are you?

LUCAS: Did you forget me already? Dios em chaniabu!

MAMA CHU: (*Amazed.*) Chiokie! Is that you, Lucas Flores? Bendito
sea Dios . . . You look exactly the way you did the day we first met.
A lifetime ago!

LUCAS: Pos sí. I'm new again . . .

MAMA CHU: How is it possible?

LUCAS: If death is real, anything is possible.

MAMA CHU: I don't believe you.

LUCAS: You got old, vieja . . .

MAMA CHU: Yes, but I'm not dead. (HE *extends his hand as if invit-
ing her to join him.* SHE *reaches for him tentatively, but fails to
touch him.*) You always had such hot heavy hands. The hands of a
troublemaker. Now I can hardly feel them.

LUCAS: (*With self-deprecating humor.*) Ni modo. I was only your husband *número* three.

MAMA CHU: You died too young, Lucas Flores . . . I told you not to
go back to Sonora. Your Yaqui dances got you killed.

LUCAS: It wasn't the dancing that killed me, Chu, it was the Revolución.

MAMA CHU: The pinche Revolution. What good did all the killing do?

LUCAS: I did what I had to do . . . So the Yoris would know we're not
animals.

MAMA CHU: They shot you dead like a dog in the dust!

LUCAS: It was the price to be paid.

MAMA CHU: For what? What did you accomplish? ¡Ni madre! You
left me.

LUCAS: I left you my blood . . . What did you do with it? You spilled it.

MAMA CHU: I never spilled it! Your daughter threw away her own life.

LUCAS: Your life's candle is burning low, mi Chu. You can't die without making peace with your muertitos.

MAMA CHU: (*Suddenly alarmed.*) ¡Oyes! Who said anything about dying? I see now. ¡Condenado! Is that why you're here, to take me away!

LUCAS: I'm here . . . to escort the Deer.

MAMA CHU: (*Shocked.*) What . . . deer . . . where to?

LUCAS: The wilderness world. Resurrection. (HE *shakes a rattle.* CAJEME *enters swiftly, rattling his gourds.*)

MAMA CHU: Cajeme, get back! ¡¿Qué estás loco?! (*To* LUCAS.) There's no candle for the dead here. God knows my sins because I've confessed to Him, but only to Him! You're nothing but a ghost. Get out! ¡Déjame en paz!

LUCAS: En paz descansa. (LUCAS *retreats.* CAJEME, *intrigued, starts to chase him.*)

MAMA CHU: ¡Oye, tú! Where do you think you're going? Come back here! Do you want to die? You're going to be the death of me. Then where will you be? We'll be going home soon . . . together! Now go to sleep. ¡Por el amor de Dios! (SHE *lies back.* CAJEME *snuffs, arguing back and runs out.*)

Fade to black.

SCENE SEVEN

Exterior night. The siren of an ambulance arriving. ARMIDA *walks beside* PROFE, *downstage, outside of the hospital.*

ARMIDA: Hospitals, I hate hospitals. They remind me of jail . . .

PROFE: How do you know what jails are like? (SHE *gives him a look.*) Skip it . . . Oralia's making herself at home. When she moved in with Tilly . . . "to take care of Mama Chu," she said . . . she gave me twenty bucks for food . . . That was a month ago. They ate everything in the house! We're down to instant coffee and hard tortillas. Now they eat out . . . Mama Chu's boarding house is closed!

ARMIDA: It must be really empty. It's a big house.

PROFE: Your Tía's always had her eye on it. . . She's already staking her claim.

ARMIDA: She's already got a home . . . She's not separated from Uncle Jack again?

PROFE: Mama Chu got sicker. That's all I know. Oralia's wanted to put her in a home and sell the house for years.

ARMIDA: I shouldn't have said what I said . . . about Mama Chu, I mean. She's not a racist . . .

PROFE: ¡N'ombre! She's the darkest one. Sweet as a Hershey bar.

ARMIDA: . . . even though when I was little, she was always yelling at me to stay out of the sun. She said I'd never amount to anything.

PROFE: Did you believe her?

ARMIDA: No. She only made me try harder in school.

PROFE: There you go. She knew what she was doing.

ARMIDA: (*Deeply disturbed.*) I'd like to believe that. Sometimes she can be loving. Sometimes not. She runs hot and cold . . . like my love life . . . How did Mama Chu manage to have twenty children?

PROFE: She got married.

ARMIDA: What happened to them? I mean, I know one of them was my mother, then there's you and Tía Oralia. What about the rest?

PROFE: They died. Some in the Revolution. Others in the small pox epidemics. They came and went. Babies mostly.

ARMIDA: (*Touched.*) It must have been terrible for her.

PROFE: She was what they called a soldadera . . .

ARMIDA: I know. A soldier woman. "An angel in the battlefield . . ." I love those old stories about grandma . . . What I can't figure out is how she had the time to have all those babies.

PROFE: She had three husbands. Outlived them all, too.

ARMIDA: She's amazing.

PROFE: She loves you, you know . . . Mama Chu raised you like her own daughter.

ARMIDA: (*Ironically.*) Agustina? Or Oralia?

PROFE: ¡No, qué Oralia! She's her father's daughter. Don Güero was a coño.

ARMIDA: (*Shocked but amused.*) A what?

PROFE: Listen to me. Oralia wants Mama Chu's house. She wants to sell it and cash in on it, as soon as grandma dies . . .

ARMIDA: What about you?

PROFE: What about me? I don't own the house. Neither does Oralia . . . You do.

ARMIDA: Me?!

PROFE: The papers are in your name.

ARMIDA: Since when?

PROFE: Since you were born. . . . Promise me you'll never tell Mama Chu.

ARMIDA: I promise.

PROFE: Your mother made the down payment. I kicked in my Navy money. She wanted you to have it.

ARMIDA: Where was my father in all this?

PROFE: Cosme Bravo? Phfft. He was long gone.

ARMIDA: (*Emotional pause.*) Why did she do it, Profe?

PROFE: Buy the house?

ARMIDA: Commit suicide.

PROFE: How should I know?

ARMIDA: She must have hated her life . . .

PROFE: No. There were good times, too. Especially when you came along.

ARMIDA: That's bullshit. I was her only child. Why did she bother having me?

PROFE: Does it matter?

ARMIDA: She's been ticking inside of me all my life . . . one of these days I'm afraid she'll explode like a time bomb.

PROFE: Stop acting like Agustina.

ARMIDA: What are you hiding? Was my mother a Tijuana prostitute or what!

PROFE: Leave it alone, godammit! You don't know what you're getting yourself into.

ARMIDA: I have a right to know! And you have a responsibility to tell me, Tío. Can't you see that?

PROFE: (*Stamping out cig.*) I've told you about the house. That's all you need to know. It's getting late. Mama Chu's going in early in the morning. Let's go inside. Those hard couches in the waiting room are starting to look good. (HE *turns and goes.* ARMIDA *watches him go incredulously.*)

ARMIDA: Profe! You're really not going to tell me? And you call me stubborn? What is this, a family trait or something? Profe! (SHE *pursues him.*)

Fade to black.

SCENE EIGHT

The operating room. MAMA CHU *is wheeled into place by* NURSE/ANESTHESIOLOGIST. DOCTOR *steps up to her under bright lights.* MAMA CHU *looks barely awake. We hear her heartbeat.*

NURSE: Good morning, Doctor. Ready?

DOCTOR: This patient is wrong side up, Nurse.

NURSE: Your procto exam is later, Doctor. This is your grapefruit tumor.

DOCTOR: (*Without skipping a beat.*) I knew that. Of course . . . Mrs. Reyes . . . are you there? Speak to me, Mrs. Reyes.

NURSE: It's Flores, Doctor. Sorry.

DOCTOR: (*Grinning chagrin.*) Flores . . . Yesss. I'm afraid I'm a bit off my game this morning, Blanche. My second wife is suing me for divorce.

NURSE: (*Dripping sarcasm.*) Oh, Dick, what happened? Another slip of the Dick?

DOCTOR: That's beneath you, Nurse.

NURSE: Every nurse on every floor of this hospital has been beneath you, Doctor. I should know. . . It goes with the job.

DOCTOR: Can you hear me, Mrs. Flores? I'm Doctor Jory. My anesthesiologist is going to put you under now, so we can proceed with your exploratory surgery, your bi-oopsia, did I say that right? We're going into that bola that the X-Rays revealed in your panza. We're going to excise un poquito. Then we'll be finito. Okey doakie? Superb. (MAMA CHU *mumbles something indecipherable.* DOCTOR *leans in.*)

MAMA CHU: Doctor Yori . . . ¿dónde está el Cajeme?

DOCTOR: What's that, Mrs. Flores?

MAMA CHU: No encuentro al yaqui . . . No lo siento . . . ¡Se me perdió el Cajeme!

DOCTOR: (*Simultaneously.*) Hmmm, I see . . . You don't say . . . Aaah, superb.

NURSE: What's she saying?

DOCTOR: How the fuck should I know? The old bag is rambling. Take her under. (DOCTOR *pinches* NURSE's *bum.* SHE *places a gas mask on* MAMA CHU.)

NURSE: And awaaay we go. (*Lights dim to black, as we begin to hear the pounding of* MAMA CHU's *heart. Scrapers and rattles in background. Upstage center. Lights reveal a miasma of veins and arteries throbbing with blood. Rowdy circus music. Spotlights slash across* MAMA CHU's *bed.* CAJEME *comes out running, rattling, aroused by the commotion.*)

COSME: (*O.S.*) ¡Señores, señoras, señoritas, y lo que quede! El Circo Azteca proudly presents an Impossible Act of Love: ¡Agustina, La Mariposa fina, y El venaditoooo! (COSME *appears, with a small piñata deer head on his crown.*)

Soy un pobre venadito
que habito en la serranía
aunque no soy tan mansito-o-o
no-o-o bajo al agua de día
de noche poco a poquito
y en tus brazos, ¡vida mía!

(CAJEME *calms down, mesmerized by her . . .*)

COSME: La Mariposa, that most beautiful of los insectos . . . began her life as a caterpillar . . . a sexy black gusano with jazzy red horns. (AGUSTINA *appears dancing to the "St. Louis Blues," wearing a scant costume c. 1936.* AGUSTINA *dances.* COSME *plays puppeteer.*) Un día when she was munching on a leaf, she ran into a Deer. He was speechless, in fact, he was a mute, but ¡Caray! It was love at first sight. They had lunch together. (COSME *plays the deer, holding out a prop leaf to feed* AGUSTINA. HE *lifts a crow puppet and attacks* AGUSTINA, *the caterpillar.*) Suddenly, out of the blue, Don Cuervo swooped down ready to eat the worm. The Deer, fighting to save her, slashed his horns at the crow. ¿Y saben qué? He won! (HE *skewers the crow on his horns.* AGUSTINA *withdraws into her black chemise flapper dress.*) The next day the worm buried herself in a cocoon y el venadito thought she was dead. ¡Pero no! She was reborn as a beautiful butterfly. (AGUSTINA *emerges with spectacular wings.* COSME *strokes her.*) Little did he know, she was doomed to die young. But the sex was unbelievable! (*Circus fanfare.*) The Butterfly and The Deer! (*Squinting from her bed,* MAMA CHU *confuses* COSME *for* CAJEME.)

MAMA CHU: Agustina! What are you doing? Cajeme doesn't belong in your filthy circo!

AGUSTINA: Oh, no? Where does he belong?

MAMA CHU: Don't touch him like that.

COSME: Señora, you're screwing up the act.

AGUSTINA: ¿Qué le pasa, Mamá? Having troubles with your little deer? He's not getting horny on you, is he?

MAMA CHU: ¡Cómo serás! Is there no respect for madres in this world anymore?

AGUSTINA: That depends on the madres. Madres puras are not the same as puras madres.

MAMA CHU: You have no shame!

AGUSTINA: You were the one who held the family together, Mama Chu. Sometimes we all slept in the same bed, shivering under one blanket, but we were happy . . .

MAMA CHU: We were a family . . . Bendito sea Dios . . . without a father.

AGUSTINA: (*Sweetly sarcastic.*) Not even Papá Lucas? Or Papá Güero?! You remember Oralia's daddy, don't you, Mama Chu?

MAMA CHU: Don't mention Güero Azul to me.

AGUSTINA: Then there were the off days, when you got into one of your killer moods, and we never knew who was on your shit list. Most of the time, it was me.

MAMA CHU: Ay, Agustina, what you put me through! You made me suffer la pena negra.

AGUSTINA: I grew up washing the calzones of strangers.

MAMA CHU: Don't talk to me about men's calzones!

AGUSTINA: It's not like you don't know what hangs inside them. . . . after three husbands. I knew what was going on, even as a kid.

MAMA CHU: We took in laundry, we cooked for the men, that's all that was going on! I crossed the border and raised my children by myself, like a decent woman, ¡gracias a Dios! None of my so-called husbands helped me. My son helped me to buy my house.

AGUSTINA: You ran a hellavu boarding house, Mama Chu. Oralia was the bait, and I was the maid. Guess who got screwed? Cinderella.

MAMA CHU: Malcriada . . . that was that hot yaqui blood of yours . . . That's why you left me! You got hot and ran off with that goddamm clown!

AGUSTINA: I never asked you to follow me.

MAMA CHU: How dare you. I told you that hijo de la chingada would abandon you. (COSME *waves from upstage center, where he has been inticing* CAJEME *with his prop of green leaves.*)

AGUSTINA: No. I abandoned him. You made me despise him. . . . But through all those years, you never told us you had a dirty little secret, did you, Mama Chu?

COSME: The Crying Woman of the Revolution.

MAMA CHU: ¡Cállate la boca!

AGUSTINA: I had a dirty little secret of my own. It's hard to be a santa madre if you don't spread your legs.

MAMA CHU: Shut up, I tell you! Go away!

AGUSTINA: You knew what was going on, but to admit that was to uncover all of your own lies.

MAMA CHU: Liar! ¡Mentirosa!

AGUSTINA: Don't be a hypocrite, Mama Chu. It was you who turned me into a puta. (AGUSTINA *lies back on* MAMA CHU's *bed, lifting her legs.* CAJEME *innocently appears upstage between her legs.* AGUSTINA *stands and pulls him out provocatively.*)

MAMA CHU: WHAT! Shameless demonios!! What are you doing? Under my very eyes! You will burn in Hell forever! (THEY *rush into the shadows.* COSME *retreats.*) (*Horrified.*) Cajeme! Yaqui desgraciado, you godammit! You are brother and sister!

Blackout.

SCENE NINE

The cafeteria. The next morning. ORALIA *and* TILLY *enter, carrying a bag of coffee and donuts.*

ORALIA: Where is everybody? Isn't anybody here? Don't tell me! I'm the only one who gives a damn about Mama Chu?

TILLY: (*Opening the bag.*) They spent the night. Maybe they already had breakfast.

ORALIA: Look at the size of that cinnamon roll. Are you starting to show? Pull in that panza, ¡ándale! I don't want anybody to know about this, especially Mama Chu . . . you hear me? The shock would kill her. You're her angel . . .

TILLY: It's gotta come out sometime.

ORALIA: You little slut! Do you want to kill your grandmother? It'd be different if it was your putita cousin, Armi . . . (ARMIDA *enters with* PROFE. *Without missing a beat* ORALIA *says.*) Mira, mira. There you are! Boy, you two look beat. I didn't sleep a wink neither. Tossing and turning . . . turning and tossing. Tilly, crack out the coffee and donuts.

TILLY: (*Dispensing.*) How's Mama Chu?

ARMIDA: Just out of the O.R.. The doctor said he'll come talk to us as soon as he can.

PROFE: No coffee for me. My nervous stomach.

ORALIA: I thought it was a weak bladder.

TILLY: So you met Doctor Jory?

ARMIDA: I spoke to the nurse.

ORALIA: Wait till you meet the doctor . . . looks just like, éste, cómo se llama . . . the one on TV? El Doctor Kildaire, hombre.

TILLY: Richard Chamberlain?

ORALIA: ¡Ese mero! Don't you think the doctor looks like your dad when he had hair?

TILLY: I didn't know my dad when he had hair.

ORALIA: He was a handsome güerote . . . with blue grey eyes like a wolf . . . born in Mexico. That's his weakness.

ARMIDA: Since when is being a handsome güerote a weakness?

ORALIA: You know how machos are! We haven't been married for the last thirty years for nothing . . . Why? What have you heard?

ARMIDA: About what?

ORALIA: About nothing! Jack's a good provider . . . Running his plumbing business. Laying pipe all over town . . . Men are pigs.

TILLY: Here comes the doctor! (DOCTOR *enters, with a cup of coffee.* HE *starts to light a cigarette. His toothy grin and nasal tones evoke a superior air.*)

ORALIA: That's the kind of piggy I want for you. Oye, Doctor Kildeer, over here.

DOCTOR: Superb. Yes . . . may I sit down?

ORALIA: Not unless you wanna lay down . . . Just kidding, hombre, just kidding! (PROFE *frowns as* ORALIA *guffaws.* TILLY *rolls her eyes.*)

TILLY: You want some sticky roll, Doctor?

DOCTOR: (*Holding his unlit cigarette.*) No, thank you . . . Let me get
right to the point. Here's the situation. I have some good news and
some bad news. The good news is the tumor isn't malignant. Or
benign. It's not the big C. It's not even a tumor.

ORALIA: Oh, thank God! Thank you, Jesus!

PROFE: ¡Gracias a Dios!

TILLY: Does that mean grandma's gonna live?

DOCTOR: Barring other complications . . .

TILLY: What complications?

DOCTOR: Uterolgia . . . eclampsia . . . osteoporosis. The possibilities
are legion.

ARMIDA: What's the bad news?

DOCTOR: The bad news is that there's still a rather sizable growth in
her corpus, not abdominal but uterine.

ARMIDA: In her uterus?

DOCTOR:In her matrix, yes. Such as it is. It's hardly unnatural, but
long overdue for obstetric extraction.

ARMIDA: (*Brightly.*) What are you saying? Are you saying what I
think you're saying?

DOCTOR: What do you think I'm saying?

ARMIDA: She isn't . . . is she?

DOCTOR: (*Impressed.*) Yes, as a matter of fact, she is.

ARMIDA: You can't be serious!

DOCTOR: Oh, yes!

ARMIDA: That's impossible!

PROFE, ORALIA, TILLY: WHAT?

ORALIA: What's impossible? What the hell's the matter with Mama
Chu!

ARMIDA: She's pregnant!

TILLY: Grandma?! (*A breathless pause in silence. Then the shocked
exhalations.*)

ORALIA: Naw-uhhh! How can she be pregnant?!

PROFE: She's 84 years old! More or less.

DOCTOR: I'm aware of her age. Más o menos.

TILLY: This is ridiculous!

DOCTOR: I need to explain something . . .

ORALIA: Mama Chu having a baby? Somebody godamn well better explain something!

DOCTOR: The fetus is mummified. (*The family members look at the* DOCTOR *with disbelief.*)

ARMIDA: What do you mean . . . mummified?

DOCTOR: Perfectly preserved. About two pounds. Deceased, of course.

ORALIA: Inside Mama Chu?

DOCTOR: Cradled into a tight fetal position no larger than a bloated softball.

TILLY: Male or female?

DOCTOR: Hard to say. It's been that way for quite some time.

PROFE: For how long?

DOCTOR: We're running some tests, but it appears perhaps as long as sixty years . . .

PROFE: Sixty . . . years?!

TILLY: How can that be?! How could it be inside of her for so long and nobody know it?

DOCTOR: (*Grinning.*) Obviously, she hails from Mexico, yesss?

ARMIDA: The real question is did Mama Chu know it? And why would she keep it a secret? How can a pregnant woman not give birth? (DOCTOR *looks at* Armida, *appraising her smart demeanor.*)

DOCTOR: Some things defy medical logic, Miss Flores, especially south of the border.

ARMIDA: Miss Bravo. I'm her granddaughter. And I don't appreciate being condescended to, Doctor. I'm a graduate student at Cal Berkeley.

DOCTOR: I see . . . Who is being condescending to whom, Miss . . . Bravo?

ORALIA: Oye, Doctor. Where does this leave Mama Chu? What's gonna happen to her?

DOCTOR: Our options are only two really. One is a standard C section, remove the fetus surgically, cleanly, and hope for the best. Or . . .

ARMIDA: Let the fetus stay where it is.

DOCTOR: Exactly.

ORALIA: Can't you just yank that little sucker out of there?

DOCTOR: Well, yes, a Caesarean is easy enough, even at her advanced age . . . but either way her prognosis is not good.

TILLY: Is it bad? (THEY *all look at her.*)

DOCTOR: There's no guarantee there won't be any complications. A simple C-section isn't normally life threatening, but she has heart disease, diabetes, emphysema and arthritis. Throw in a little kidney failure and you've got bingo.

ARMIDA: You mean she could . . . ?

ORALIA: Die?!

DOCTOR: I didn't say that. We can stablize her post-operative pain and put her on antibiotics, naturally . . . but she's got to fight. That depends on her will to live. (*The family exchanges glances.*)

PROFE: What do you recommend, Doctor?

DOCTOR: I'd like to go for a C-section immediately. It's clean, efficient, and quick. We can be in and out before she knows it.

ARMIDA: (*Incensed.*) You can't operate!

ORALIA: Yes, he can! He's got to!

ARMIDA: How do we know it won't kill her . . . to lose the fetus she's been carrying for sixty years! Shouldn't we ask Mama Chu how she fucking feels about it?

ORALIA: Don't you use that language with me!

ARMIDA: It's Mama Chu's choice, Tía! This is almost like an abortion.

DOCTOR: You may be right. She's lived with the fetus for this long, perhaps it's best to let sleeping dogs lie.

ARMIDA: (*Sarcastic.*) Did you suddenly turn into a veterinarian, Doctor?

DOCTOR: I beg your pardon?

ARMIDA: How many Third World women have you spayed?

DOCTOR: (*Rolling his eyes.*) I recommend that you discuss this among yourselves. As far as I'm concerned, the decision to operate or not is up to you, her family, in consultation, of course, with the patient. We're taking her back upstairs, where you can speak to her as soon as she is conscious. Yes? Superb. (DOCTOR *starts to exit, finally lighting his smoke, but* ARMIDA *waylays him to one side.*)

ARMIDA: Doctor?

DOCTOR: Miss Bravo?

ARMIDA: One more thing . . . If Mama Chu has carried this fetus for sixty years, what are the implications for the rest of her family?

DOCTOR: Above or below the equator. Can you be more specific?

ARMIDA: Could she have given birth to . . . her later children?

DOCTOR: Is this a trick question?

ARMIDA: Just answer yes or no.

DOCTOR: I think you know the answer.

ARMIDA: She'd be sterile, wouldn't she?!

DOCTOR: Frankly, my dear . . . I wouldn't worry about it.

NURSE: (*O.S.*)(*On the intercom.*) Doctor Jory. Calling Doctor Jory. You're wanted in the O.R., Doctor.

ARMIDA: Do you know where that leaves us?

DOCTOR: I have a rectal exam waiting. More than that I'd rather not say. (DOCTOR *goes. The others turn, with fearful concern.*)

ORALIA: Wait a minute, what the hell are you driving at, prieta?

PROFE: Sterile! What are you saying?

TILLY: She just likes to use big words.

ARMIDA: How old are you, Tía?

ORALIA: What the hell does that have to do with anything!

ARMIDA: Fifty?

ORALIA: Forty-nine! I was born in 1920.

ARMIDA: And my mother would have been fifty-one because she was born in 1918. Five years after Profe!

PROFE: So the hell what?

ARMIDA: You're only fifty-six, Tío. If Mama Chu's been pregnant for sixty years, how could she have given birth to you or to any of her children, including . . . my mother? (*There is a stunned silence.*)

TILLY: Are you saying Mama Chu's not really our grandmother?

ARMIDA: I don't know, but if it's true . . . we're not Mama Chu's flesh and blood . . . are we?

ORALIA: Enough! ¡Ya basta! Shut up, just shut up! Go away! You've never wanted to be part of this family. I don't what to hear anymore of this shit!

TILLY: Me neither! You're a real bitch, Army. You think you're so smart. (ORALIA *and* TILLY *hurry out.* ARMIDA*'s mind is racing.*)

ARMIDA: (*Desperately.*) I want the truth, Profe, once and for all. I need to put the pieces together. I need dates, facts, names! Everything you can remember. Do you now understand how important this is?

PROFE: It's all or nothing . . .

ARMIDA: The mummified fetus puts us all in limbo. This is worse than a death in the family. It's the death of the family. Cut off at the root! Who are we, Tío?

PROFE: (*Under his breath.*) Los hijos de La Chingada . . .

Fade to black.

ACT TWO

SCENE ONE

Darkness. The wail of the train, approaching from a distance. Lights upstage on MAMA CHU, lying unconscious in her hospital bed, attached to the life support equipment blinking, beeping and hissing in the dim light.

PROFE: I never knew my father . . . he was killed before I was born. It was always just Mama Chu and me . . . (*Downstage, PROFE is sitting with ARMIDA in the waiting room, strumming on his guitar.*) We came out of the Revolution . . . we came in a Yaqui troop train. Mama Chu was a five-year veteran of the war by then. Besides being a widow, she had already lost most of her snotnoses in Mexico . . . only one survived. Her only mocoso, me. (*Upstage. A boisterous crowd enters. Among them is CAJEME, without deer horns, as PEDRITO. The crowd climbs on MAMA CHU's bed, doubling as the top of a boxcar. PEDRITO gets lost.*)

MAMA CHU: Pedrito? Pedrito, mijito, up here!

PEDRITO: (*Running to her, stuttering.*) ¡M-m-ma . . . m-maá! (*Music. MAMA CHU sits PEDRITO beside her, a stoic icon in a rebozo, as the train sways, a moving image from the Mexican Revolution, c. 1916. "La Marcha de Zacatecas" plays.*)

PROFE: The indio rebels were about to attack Nogales, so the Mexican Government sent Yaqui draftees to the border to fight their own people. Mama Chu and I came all the way from the Yucatán. . . (*Troop train steams into a station, whistles blowing.*) The raza was coming across the border like a human flood pouring into Tucson . . . so that's where we went . . . just Mama Chu and me . . . into the teeming barrios. (*The cacophony of the station. MAMA CHU climbs off the bed and maneuvers through the moving crowd.*)

MAMA CHU: Pedrito, stay with me, my son.

33

PROFE: I was late in learning to talk. I don't know why. Words just wouldn't come out.

ARMIDA: How old were you, Profe?

PROFE: I was five. Musta been about 1916, 1917, más o menos. Mama Chu was around thirty.

ARMIDA: I can't imagine Mama Chu so young. (MAMA CHU *turns to* PEDRITO, *scrubbing clothes in a washtub.*)

MAMA CHU: Pedrito, por dios, get out of the sun, ¡chamaco! You're turning black as zapote! How many times do I have to tell you? The gringos will eat you alive!

PROFE: She hasn't changed . . . except she's toothless now. I remember when she still attracted men. Lots of men. She made good money.

ARMIDA: You don't mean . . . Mama Chu sold her body?

PROFE: Well, no, but she rented it a little. Back then she was chichona enough to work as a wet nurse. The amazing thing is she always had milk. If she wasn't feeding babies, she was bringing them into the world. That's how she met your Tata. (*Dogs bark in the distance.* LUCAS FLORES, *38, appears, dressed in miner's clothes, carrying a woman in his arms.*)

LUCAS: (*Whispering.*) ¡Señora!

MAMA CHU: Who's there?

LUCAS: Lucas Flores!

ARMIDA: My grandfather?

PROFE: He came in the middle of the night . . . (LUCAS *is desperate, walking in the crumpled figure of his wife.* HE *removes his straw hat with a candle riding on the brim.*)

LUCAS: Doña Chu, please excuse this molestia. They tell me you're a midwife. My woman is about to . . . part with child.

MAMA CHU: Come in. Lay her down on the bed. (LUCAS *lays his wife on the bed.* MAMA CHU *examines her.*)

PROFE: Back in Sonora, he had been a Pascola dancer in the Yaqui Easter Ceremony. Now he was just another refugee, a miner from up around Bisbee. A labor agitator.

MAMA CHU: Why did you wait so long to bring her?

LUCAS: La huelga. We're on strike in the copper mines. You must know how it is.

MAMA CHU: I don't know anything. I don't want trouble.

LUCAS: Can you deliver her?

MAMA CHU: This woman doesn't have the strength to give birth! It'll kill her.

LUCAS: No. She's come a long way. She can't desert me now . . . Save her, please, even if we lose the baby. Just don't let her die!

MAMA CHU: That's not up to me, it's up to God.

LUCAS: She would want God to save the child . . . Do what you have to do.

MAMA CHU: (*Sign of the cross.*) ¡En el nombre sea de Dios! (WOMAN lets out a terrible scream. MAMA CHU goes to work.)

PROFE: Mama Chu delivered the baby, but the woman died, giving birth to a daughter. Don Lucas was beside himself with grief . . . Before dawn, he took his dead wife out to bury, leaving the baby girl with Mama Chu. (LUCAS *picks up the woman's body and takes her out.* MAMA CHU *lies down with the baby.* PEDRITO *sleeps on the floor.*) Her milk started to flow as soon as she lay down so she fed the child her breast. The child fed and slept in her arms for a day and a half. The following night Lucas returned, drunk with grief. . . . (LUCAS *touches* MAMA CHU *in bed with the baby.* SHE *abruptly sits up, aware of his urgent sexuality.* PEDRITO *wakes and listens.*)

MAMA CHU: ¡Epa!

LUCAS: Did I scare you, Doña Chu? Sorry. I was just looking for my daughter.

MAMA CHU: What for? What are you doing?

LUCAS: I'm going back . . . to Sonora. Tonight.

MAMA CHU: Are you crazy?

LUCAS: The gringo sheriffs are looking for me.

MAMA CHU: What??

LUCAS: There's a warrant out for my arrest.

MAMA CHU: (*Gets up,* PEDRITO *crawls into bed.*) Why?

LUCAS: They're deporting all the yaquis who aren't sheep. All the rebels and troublemakers wanted by the Mexicans. If they catch me here . . .

MAMA CHU: (*Fear turning to rage.*) They'll deport all of us! What have you done? Me lleva la triste chingada . . . Get out of my house! ¡Ándale, hombre! Go!

LUCAS: I'll be executed . . . unless I can get to the Bacatete Mountains and join the Yaqui resistance. (*The baby wakes up crying.* MAMA CHU *breast feeds her.*)

MAMA CHU: Don't talk to me of yaquis! We aren't yaquis here! We're fish out of water, gasping to breathe, and drowning in the air . . . maids, farm workers, mano de obra. We're invisible . . .

LUCAS: We're indios. On both sides of the border.

MAMA CHU: I don't want trouble. That's why I left Mexico. I'd rather be invisible.

LUCAS: You are a woman.

MAMA CHU: You are a godemeh fool.

LUCAS: Better to die like a dog fighting for our Yaqui lands in Sonora than to live here . . . like a dog . . . Eating the scraps of gringos.

MAMA CHU: At least we aren't dodging bullets in the deserts. No, gracias a Dios, we're here . . . in los Estados Unidos . . . and here we are Mexicans not indios!

LUCAS: (HE *stares at his daughter.* PEDRITO *looks at him curiously.*) What about my daughter?

MAMA CHU: She's asleep, can't you see?

LUCAS: I see you've been feeding her.

MAMA CHU: Would you rather she starve to death?

LUCAS: After what her mother went through . . . don't be heartless. What if . . . I leave her with you?

MAMA CHU: For how long?

LUCAS: (*Shrugs.*) Sepa. I'll be back to claim her when it's safe. . . . Then I'll pay you.

MAMA CHU: Pay me now.

LUCAS: I have no money.

MAMA CHU: I don't give credit.

LUCAS: Then she's yours . . . if I don't come back.

MAMA CHU: (*Ambivalent.*) She's a pretty little monkey, but I know my people. She's going to need the kind of discipline only a Yoeme mother can give.

LUCAS: Aren't you a Yoeme mother?

MAMA CHU: (*Bluntly.*) My entire familia was killed in the war, señor. I came all the way from the Yucatán with my little son, and never looked back. You don't know what I've been through.

LUCAS: We're all orphans of the storm, mi Chu . . .

MAMA CHU: Leave her then.

LUCAS: I don't want her baptized, but I want her to have her mother's name. Armida . . . Do you understand? Armida!

MAMA CHU: You'd better go. (LUCAS *shrugs, leans over and kisses the baby.*)

LUCAS: Adiós, mi'jita. . . . I'll be back. Pronto. I promise you.

MAMA CHU: Don't promise. Just go! (LUCAS *exits. Lights crossfade upstage to downstage.*)

PROFE: So! That's how your mother was born . . . Of course, Mama Chu named her Agustina. Not Armida. That's your name.

ARMIDA: Hold it, Profe. Agustina, daughter of Armida . . . Are you saying I was named after my biological grandmother?

PROFE: Más o menos.

ARMIDA: Then my mother must have known about her!

PROFE: What makes you say that?

ARMIDA: Why else would she name me after her? She must have done it to spite Mama Chu. How did she find out about her?

PROFE: You're getting ahead of the story . . . (*Pause.*) Lucas went back to fight in the Revolution, and Mama Chu waited for his return. He didn't come back . . . for fifteen years.

ARMIDA: Fifteen years!

PROFE: The federales caught him, sentenced him to hard labor in a Yaqui prison.

ARMIDA: What did Mama Chu do?

PROFE: She washed clothes . . .

Cross-fade.

SCENE TWO

MAMA CHU *scrubs clothes in a washtub, c.1918–20.* AGUSTINA *rides in on* PEDRITO's *back, giggling with delight.*

PROFE: While Mama Chu worked, I watched over Agustina . . . We were alone, but we had each other, so we grew up . . . real close. Like brother and sister. After a few years in Bisbee, we moved on to La Mesa outside of Phoenix. Mama Chu never got around to telling Agustina the truth.

ARMIDA: (*Glaring at him.*) You knew! Why didn't you tell her?

PROFE: She was still a little girl. Besides, we thought Lucas Flores was dead . . .

MAMA CHU: Pedrito, Agustina . . . Settle down!

PROFE: And a new stepfather came into our lives. (*Spanish music. Enter* DON GÜERO *sporting a flaring mustache, dressed in black from his hat and cape to his boots.* HE *carries a small bundle in a blanket.* MAMA CHU *waits expectantly.*) He'd made a lot of money in the weapons trade, selling German Mausers below the border and hauling back freight. Mama Chu got to cooking and cleaning for him . . . (DON GÜERO *stops before* MAMA CHU, *who bows flirtatiously.*)

MAMA CHU: Don Güero . . . what do you have there . . . your laundry?

DON GÜERO: A sunflower, Doña Chu . . . (MAMA CHU *opens the blanket and gasps.* SHE *takes the baby.*)

MAMA CHU: ¡Pero qué chula! She looks just like . . . a little angel.

DON GÜERO: . . . As fair-skinned as my sainted mother in Vienna. They tell me your breasts always have milk. Would you be so kind as to . . . give her suck?

MAMA CHU: (*Overwhelmed.*) Cómo no, Don Güero. . . . with pleasure. Pase Ud, niños go play. (PEDRITO *and* AGUSTINA *exit.*) What's the beautiful angelito's name?

DON GÜERO: I didn't ask. I came back from Texas to find all my servants dying . . . including my mistress. You Yaquis must be immune. The Spanish flu epidemic is killing everybody. (MAMA CHU *sits on the bed to breastfeed the baby.* DON GÜERO *eyes her with rising interest.*)

MAMA CHU: ¡Ay, santo! Such a hungry little mouth. I'm going to call her . . . Oralia!

DON GÜERO: Call her what you like. You are truly . . . generously endowed, Doña Chu. But you're letting God's gifts go to waste.

MAMA CHU: Ay, Don Güero. Babies are the true gifts of God. One only serves the Señor. . . speaking as a widow.

DON GÜERO: Vale. Vale. You're too young to be a widow. I own a private house in Phoenix. Are you open to more permanent employment? (MAMA CHU *sits up before his devouring eyes.*)

MAMA CHU: What are you proposing, señor?

DON GÜERO: I need servants. The child needs a wetnurse. You can live in my house, and bring your son and daughter. They can work for their keep. What do you say—¿juega?

MAMA CHU: I can cook, clean, nurse, wash, and sew. What else do you expect from me?

DON GÜERO: (*Bluntly, his nostrils flaring.*) Piety and breeding . . . privileges. For myself.

MAMA CHU: I can give you all the services of a good wife, señor . . . providing, of course, you make me a decent proposal of marriage.

DON GÜERO: (*Bemused.*) Marriage? ¡Coño! Why would a cristiano like me want to marry his Indian servant? Who do you think you are?

MAMA CHU: (*Fiercely proud.*) I was raised in a French household in Guaymas, Don Güero.

DON GÜERO: Don't be foolish. This is an opportunity. Maids sell by the ton along the border.

MAMA CHU: I'm not a Yori puta!

DON GÜERO: You're making a big mistake.

MAMA CHU: Better alone than in bad company, señor. This is los Estados Unidos.

DON GÜERO: ¡Mira, mira! Don't put on airs with me, eh? You came to los Estados Unidos by the grace of God, through the asshole of the country. ¡Carajo! . . . You arouse me, prietita. I can smell your raw womanhood. You and I could breed sons together.

MAMA CHU: Bastard sons?

DON GÜERO: Half breeds. So they can work for me.

MAMA CHU: For half pay? I'm not interested. Even for the sake of this beautiful angelito. Here, take her. (SHE *holds out the baby to him. The baby starts crying.* DON GÜERO *fingers his loaded revolver, darkly, insanely.*)

DON GÜERO: Very well. ¡Coño! I'll marry you . . . on my honor as a *caballero.* By the power vested in me by the Common Law . . . (HE *pulls the pistol up to her head.*)

MAMA CHU: Don Güero, por favor.

DON GÜERO: I hereby pronounce us man and wife! En el nombre del padre, del hijo, y del espíritu santo. ¡Amen! (HE *makes the sign of the cross with his gun, laughing.*)

PROFE: So that's how Mama Chu ended up in her second marriage . . . She fell in love . . . with your tía! Fat and pink and pretty, right? A real Cupie Doll . . . My stepfather, unfortunately, turned out to be a real hijo de la chingada. (PEDRITO *comes forward, curiously nosing about the baby.*)

DON GÜERO: ¡Oye, tú! Animal, get away from that baby. And get off your lazy culo, eh? ¡Indio huevón! Go to work! (DON GÜERO *throws a rock, which* PEDRITO *ducks, as he runs out.*)

PROFE: His name was Güero Azul . . . because of his one blue eye. Thanks to my padrastro, I grew up fast, real fast, waking up to his two finger whistle every morning, ducking his rocks and feet. . . . He was one stingy desgraciado lemme tell you . . . coming and going to Texas and Mexico all the time. We lived in his house like servants. We didn't starve . . . but we were always hungry. (DON GÜERO *walks up to* MAMA CHU, *carrying a gunny sack.*)

DON GÜERO: ¡Ándale! Make me something to eat.

MAMA CHU: (*Feisty.*) Bring me something to cook, señor.

DON GÜERO: (*Tossing the sack.*) Here! Meat! ¡Garbanzo, frijol! A week's provisions. (PEDRITO *and* AGUSTINA *re-enter, looking hungry.*) Did your starving mocosos eat everything again? I want that boy to go to work.

MAMA CHU: This won't last two days. I'm going to start taking in washing again.

DON GÜERO: Scrubbing other men's clothes like an india patarajada? ¡No, mi señora!

MAMA CHU: I've got to feed my children!

DON GÜERO: Let them suck on your fountains of milk and honey.

MAMA CHU: Don't be crude.

DON GÜERO: Your little brown bastards are not mine, *¿me oyes?* It's been a year . . . Why aren't you pregnant yet?

MAMA CHU: Maybe you're shooting blanks.

DON GÜERO: (*Incensed.*) Get into bed.

MAMA CHU: In the middle of the day?

DON GÜERO: Now!

MAMA CHU: No! The children. Niños, go outside. (SHE *gives them bread.* PEDRITO *and* AGUSTINA *exit.*)

DON GÜERO: I'll give you some blanks! (HE *flings her onto bed, and bends her over, lifting her skirts.*)

MAMA CHU: Güero, ¡por el amor de Dios!

DON GÜERO: (*Sign of the cross.*) En el nombre del padre, del hijo, y del espíritu santo. Not for lust, señor, and not for pleasure, but to serve thy will! (DON GÜERO *thrusts, plunging like a bull. Lights down.*)

PROFE: He wanted a son of his own loins, you see? Unfortunately, year after year passed and Mama Chu couldn't get pregnant. Don Güero's eye began to wander. Mama Chu ignored his philanderings and took care of his house, happy we were living like gringos. We even had running water and electric light. (*A light bulb glows upstage, dimming up to full.* MAMA CHU *and her children gather round the bulb, c. 1927, oohing and ahhing.*) Then, after nine years together, Don Güero's eye finally landed on Agustina. (DON GÜERO *leers at ten-year-old* AGUSTINA *playing with* PEDRO.)

DON GÜERO: ¡Coño! This little one is almost ready for the . . . chínguele, chínguele. (*Pulls out a candy cane and whispers.*) Agustina . . . see? For you, mi'jita. (AGUSTINA *goes for it.* MAMA CHU *glares at him.*) ¡¿Qué?! (AGUSTINA *runs out.* DON GÜERO *follows her.* MAMA CHU *turns away. Downstage* ARMIDA *stares incredulously at* PROFE.)

ARMIDA: No.

PROFE: Yes.

ARMIDA: He molested my mother?!

PROFE: For years.

ARMIDA: Years! Where the hell was Mama Chu? Couldn't she tell what was going on? (PEDRITO *goes after* AGUSTINA.)

PROFE: Mama Chu was blind to everything but Oralia. She was afraid to lose her. . . . Times were hard . . . People did what they had to do just to survive. Don Güero always had money, and he spoke inglés.

DON GÜERO: You little son of a bitch, get OUT! (DON GÜERO *slaps* PEDRITO *and kicks him back out, onstage.*)

ARMIDA: What a bastard . . . (AGUSTINA *emerges wounded.* PEDRITO *tries to console her.*)

PROFE: In the end, after years of taking his insultos y patadas, your grandma found out he had six other wives and dozens of children in Mexico and Texas. (DON GÜERO *appears with a bigger lollipop.*)

DON GÜERO: Oralia! Shhh! Ven aquí . . . (ORALIA *runs out, chasing after* DON GÜERO *and the lollipop.* MAMA CHU *notices she is missing.*)

PROFE: Then she caught him trying to molest little Oralia.

ORALIA: (*Running out frightened.*) Ma-MAAA!

ARMIDA: You gotta be fucking kidding me!

PROFE: Cállate. That was the last straw. She locked him out of the house . . . (MAMA CHU *moves the bed to block the door.*)

DON GÜERO: (*O.S.*) ¡Doña Chu! Open the door, señora! I'm here to take my daughter where she belongs. With my civilized white wife in Texas.

MAMA CHU: No, señor! Go back to your civilized bolillas in Texas! Niños, quickly come to me! (DON GÜERO *breaks down the door and enters, seething with rage.*)

DON GÜERO: ¡Arrastrada, india babosa! (PEDRITO *comes out of the shadows and jumps on* DON GÜERO.)

PEDRITO: NOOOO! (DON GÜERO *throws* PEDRITO *to the floor*).

DON GÜERO: ¡Hijo de perra! You wouldn't do that if you were my flesh and blood. Twelve years, mujer! Twelve long years, wasted, without a son. It isn't me. It's you! A curse has dried up your insides! Worthless cunt! (*Pulling out his pistol.*) ¡Yaqui seca! I'm going to shoot you and your savages in the head, right here, right now . . . Who'll give a damn? Like killing animals! (HE *points the gun at* PEDRITO *then at* AGUSTINA.)

MAMA CHU: ¡DESGRACIADO! (MAMA CHU *hits* DON GÜERO *over the head with something and sends him reeling.* PEDRITO *kicks him. Both pummel him unconscious.* PEDRITO *picks up the gun and points it at* DON GÜERO *on the ground.*) Pedrito, no! (PEDRITO *comes to his senses and drops the gun.* MAMA CHU *gathers her children and hugs them desperately.*)

PROFE: Mama Chu packed up our belongings, and we left Don Güero's house that very night . . . We took Oralia with us. She never saw her father again . . . He died a year later. One of his mules kicked him in the head. (*There is a pregnant pause.*)

ARMIDA: This is really screwed up . . . I mean, how can I ever look at Tía Oralia the same way again?

PROFE: You wanted to know . . .

ARMIDA: Does she know?

PROFE: She wants Mama Chu's house . . . That's all she knows. She's Don Güero's daughter.

Fade to black.

SCENE THREE

MAMA CHU'*s room. Late morning.* ORALIA *and* TILLY *are sitting next to* MAMA CHU, *who is lying in her bed drifting in and out of consciousness.* ARMIDA *and* PROFE *join them.*

ORALIA: She's opening her eyes . . . I think she's coming to! Mama Chu, can hear me? We're all here, Mama Chu. Me, Tilly, Profe, and

look here, even this one. Do you recognize her? I forced the renegada to come see you! (ORALIA *pulls* ARMIDA *over to the bed.*)

ARMIDA: Hello, Mama Chu.

MAMA CHU: ¿Quién eres tú?

ARMIDA: (*Taken aback.*) Armida.

PROFE: Agustina's daughter.

MAMA CHU: (*Baffled.*) Who?

ARMIDA: Go ahead and be mad at me, if you want to, Mama Chu . . .
but we're all here because of you. We just want you to get well.

TILLY: We love you, Grandma!

ORALIA: Apologize to her.

ARMIDA: For what? I'm not sorry for wanting my own life.

PROFE: Like mother, like daughter.

MAMA CHU: (*Looking at everybody.*) ¿Cájeme . . . dónde está
Cájeme?

TILLY: What's she saying?

MAMA CHU: (*Disoriented.*) ¿Dónde estoy yo?

ARMIDA: You're in the hospital, Mama Chu. We have an important
decision to make. About your health. Do you understand?

ORALIA: Armida! You're wearing her out. Step back. Don't hog her
attention. Let others talk to her.

ARMIDA: (*Whispering.*) Somebody has to tell her what's going on.

PROFE: (*Whispering back.*) Who's gonna tell her? Are you gonna tell
her? I'm not gonna tell her.

ORALIA: How are you feeling, Mama Chu? Are doing okay? The doctor says you're going to be fine. Nothing to worry about. We'll have
you back in your casa in no time.

MAMA CHU: ¿Cuándo? ¡Yo quiero irme a mi casa!

TILLY: They can't let you go home yet, Grandma.

MAMA CHU: ¡Home! ¿Por qué no?

PROFE: Doctor's orders, Mamá. They've gotta fix you up real good
first. Take out the . . . gas.

ARMIDA: The doctor says you're carrying a fetus, Mama Chu. He says
you've been carrying it for sixty years. Do you want to tell us about it?

ORALIA: What the hell are you doing?

ARMIDA: Telling her the truth.

ORALIA: You wanna give Mama Chu a heart attack? Don't talk about
that thing right now.

TILLY: It's not a thing, it's a baby.

ORALIA: It's a mummy, dummy. You stay out of it. (TILLY *is suddenly insulted.* SHE *glares at her mother.*)

MAMA CHU: (*Sitting up.*) Ya pues, stop fighting all of you! What are you talking about?! I want to go home! ¡Yo quiero irme a mi casa! Do you hear me? (MAMA CHU *gets out of bed, and looks back at the family still gathered around the bed.* THEY *do not see her.*)

ORALIA: Oh oh . . . I think she's asleep again.

MAMA CHU: Can't anybody hear me? Is anybody there? ¿Halo? Me lleva la triste tiznada. (NURSE *enters, smiling through her teeth.*)

NURSE: Excuse me, what are you all doing here?

ARMIDA: We're visiting with my grandmother. That a problem? This is a private family discussion.

NURSE: The rules say no more than two visitors at a time.

ARMIDA: This is the first time we've talked to her since the biopsy! (MAMA CHU *walks around, observing, out of the loop.* NURSE *checks the empty bed, as if the absent patient is still there.*)

NURSE: Exactly. She's still lapsing in and out of consciousness. Yep. She's out again. Two of you have to go. ¡Pronto!

ORALIA: Tilly and I will take the first shift. You and Armida scram, Profe.

PROFE: Ni modo Quasimodo.

ARMIDA: No, wait a minute, Profe. I'd like to stay. All right with you, cuz?

TILLY: (*Defiantly looking at her mother.*) Sure. Why not?

PROFE: We're all familia, ¿qué no?

TILLY: We'll be down in the cafeteria. Eating. (PROFE *and* TILLY *exit.* NURSE *turns to* ORALIA. MAMA CHU *comes up to* ARMIDA *but her granddaughter cannot see her.*)

NURSE: Doctor Jory just called. He needs to know what the family has decided to do about the patient's condition. Should we prepare her for surgery mañana . . . or release her with a hot water bottle?

ORALIA: Surgery.

ARMIDA: No, release!

ORALIA: Do you want her to die?

ARMIDA: No, do you want to kill her?

NURSE: I'll tell him you're still working on it. (NURSE *exits.* MAMA CHU *comes back to her bed.*)

MAMA CHU: They're leaving! Is everybody leaving? ¡No se vayan! I
feel anger . . . and suspicion . . . Why can't you hear me? I hear
everything. . . .

ARMIDA: Sixty years ago, Mama Chu was my age . . . That was in
1909, can you imagine? She was still in Mexico. The vagueness of
our family history has always bothered me, but this is ridiculous.
It's like spilling an unfinished puzzle and having to start all over
again . . .

ORALIA: ¡Ay! Stop exaggerating.

ARMIDA: None of these implications seem to affect you, do they, Tía?

ORALIA: You've always been too damn smart for your own good,
mi'jita. You don't know when to keep your hociquito shut.

ARMIDA: I have a right to express my own opinion. This is a family
crisis!

ORALIA: How can there be a family crisis if you wipe out the whole
godamn family? ¡Qué cosa! Asking the doctor if Mama Chu is sterile . . . have you no respect? Don't you dare say that to your grandmother.

ARMIDA: What are we going to tell her?

ORALIA: We'll tell her the doctor said King Tut has to come out and
that's it! This is a matter of life and death.

ARMIDA: So now you admit it?

ORALIA: I don't admit nothing. Mama Chu's had these dolores de
panza for years, and it's gotten worser. That's all.

ARMIDA: But you've known all these years.

ORALIA: I didn't know she had an aborto in there. I knew she had
something, but not that. All I knew is my daddy left her because she
couldn't give him the sons he wanted.

ARMIDA: He didn't leave her, she left him.

ORALIA: (*Guardedly.*) What do you know about it?

ARMIDA: Profe told me about Don Güero.

ORALIA: What did that old wino told you?

ARMIDA: About your father . . . and my mother.

ORALIA: (*Gasps, chokes, spits it out.*) Those are nothing . . . but dirty
lies! . . . and rumors. ¡Mentiras! Profe had no business telling you
that! My daddy was a rich man. He had money and property. He
didn't have to go around doing that! He gave Mama Chu the best
years of her life. Those filthy lies were started by Agustina to get
back at me, because I was Mama Chu's favorite!

ARMIDA: Why was that, Tía?

ORALIA: (*Wiping crocodile tears.*) Because God made me . . . her
    angel. Because when Papá Lucas came back from Mexico to live
    with us, he paid more attention to me than his own flesh and blood
    daughter . . . Because even then Profe was always lying for her and
    protecting her, and I could already tell there was something fishy
    going on between them.
ARMIDA: What the hell are you saying?
ORALIA: Why do you think your mother committed suicide, mi'jita?
    Because of your father.
ARMIDA: Cosme Bravo?
ORALIA: The Butterfly and the Clown! Right. And Profe the monkey's
    uncle.
ARMIDA: Tell me about it, Tía . . . and don't pull any punches.
MAMA CHU: ¡Por el amor de Dios! No! I don't want to hear anymore!

Cross-fade.

SCENE FOUR

LUCAS FLORES *enters, an old limping ex-con, in hat and Levis.*

ORALIA: Papá Lucas came back from Mexico in 1933, and picked up
    where he left off fifteen years before . . . he moved in with Mama
    Chu. (MAMA CHU gets out of bed, and hugs him in an emotional
    moment.)
MAMA CHU: Lucas Flores, I thought you were dead.
LUCAS: Not yet. (THEY *are joined by* AGUSTINA, *16, and* PEDRI-
    TO, *21.*)
MAMA CHU: This is your daughter.
LUCAS: Armida?
MAMA CHU: No. Agustina, say hello to your father.
AGUSTINA: (*Afraid of him.*) I don't have a father. (SHE *hides behind*
    PEDRITO, *who shields her.*)
MAMA CHU: Don't be silly. He's your Papá Lucas. (*To* LUCAS.) This
    is my son. Say something, Pedro.
PEDRITO: (*Extending his hand.*) Pa-pá Lucas. (AGUSTINA *runs out,
    and* PEDRITO *protectively follows her.*)
MAMA CHU: Give her time to get used to you.
LUCAS: You didn't name her Armida.

MAMA CHU: (*Guilty.*) She doesn't know . . . about your wife. She thinks I'm her mother.

LUCAS: You never told her . . . why?

MAMA CHU: I had Pedro, Oralia, and your renegada daughter, Agustina. I had to put food in their little bellies every day. I fed them, I clothed them, I put them to bed every night. Where were you? What did you care if they lived or died? You were off in your pinche Revolución.

LUCAS: I was a prisoner of war.

MAMA CHU: You said if you didn't come back, she was mine . . . Are you going to tell her?

LUCAS: What have we got to lose?

MAMA CHU: A family. (PEDRITO *comes back in with* AGUSTINA. SHE *sheepishly hugs* LUCAS.)

ORALIA: It was in the depths of the Depression, and we were starving, but Lucas took the whole family to the circo! (*Circus music. The family goes to the circus, sitting on the bed.*) Agustina's eyes were like saucers that night, but all eyes were on me. . . . I was glowing like a white dahlia in a bed of manure. (AGUSTINA *is fidgeting and blocking* ORALIA, *who is preening herself, totally aware all eyes are upon her.*) Sit down, will you, prieta!

AGUSTINA: Don't you love this, Oralia? Isn't it exciting? A Mexican circus!

ORALIA: I'd rather be at the talkies.

AGUSTINA: Everybody's looking at you. Like a star!

MAMA CHU: My head hurts. These hard benches are hurting my nalgas. And I'm feeling fleas.

LUCAS: We just got here. Relax.

MAMA CHU: I feel a bad presentimiento . . . there's something evil in the air. We shouldn't have come! I told you, señor, te dije! But would you listen to me?

LUCAS: We're here for the jobs, mi Chu. They'll be hiring to pull down the tent tonight after the last show.

MAMA CHU: Don't you see how the men are staring at Oralia? Like lions waiting for the meat!

LUCAS: ¡Carajo! Word must have gotten out.

MAMA CHU: My angel is not for these animals! I hate this chingado rascuachi circus. Too many machos . . . verijones. ¡Vámonos! (MAMA CHU *gets up to go, as family members resist. Fanfare.*)

COSME: (*O.S.*) ¡Señores, señora, señoritas, y lo que quede! El Circo Azteca is proud to present COSME "El Paleolítico" ¡BRAVO! (COSME *enters, wrapped in a serape, wearing a caveman mask with a Spanish hat and a costume of animal skins, juggling balls and clubs. They fall, he ducks.*) ¡Ay, Chihuahua, raza! I lost my pelotas . . . but I still have my macanota, no? (HE *razzes the audience with his club.* MAMA CHU *has a flash.*)

MAMA CHU: Who's the payaso?

LUCAS: The man with the jobs.

MAMA CHU: I've seen him before . . .

COSME: I am Cosme the Caveman, ¡El Paleolítico! I may look like a stinking indio, but . . . (*Lisping.*) ¡Soy español! Vale, vale. ¡Una blanca rosa! Señorita, ¿cómo está usted esta noche?

ORALIA: Fine. Gracias. I'm Oralia Azul Flores.

COSME: ¡Coño! The flower of Spain . . . (HE *doffs his hat and kisses* ORALIA*'s hand.* MAMA CHU *slaps him.*) ¡Epa! Play along, vieja. No se haga.

LUCAS: Chu, what are you doing?

COSME: My mother-in-law, The Kickapoo Nana!

MAMA CHU: (*Trying to place him.*) ¡Qué kickapoo, baboso! Your clown face doesn't fool me . . .

COSME: ¡Ay, jijo de la guayaba! An old lover! And it was pretty old, lemme tell you.

MAMA CHU: Condenado . . . I know you. . . Who are you?

COSME: ¡El Paleolítico, señora! Here to tell the true story of how our beloved raza came to be like it is today, all colors, all shapes and all sizes. But I will need the assistance of a young moza fina. (ORALIA *stands,* MAMA CHU *pulls her back.*) Gracias, mi flor, but you are too beautiful and refined for a cave woman. The prietita there behind you will do. Yes, you, ¡véngase! What's your name, ¿chula?

AGUSTINA: Agustina.

COSME: A big aplauso for Agustina! (LUCAS, ORALIA *and* PEDRO *applaud.* COSME *picks up a prop club, and takes* AGUSTINA *upstage, whispering directions in her ear.*)

LUCAS: Sit down, Chu. You're spoiling our chances.

MAMA CHU: (*Deeply perturbed.*) I know him, I tell you . . . I've seen him before . . . someplace terrible . . .

COSME: (*O.S.*) Tan taran, tan. ¡Chile con pan! ¡Y ahora! For the anal-
fabetos among you El Circo Azteca presents: La historia de la
humanidad, in the Especta-CULO de ¡LOS PAAALEOOOO-LIII-
TI-COOOS! (*Music. "The March of the Giants." Two* CAVEMEN
and two CAVEWOMEN *enter.* COSME *walks downstage on giant
hairy boots.*) About a million years ago . . . in the days of Los Paleo-
líticos, the cavemen were all big hairy brutos over 15 feet tall,
even the women. They were all giants. (AGUSTINA *walks in on
her own hairy boots.*) But life, caray, life was short and hard. So if
a caveman wanted a vieja, ¡Zas! he just hit her over the head and
dragged her into his cave. No fijations, no notations. (COSME *hits*
Agustina *over the head and a* CAVEMAN *drags her away.* MAMA
CHU *reacts, but* LUCAS *stops her.* PEDRITO *runs onstage and
blocks him.*) That's how babies got made . . . One day, quién sabe
qué pasó, a midget was born. ¡El enano mexicano! (*Fanfare.*) You!
PEDRITO: Mm-me?
COSME: Yes, y-you! ¡Tartamudo! (COSME *yanks* PEDRITO *reluctantly into the act.*) It was a miracle the midget even survived. He
was only this tall when he was full grown. So the other cavemen
looked down at him and laughed. And all the cavewomen kicked his
fundis, if he laid even one dedo on any of them. En fin, he was a sad
joke. (AGUSTINA *starts kicking him around, enjoying herself.*
PEDRITO starts to respond by getting into his part. They play
along.*) ¡Bueno pues! One day the midget was sitting up on a rock,
playing with himself, when he saw a big, blond mamasota coming
from the river. When she passed under his boulder, he whispered
psst . . . The cave woman stopped and turned . . . ¿Adió? Psst! She
looked up and saw the midget wiggling his nose and making eyes
at her . . . wiggle your nose, baboso. (PEDRITO *fails to take direction. So* COSME *fills in for him.*) He was puckering his lips, blowing silent kisses. In no time he had her behind the boulder, ¡Zas,
zas, zas! Short but quick. (COSME *humps* AGUSTINA. MAMA
CHU *gets up again.* LUCAS *holds her.* COSME *sotto to* AGUSTI-
NA.) You're good. You're very good . . . (*To the public.*) ¡Pos! . . .
the cavewoman came out gorda. After a while, the other cavemen
begin to notice that more and more of their viejas were giving birth
to short, stumpy midgets in all colores and shades, pero . . . ¿por
qué? (PEDRITO *drops his act and starts arguing with* AGUSTI-
NA.) A year later, somebody caught the enano on his rock molest-
ing another cavewoman. Grabbing their macanas, the giants sur-

rounded the boulder and beat the little midget to dinosaur cuacha, right then and there! (*The* CAVEMEN *circle and beat* PEDRITO *to the floor with their clubs, creating an image that horrifies* MAMA CHU *into silence.*) . . . They scattered his short huesos to the four winds, then they killed as many of his stumpy ugly children as they could catch! (MAMA CHU *gasps at a sudden painful flash of memory.*) In time nobody remembered the midget had even existed . . . pero chingado . . . look around you, raza . . . look at how he left La Humanidad! (*Musical fanfare.* COSME *pulls out* ORALIA *then* AGUSTINA *for a bow.* HE *smooches* AGUSTINA. PEDRITO *seeing red attacks* COSME, *causing a melee.* MAMA CHU *stands, cutting loose like a machine gun.*)

MAMA CHU: (*A bloodcurdling cry.*) ¡Ayyyy! ¡Desgraciado, indio, patarajada! I know now. I remember who you are. You're the traitor, the murderer, el torocoyori who KILLED MY CHILDREN!!! (*Sfx. Distant machine gun fire. Upstage blackout. Lights up downstage on* ARMIDA *and* ORALIA.)

ARMIDA: What! Who killed whose children? What are you saying? Mama Chu recognized him . . . from before?

ORALIA: She knew Cosme Bravo, yes . . . from Sonora. He was already in his forties, but the moment she laid eyes on him, she smelled blood . . .

ARMIDA: You're talking about my father, Tía.

ORALIA: No, I'm not. The clown wasn't your father.

ARMIDA: (*Breathless pause.*) What!?

ORALIA: Don't act so shocked. I know you've had your suspicions since you were little . . . (ARMIDA *looks at* ORALIA *with wonder.*) You know who your real father is . . . You've lived with him almost your whole life. He has a nickname, but his name is Pedro. (CAJEME *and* PROFE *enter and face each other for a beat.* CAJEME *exits,* PROFE *remains.*)

ARMIDA: (*A thunderbolt.*) Profe?!

Blackout.

SCENE FIVE

The waiting room. ARMIDA *and* PROFE *are in the middle of an anxious pause.* ARMIDA *is pacing.* SHE *stops, distressed.*

ARMIDA: So it's true?

PROFE: Más o menos. Don't look at me like that.

ARMIDA: Why didn't you ever tell me! You let me grow up living a lie?

PROFE: (*Angering.*) You had food, clothes, a roof over your head!

ARMIDA: You're my father, Tío!

PROFE: Is that so bad?

ARMIDA: My mother was your sister!

PROFE: We were always close . . . but we weren't the same flesh and blood. After the nightmare with Don Güero, Agustina and I got closer than ever. Too close. If you know what I mean. She got really depressed and blamed herself . . . She was terrified of Mama Chu. She thought she was really going to burn in hell. So I told her the truth.

ARMIDA: You're weren't brother and sister?

PROFE: Pos no. I'm not Yaqui, I'm Maya Yucateco. To your mother that only meant that Mama Chu was not really her mother. Then Lucas came back, out of the blue, saying he was her father. She ran away with the circo.

ARMIDA: I can't say I blame her. . . .

PROFE: We all went after her . . . Mama Chu had Lucas negotiate the deal with Cosme: no family, no Agustina. That's how we all joined the circo.

ARMIDA: (*Cynically.*) What about my father—I mean, Cosme— killing Mama Chu's children? Didn't that get in the way a little?

PROFE: Agustina didn't believe her. Cosme made her a big star. Mama Chu settled for the boarding house in Logan Heights.

ARMIDA: Then it's not true . . .

PROFE: Does it matter?

ARMIDA: We're not a family anymore. . . . It was all an illusion.

PROFE: You were born . . . was that an illusion?

ARMIDA: You're not my tío anymore.

PROFE: I'm your pinche padre. Okay?

ARMIDA: Tell me something, Pop . . . why didn't Mom just get an abortion? It might have saved her life.

PROFE: Having you didn't kill her. . . you were her last hope.

ARMIDA: (*Soulful pause.*) There's something I have to confess, too . . . that was me you saw in Tijuana about a year ago.

PROFE: I know. Who was that hippy with you?

ARMIDA: Cage, my boyfriend. . . . He brought me to Mexico in his Volkswagen van . . . He's not the one who got me in trouble. He was just a friend then . . . but I asked him to help me to find a Mexican doctor who performed an abortion on me. . . . I couldn't stop and see the family after that, especially Mama Chu. I was afraid she'd see right through me. (PROFE *tenderly embraces ARMIDA.*)

Cross-fade.

SCENE SIX

MAMA CHU*'s room. Music.* COSME *comes rolling onstage, pushing his legless torso on a low cart and carrying a small bundle in his arms.* MAMA CHU *looks down at him from her bed.*

COSME: (*Singing.*) Soy un pobre venadito. . . que habito en la serranía. . .
MAMA CHU: (*Warily.*) Cosme Bravo! . . . what are you doing? What are you bringing me . . . Is that . . . ?
COSME: My laundry, Doña Chu. My stinking socks, my guardapedos . . . my silk shirt. My dirty underwear . . . stained with misfortune.
MAMA CHU: (*Taken aback.*) You expect me to clean your dirty calzones?
COSME: You are the only one who can . . .
MAMA CHU: ¡Demonio! You died of syphilis.
COSME: Órale, Doña Chu . . . I died of diabetes. Both legs chopped off at the knee. I lost the circo. I lost my wife. I lost my daughter. . . . But why bring that up? What did I ever do to you . . . ? And don't say I killed your mocosos.
MAMA CHU: You deny you destroyed Agustina!
COSME: You're the one who called her a yori puta. Let's be honest. La Mariposa bought your mojado boarding house.
MAMA CHU: You're lying. Profe gave me the money.
COSME: Which he got from Agustina . . . simón limón. Don't act like you didn't know.
MAMA CHU: You made her drink and smoke marijuana!
COSME: It relaxed her on the trapeze. There are worse things . . .
MAMA CHU: Like prostitution?!
COSME: (*Derisively.*) She was my vieja, señora. Because of your Yaqui lies and suspicions, she stopped sleeping with me. To spite me, she openly began to see other men. To save my pride, I had to spread the rumor I was whoring her. Do you blame me?

MAMA CHU: You know who you are and so does God!

COSME: God, yes, but do you? And who are you to accuse me? Admit it. We all put on masks when we crossed the border. We left an ugly revolution behind. If you know who I was in Sonora, then I must know who you were . . .

MAMA CHU: Who was I?

COSME: (*Unctuously devious.*) Sepa. How would I know? Perhaps La Llorona . . . the Crying Woman of the Revolution. (HE *puts on a military hat.*)

MAMA CHU: You were the bastard son of the general!

COSME: The son of the Priest. Some are born to the cross, some to the double cross. (*Braying like a jackass.*) Eee-haww! (COSME *stands, extending his legs to full stature.*)

MAMA CHU: Payaso desgraciado, you dare to mock God?

COSME: We all serve as we are called, Doña Chu.

MAMA CHU: Judas! You know what happened. God was there. You did kill my children!

COSME: (*Mockingly.*) ¿Pero cómo, Doña Chu? If what you say is true, I must be the father of the horny one you never had . . . That's ugly. (*Two* SOLDIERS *enter in a military column.* THEY *search.*) Let's say, just for *chiripas,* there was a Yaqui woman with three whelps . . . a boy and two girls. . . . One day, the Army came looking for her husband, who was wanted by the government. (MAMA CHU *retreats defensively to her bed.*) To keep her children out of the hands of the raping soldiers, she killed them. . . . So after that, the woman wandered all through the Revolution, crying for her lost mocosos . . . mis hijo-o-o-s.

MAMA CHU: Enough of your lies. ¡Demonio desgraciado! Killer of your own people. ¡TOROCOYORI!

COSME: (*Striking military stance.*) Your first husband, Pedro Coyote, was a deserter from the federal army and a turncoat Yaqui spy!

MAMA CHU: ¡Demonio! It was you . . .

COSME: If you insist. Your son is under arrest.

MAMA CHU: Son? What son. Profe?

COSME: The deer dancer! (*Music. Flute and drum.* COSME*'s SOLDIERS wait expectantly, ready to catch the* DEER DANCER *as he runs in. Nobody shows.*

MAMA CHU: What deer dancer? Babosos. (LUCAS *enters the scene, under the watchful eye of the* SOLDIERS.)

LUCAS: You never told Agustina the truth, did you, Chu? You let her believe Cosme's ridiculous lies about you.

MAMA CHU: She married him! To spite me, don't you see? Who else was she going to believe! She was in the hands of the demonio.

LUCAS: So were you. If you sleep with devils, you're bound to get burned. Only in the case of Don Güero, it was my daughter. (MAMA CHU *stares at him incredulously, with residual anger. CAJEME enters without his deerhead.*)

MAMA CHU: We were alone!

LUCAS: You were never alone. You had your people. You chose to go your own way.

MAMA CHU: The old ways were dead . . . and so are you!

COSME: ¡Pelotón, atención! Medio paso doblado: uno-dos, uno-dos, uno-dos! (COSME *marches his soldiers into a firing squad line.*)

LUCAS: Ni modo. You've outlived me by thirty years. My mistake was going back to Mexico again. The Revolutionary Government was promising to return our lands to the Yaqui nation. Who knew it was a plot to wipe out the leaders of the resistance?

COSME: ¡Preparen armas!

MAMA CHU: What are you talking about?!

COSME: ¡Apunten!

LUCAS: Killing the deer.

COSME: ¡Fuego! (LUCAS *open his arms and the firing squad fires. HE falls.*)

MAMA CHU: Pedro!

Blackout.

SCENE SEVEN

MAMA CHU*'s room. Suddenly one of the monitors starts to beep, blinking its red light, panicking* TILLY *and* ORALIA.

ORALIA: What the hell is that?

TILLY: It's the heart monitor. Something's going on. It's not good. Nurse!

NURSE: (*Entering.*) What's happening here? Did either of you touch any of the equipment? What's happening to Grandma?

ORALIA: It's her heart!

NURSE: No. She's gone into a coma. (ARMIDA *rushes in.* MAMA
    CHU *observes unnoticed.*)
ARMIDA: What is it? What's happening?
TILLY: Grandma's in a coma.
ARMIDA: Coma?!
NURSE: Just a mild diabetic coma. We've had her on the IV. Her body's
    wasn't getting enough insulin for some reason. Now she's had a bit
    too much.
ARMIDA: You mean she's odeeing?
NURSE: Listen, hon, that little lady has a million things that could go
    haywire.
ARMIDA: What the hell are you talking about? That's why she's in the
    hospital! How incompetent can you get?
NURSE: (*Feathers flustered.*) All right, everybody, out. NOW.
ORALIA: ¡Cállate la boca! ¡La vas hacer enojar!
ARMIDA: Don't tell me to shut up. I don't give a damn if she gets mad.
    Fuck! I can't believe this! How can you trust a racist institution to
    do its best for somebody like Mama Chu? Does the system give a
    damn if she lives or dies? Or who she is or was or ever will be . . .
    (MAMA CHU *follows the family out into the corridor.*)
TILLY: Are you worried about Mama Chu or making a speech? (THEY
    stand outside MAMA CHU*'s room, looking through the window.*)
ORALIA: She's gotta have that godamn operation, and that's all there
    is to it!
ARMIDA: Mama Chu has to tell us what she wants.
TILLY: (*Emphatically.*) She wants to keep the baby. Why else would
    she keep it for sixty years? I know I would.
ORALIA: Don't be stupid.
TILLY: (*Suddenly self-possessed.*) I'm not stupid. I'm pregnant.
ORALIA: (*Mortified.*) What if it kills her?
ARMIDA: It's her choice. (*The three women hug.*)

Cross-fade.

SCENE EIGHT

Romantic music. AGUSTINA *enters* MAMA CHU*'s room, in a
hospital gown, smoking and carrying a bundle.* MAMA CHU *turns
toward her.* SHE *is escorted in by* CAJEME, *who stops and waits.*

AGUSTINA: (*Singing.*)

Yo ya me voy, al puerto donde se haya
la barca de oro, que debe conducirme
yo ya me voy, sólo vengo a despedirme
adiós, mujer, ¡adiós para siempre adiós!

(AGUSTINA *continues advancing on* MAMA CHU.)

MAMA CHU: Agustina, you look terrible! Half dead.

AGUSTINA: I was just about to say the same thing about you. . . . I had a baby, Mamá. A beautiful baby girl, remember? (AGUSTINA *coughs, holding out her baby.* MAMA CHU *turns away.*) Don't you want to see my baby? Look at her!

MAMA CHU: Who's the father?

AGUSTINA: A soldier. An American G.I. fighting far away, overseas, in Germany. That's why I'm calling her Army.

MAMA CHU: ¡Yori puta!

AGUSTINA: That doesn't work anymore, Mama Chu. I know your secrets. All those years with Papá Güero . . . you knew what was going on, didn't you?

MAMA CHU: I was trying to protect you.

AGUSTINA: Me . . . or your angel, Mamá? Only you aren't my Mamá! If you were, you would have stopped Papá Güero!

MAMA CHU: (*Turning away.*) I didn't know, mi'jita! I swear to you.

AGUSTINA: Look at me! You don't have to look the other way anymore. . . . You know who the father of my baby is. Only you're afraid to admit it. . . because if you do, our whole life will be a lie.

MAMA CHU: What lies have I ever told you?

AGUSTINA: What lies didn't you tell us? I don't even know you. Who are you? What have you done to us?

MAMA CHU: How can you say that . . . to me? You think I don't know what went on between you and your brother. It was a sin before almighty God!

AGUSTINA: The truth is buried deep inside you, and it's time for it to come out, Mama Chu . . . even if it kills you.

MAMA CHU: ¡Maldecida! I curse you. From the bottom of my heart, ¡te doy la maldición de tu madre!

AGUSTINA: You aren't my madre . . .

MAMA CHU: How dare you!

AGUSTINA: You never wanted to let any of us live our own lives. We

never went out. We never had friends. Even Profe. You had him tied
up like a family dog, until I got him to join the Navy. What in the
world were we hiding from?

MAMA CHU: The world. ¡Las inmundicias del mundo!

AGUSTINA: (*With ancient anguish.*) Where did Profe come from, Mama
Chu? Did you steal him too, like me and Oralia? Why couldn't you
have any of your own?

MAMA CHU: What lies did Cosme tell you?

AGUSTINA: Bedtime stories.

MAMA CHU: Lies!

AGUSTINA: Like the Crying Woman of the Revolution . . .

MAMA CHU: Nothing but lies!

AGUSTINA: She killed her children and went crazy, wandering from
battlefield to battlefield, stealing other people's children! Is that
who you are, Mama Chu? ¡¿La Llorona?! (*Laughs bitterly.*)

MAMA CHU: Stop, STOP! What do you know about me? What do any
of you know about me? I was in the Yucatán when the Revolution
began. One day in the battlefield, I found an orphan, a Mayan boy
sitting by his dead mother. What else could I do, but pick him up
and take him with me? . . . I named him Pedro.

AGUSTINA: Profe . . . poor Profe . . . he was so lonely. He didn't even
get to have the love of his daughter.

MAMA CHU: I'm sorry, mi'jita . . . God knows I'm sorry.

AGUSTINA: I died of la tristeza, Mamá. I tried to be happy, but the
sadness of our lives caught up with me . . . don't you want to see
my baby? (AGUSTINA *opens her bundle, and* MAMA CHU *pulls
out* Cajeme's *deer head with an audible gasp.*)

MAMA CHU: Cajeme! (AGUSTINA *exits.*)

SCENE NINE

CAJEME *approaches* MAMA CHU, *bewildered and baffled.*

CAJEME: Who am I, Mama Chu?

MAMA CHU: You are the son of a Deer Dancer.

CAJEME: Why am I here?

MAMA CHU: Don't worry, my son, don't worry.

CAJEME: Am I going to die?

MAMA CHU: No, you are already dead. . . (MAMA CHU *ties the deerhead back on* CAJEME's *head with tender but forceful resolve.*) For you there shall be nothing. . . no air, no sicknesses, no family. Nothing shall terrify you now . . . ! All is over for you, except for one thing: paradise! (SHE *kisses him gently on the lips. Drums beat.* CAJEME *undergoes a powerful transformation back to the deer.* HE *begins to dance, faster and faster, then exits.* MAMA CHU *falls back into bed.*)

SCENE TEN

MAMA CHU's *room.* MAMA CHU *is back in bed. The monitor starts beeping an erratic heartbeat.*

ORALIA: (*Rushing into the room.*) Oh, my God! Mama Chu! Mama Chu!

ARMIDA: Shouldn't you call the doctor?

NURSE: He's in Divorce court.

ORALIA: Oh, my God! Divorce court?

NURSE: Holy momma. Her blood pressure is really dropping!

ARMIDA: Do something!

TILLY: She's not dying, is she? Mama Chu! (MAMA CHU *watches* NURSE *working.* ORALIA *backs* TILLY *off.*)

NURSE: Don't die on me, Grandma, don't you die on me now . . . breathe, goddamn you, breathe! (SHE *applies CPR, then listens for a heartbeat.* SHE *looks up.*)

ARMIDA: Is it over?

NURSE: Her heart is beating like a drum . . . (*The family exchanges glances.*) No, I mean . . . like a drum. (*Lights change. Drums and rattles.* NURSE *and family exeunt.* MAMA CHU *sits up.*)

MAMA CHU: In that other life, I was just a girl, a Yaqui girl, born in Sonora, Mexico in the year Cajeme, the great war chief, was killed by the *federales* . . . My people had lived there on the Río Yaqui forever, in peace, which is all the *Yoeme* ever wanted. But the *Yoris* wanted our rich lands . . . the *Yoris* wanted everything . . . (*Drums and rattles. Sounds of Yaqui dear dance in the background.*) My first husband was a deer dancer . . . His name was Pedro Coyote. It was there in my ancient pueblo of Torim on the banks of the Río Hiaquimi, where, my children I saw him dance the Venado . . . for the last time. (*The voices of a crowd of men, women and children.*) It was noon on Easter Sunday . . . in the middle of the fiesta. The Pascolas were dancing when soldiers arrived without a warning. They set up their machine guns. At first we thought they were there to protect us . . . but they aimed at the crowd. PEDROOO! (*Machine gun fire. Screams and panic in the crowd.*) People screamed, and bodies began falling, dying in their own blood. Those still on their own two feet fled in terror, escaping into the mountains, but . . . we knew . . . it had begun . . . the war to exterminate the Yaqui! (*Sounds of women and children weeping. Soldiers' voices.*) My children and I were driven down the street like cattle. The soldiers marched us in the midday heat to the cemetery outside of town. There were hundreds of other Yoeme being held there. They were there with other men digging a pit, under the rifle barrels of the soldiers. When the pit was done, the killing began. Old men, women and children were shot into the hole. One after another . . . (*Machine gun fire and screams. Crackling fires.*) The killing went on for hours, and as the sun turned red, the cries of the Yaqui mothers and their children reached up to heaven, as the machine guns silenced them forever. Fires lit up the night sky, crackling and roaring and filling the choking air with the stench of burning flesh. (*The screams and machine guns die out.*) As dawn came, I awoke from my nightmare to discover that it was real. They didn't shoot me, but they ripped my children from my arms. I had three children. Pedrito, Agustina and Oralia. I never saw them again. The soldiers never noticed that I was pregnant. They separated the women according to our age and looks. And then they raped us. (COSME BRAVO, *20 years younger, appears in an army uniform.*) I was taken by a torocoyori turn-coat Yaqui, the bastard son of a general, who was slaughtering his own people like a rabid dog at the service of his Yori masters . . . Cosme Bravo . . . how could I ever forget his face? I spit into it. He beat me. When he tired of raping me, I thought he was going to shoot me, but he put me on the train, in a cattle car with other Yaquis, deported to Yucatán into slavery.

COSME: Adiós, mi chula prieta. (*Musical transition as* MAMA CHU *rides in the cattle car.*)

MAMA CHU: I knew I was carrying my last child, so I prayed and made a manda to God. Diosito Santo . . . I know if by some miracle my newborn survives without me, he will be a slave. So I pray to you,

Dios mío, do not let him be born a slave, please God! Do not let them
take my baby from my body and feed it to the dogs when it is dead
like dogmeat! I say this as a manda, take my baby's life, take it! but
don't let me die without it. Saying this, I did not yet know the infinite
ways of God. He granted me my manda, but in his divine wisdom. I
did not know God would make me carry it for the rest of my life. That
is my manda. To carry the son of Pedro Coyote forever.

Fade to black.

SCENE ELEVEN

The wail of a train. ARMIDA BRAVO, *54, appears downstage.
Carlos Santana's* "Farol" *plays in the background.*

ARMIDA: In the spring of 1969, my eighty-four-year old grandmother—
given the option whether or not to abort her sixty-year-old mummified fetus—chose to carry it to the inevitable end . . . Through her
manda, she made me a gift of my Yaqui-Mayan heritage and iden-
tity. Not to mention my Ph.D. in Cultural Anthropology. (*Using a
laptop with power point illustrations,* SHE *lectures.*) The Yaqui
Wars of Liberation started in 1528, four years after the Conquest of
Mexico. They continued unabated for four centuries. In the 1600's
Jesuits taught the Yaquis Christianity by blending their dances into
the Easter Ceremony. The Jesuits were expelled in 1769 for advo-
cating Yaqui atonomy. In 1777–78, the winter of Valley Forge, at
the request of General George Washington, Yaqui troops defended
the mouth of the Mississippi against the British navy in defense of
the American Revolution. Their own cries for freedom went
unheeded. (*Documentary images from the Yaqui wars appear on
powerpoint.*) In 1905, under orders from President Porfirio Díaz the
Mexican army in Sonora began to execute these final solutions for
the Yaqui problem: 1) The colonization of the Yaqui; 2) a war of
total extermination against the insurgents; and 3) the deportation of
the entire tribe, removing it from its ancestral lands in the state and
scattering it in that part of the national territory most distant from
Sonora. (SHE *turns off the laptop and gets personal.*) My own
grandmother, Jesús María Flores, whom we lovingly called Mama
Chu, was sold on the auction block in Mexico City for sixty dollars.

She was bought by a henequen plantation in the Yucatán peninsula, where slaves were needed to replace the natives killed in the Mayan rebellions or deported as slaves to Cuba. . . . She was there until the Revolution carried her north to the US Mexican border . . . (SHE *starts to leave, but pauses.*) Oh, yes. She didn't die in 1969 . . . she kept the fetus and lived for another thirty years, finally joining the cosmic dance in the fall of 1999 at the ripe old Yaqui age of 114 . . . (MAMA CHU'*s room. The family gathers round* MAMA CHU, *in a classic deathbed tableau.* ARMIDA *enters and stands beside her grandmother, with* AGUSTINA *facing her across the bed.*)

ARMIDA: Mama Chu, I don't know if you can hear me, but it's okay . . . you can let go now.

AGUSTINA: She's talking to you, Mama Chu. I know you can hear her.

ARMIDA: I finally understand. . . . You, my mother, Profe, everything. Peace, Grandma, peace.

MAMA CHU: I hear her, but I can't see her . . .

AGUSTINA: Open your eyes, Mamá, look at my daughter! Isn't she beautiful? (MAMA CHU *opens her eyes and sees* ARMIDA.)

MAMA CHU: Armida, mi'jita . . . te doy la bendición de tu ma—dre. (SHE *loses it.* LUCAS *comes up to* MAMA CHU *in bed.*)

LUCAS: Are you ready to go now, mi Chu? (*The entire family, living and dead, gathers round.*)

MAMA CHU: Look at them, Lucas. Mi familia. We all survived after all.

AGUSTINA: Give me your hand, Mamá Chu. (MAMA CHU *gives* AGUSTINA *her hand;* ORALIA *takes the other.* ARMIDA *turns downstage into a private prayer.*)

ARMIDA: Dear God . . . is it so outrageous to believe that the mummified fetus like an ancient kernel of millenial corn soaked with the waters of divine mercy and luck might yet spring to life, that something sacred and alive might come from all that suffering . . . that our entire family history is but the struggle to find our birth passage to a new world . . .

MAMA CHU: Cajeme, mi'jito, dance! (*Downstage,* CAJEME *dances. The rest of the family stays around the bed, as* AGUSTINA *sings.*)

AGUSTINA:
No volverán tu ojos a mirarme
ni tu oídos escucharán mi canto

voy aumentar, los mares con mi llanto
adiós mujer, adiós para siempre, ¡adiós!
(*The family members clutch hands, looking at* MAMA CHU *as she powerfully grips her daughters' hands in extremis.*)
ARMIDA: Goodbye, Mama Chu!
PROFE: ¡Adiós, Mama Chu!
TILLY: Goodbye, Grandma!
ORALIA: (*Bursting into tears.*) ¡MAMAAAÁ! (CAJEME *dances to a climax at the foot of the bed. With his deer head up in triumph, he collapses, lifeless.*)

Black.

Mundo Mata

CHARACTERS

Mundo Mata, 30, a Vietnam veteran
Huesos, 27, a skinny guy
Greñas, 22, a hairy guy
Vera Campos, 29, a packinghouse worker
Flaco, 35, her husband, a tecato
Güerito, 7-10, her son
Güera, 32, bar owner and Mundo's sister
Prieta, 28, her partner,
Sugar, 33, a farm worker
Tapón, 50, a feisty campesino
Botella, 45, his truculent wife
Sheriff Sam Barnes, 47
Ella Barnes, 40, his wife
Gudunritch, 37, a corporate grower
Roddenberry, 51, a local grower
Lola Mata, 61, Mundo's mother
Teodoro, 55, Mundo's uncle
Bullet "Ray" Mata, 25, Mundo's brother, a union organizer
Chuck Whittaker, 36, union organizer
Campesinos, farmworkers
Raza, Mexican Americans

TIME AND PLACE

Burlap, California, a tank town in the heart of the great central San Joaquin Valley in the Summer of 1973.

SETTING

A packing shed with empty fruit boxes sitting on pallets, which get moved and tossed around by the farm worker chorus, as they sing. Boxes are stacked and upended by the workers to form the various interiors and exteriors of the scenes in the play. Visuals and slides may or may not reinforce the reality of piece by the addition of overhanging projection screens, while enhancing the spare Brechtian approach.

Light and sound play crucial roles in establishing place and time.

ACT ONE

PROLOGUE

The packing shed. Early morning. Tractor whistle blows. Enter
FARMWORKERS, *men and women, coming to work. Enter* CHUCK
WHITTAKER *with a bullhorn, and* SALVADOR "BULLET" MATA
carrying his guitar. Led by BULLET, *the farmworkers sing "El corrido
de la unidad."*

BULLET:
> Hermanos y campesinos
> aquí les vengo a cantar
> les hablo de César Chávez
> canto de nuestra unidad.
>
> Con un dedo no haces nada
> tú ni puedes trabajar
> ni con dedos separados
> si la mano abierta está.
>
> Pero si los dedos se unen
> la mano vas a cerrar
> la unión es como esa mano
> ¡con fuerza para luchar!

FARMWORKERS: (*Singing chorus.*)
> Nuestra unión hace la fuerza
> nuestra fuerza hace la unión
> es nuestro pueblo marchando
> hacia la liberación.

WHITTAKER: Brothers and sisters, we are here today to talk about
César Chávez and our union, the United Farm Workers of America!
(*Beat.*) With one finger you can't do anything, you can hardly work.
With fingers apart you can open your hand and beg for welfare. But

67

with the fingers united you can form a fist with the power to fight back. (*Beat.*) Our union is our strength and our strength is our union. Join us in our struggle for representation by signing this petition for union elections. ¡Sí, se puede!

FARMWORKERS: (*Singing chorus.*)
Nuestra unión hace la fuerza
nuestra fuerza hace la unión
es nuestro pueblo marchando
¡hacia la liberación!

BULLET: ¡Qué viva nuestra unión! (CAMPESINOS: ¡QUÉ VIVA!) ¡Viva César Chávez! (¡QUÉ VIVA!) ¡Abajo con los rancheros! (¡ABAJO!) (*A fire door suddenly opens up with a violent slam. A squad of goons enters at rear, with* RODDENBERRY, *the grower.*)

RODDENBERRY: Okay, you red sons of bitches. It's pay day! (*The goons attack with clubs. Screams. Freeze.* BULLET *steps out.*)

BULLET: The summer of 1973 was one of the worst we ever had. The United Farm Workers were fighting for their lives, and I was fighting to stay nonviolent. (*Unfreeze action. More screams. Action freeze again.*) Órale, don't get me wrong. I was scared shitless. But it was do or die. The moment I met César Chávez on campus, I knew he was for real. Like Gandhi and Martin Luther King, you know? I just didn't know how real. (*Unfreeze action into slow motion.*) Reality is some goon kicking you in the ass. It's the shivering dawn and burning sun and four hours of sleep on a hard floor before picketing for another twelve hours on cold rice and beans. It's the taste of your own blood, before you realize you've been hit. It's what you believe. Actions, not words. That's why I volunteered. To come back to Burlap and organize campesinos. (*Goons and farmworkers exit.*) I was born here, you see—but I wouldn't exactly call it a homecoming. That summer, in the mind of my carnal, Burlap was still the belly button of the world . . . el ombligo del Mundo. (HE *exits.*)

Fade to black.

SCENE ONE

A street in Burlap. Night. "It was just my imagination" is playing on the car radio, as the batos come in lowriding, cruising. MUNDO *is driving his ranfla.*

GREÑAS: (*Stoned in the back seat.*) Muerto.

HUESOS: What's that, ése?

GREÑAS: This stinking town, man. Watcha. Deader than a cemetery.

HUESOS: La raza está roncando. O foquiando.

GREÑAS: Pinche pueblo cagalero. Nothing but perros and outhouses. (GREÑAS *cracks up.* MUNDO *pulls over the curb. Stops.*)

HUESOS: We're stopping? Óra-leh, how did you know, carnal. Tengo que hechar la agua. (HUESOS *jumps out of the car.* MUNDO *follows quietly.*)

MUNDO: Ése, Greñas, can I talk to you?

GREÑAS: Who?

MUNDO: You.

GREÑAS: Me?

MUNDO: Out here, carnal.

GREÑAS: (*Gets out.*) ¿Qué pedo?

MUNDO: Pinche pueblo cagalero, ¿eh? (*Laughs,* GREÑAS *laughs with him.*) Nothing but outhouses?

GREÑAS: (*Cracks up.*) Sirol.

MUNDO: (*Grabs him tight.*) Next time you say something about my pueblo, ¡watcha el hocico, buey!

GREÑAS: (*Startled.*) ¿Qué dije?

MUNDO: (*Deadly, menacing.*) Yo soy el Mundo, carnal, and nobody shits on my town, you dig? ¡Con safos, puto! El que me la hace, me la paga.

GREÑAS: (*Dumbfounded.*) ¡Dame quebrada, ése! I didn't know.

MUNDO: (*Grabs him by the hair.*) You've got a lot to learn, Greñas. This world's made up of shitty little towns. What hole did you come from?

GREÑAS: ¡Yo soy de Durango, Mexico, ey!

MUNDO: (*Easing off.*) Órale pues . . . Durango Kid. This time hasta aquí nomás, because we're camaradas, right?

GREÑAS: Right.

MUNDO: (*Letting him go.*) Ahí te llevo.

HUESOS: (*Off to one side.*) ¡El Mundo rifa!

MUNDO: Eh, man, don't say that with your macana in your hand.

HUESOS: Just telling Greñas. This is Burlap, Califas, carnal. Mundo's world. (*Dogs howl in the distance.*) Órale, you hear that? Pobre pinche huesuda. Sounds like they got the bitch in heat again. Ése,

Mundo, you see that dog fight out here today? Man, había como
twenty perros killing each other for that old bitch. She was in the
middle of the pack, you know? And the perros were going round and
round, throwing mordidas, bleeding, biting off hairs. Luego, from
outa nowhere, bato, comes this other perro y ¿sabes qué? He jumps
over all of 'em with his spear sticking out y zas, mano! ¡Que se la
ensarta! Just like a flecha. He did his thang ¡y se bailó, a los otros al
mismo tiempo!

MUNDO: That's my kind of perro.

HUESOS: Estuvo bruto, carnal. Then they got stuck.

MUNDO: (*Cracks up.*) Chale.

HUESOS: Y que comienza a salir la raza. Everybody in town came out.
Old ladies with hot water, chavalillos with sticks. You should have
seen the look that perra gave me.

MUNDO: She got what she deserved. Por putinga.

HUESOS: ¿Te das cuenta, Greñas? This is El Mundo de Burlap, ése.

FLACO: (*O.S.*) Oye, Mundo, ése, Mundo! (FLACO *enters looking like
death warmed over.*)

MUNDO: Órale, Flaco . . . ¿Qué pues, nuez?

FLACO: Is the drugstore open?

MUNDO: Chale. The old drugstore is closed. For good.

FLACO: I need a nickel bag, carnal. ¡Aliviáname!

MUNDO: Let me see your *nickle*.

FLACO: No seas gacho, cabrón. Give me a little credit. My old lady's
good for it.

MUNDO: Vera? . . . She's got the feria?

FLACO: Who said anything about feria? My old lady kicked me out,
ése. She's upstairs. Go for it.

MUNDO: (*Refusing him.*) Don't make me teach you a lesson, cabrón.
¡Descuéntate!

FLACO: She's not a whore, you know. She loves me. She just hates to
see me shoot up. (*Suddenly two car headlights momentarily sweep
the scene, and the action freezes. Heads follow a passing car offstage.*)

HUESOS: Órale, trucha. That's Barnes.

GREÑAS: Who?

HUESOS: Deputy Sheriff Sam Barnes, baboso.

GREÑAS: Why is he staring at us?

HUESOS: He wants your ass.

GREÑAS: Up yours, pirujo!

MUNDO: ¡Cálmenla! Ya me están agüitando. (*The others shut up.*) Barnes is just passing through. He's too chickenshit to stop at night. See? (*Watches the car go.*) Vámonos. Split, Flaco. A tu chante. (MUNDO *heads back to the car. FLACO follows him closely.*)

FLACO: What about my fix, ése? (*Lights of another passing car.*)

HUESOS: Trucha. Here comes another ranfla.

GREÑAS: ¡Gatos güeros! A blondota in a Cadillac. Mamasota . . . What's she doing in town?

HUESOS: She's looking for pedo, Mundo.

GREÑAS: She's looking at you like she knows you, carnal.

MUNDO: Chale. She's the Deputy Sheriff's ruca. No sean mensos. The growers are meeting over at the Elks Club. Something's up.

HUESOS: What?

MUNDO: What do you care? I don't see your brown ass out in the fields! (GREÑAS *cracks up, humiliating* HUESOS.)

HUESOS: Chale. We're part of the downtown merchants. The Burlap Mafia.

FLACO: What about it, ése? Capea. (MUNDO *stares at* FLACO, *withot betraying emotion.*)

MUNDO: Pinche Flaco. (HE *slaps a nickel bag into* FLACO'*s palm.*)

FLACO: Pinche Mundo. (FLACO *leaves quickly.*)

GREÑAS: ¡Ora-LAY! How many rucas does this bato have? Ése, carnal, no me digas, pero did Flaco just pimp you his old lady, man?

MUNDO: (*Darkly.*) What?

GREÑAS: Nada . . . Like I said, no me digas.

MUNDO: You think I'd screw my best friend's old lady behind his back?

GREÑAS: Well . . .

MUNDO: Well, what?

GREÑAS: It wouldn't be behind his back.

MUNDO: (*Stalks him.*) Do I look like a motherfucker to you?

GREÑAS: ¿Sabes qué? I don't want any pedo.

MUNDO: I told you, bato. ¿No te dije? (*Knocks him dowm.*) This is my pueblo, mi raza, buey! (*Kicks him.*) ¡Mi madre seca! You're going to learn some respect. ¿Me entiendes cómo?

GREÑAS: Simón.

MUNDO: Get up. (GREÑAS *gets up.*) You're still one of my soldados, cabrón. (*Gives him an abrazo.*)

GREÑAS: Órale.

MUNDO: Get in. (MUNDO *and* GREÑAS *get into "The Car."*)

HUESOS: A toda madre. That's the way it should be entre camaradas. Nos chingamos, luego nos abrazamos. You'll learn, Greñas. This bato's not called Reymundo, for nothing. (*Gets into car.*) In this town, he's the king of the world. (*The batos drive off cruising to a mariachi ranchera: "El Rey."*)

Fade to black.

Set transition: FARM WORKERS *enter singing along with "El Rey" and begin throwing boxes around, creating the next setting.*

SCENE TWO

"La Divina Garza" cantina. Music on the jukebox. People dancing, drinking cerveza. PRIETA *and* GÜERA *are serving food and beer.* FLACO *has locked himself in the men's room.*

TAPÓN: ¡Ésa, Güera!

HUESOS: Bring us a couple more, bato.

GREÑAS: Dos Coors y una Hamms.

PRIETA: ¿Menudo? Who ordered menudo?

TEODORO: Aquí mero.

GREÑAS: ¿Y mis carnitas?

PRIETA: They're coming.

HUESOS: ¿Y las tortillas?

PRIETA: Un momento.

GREÑAS: Ay, mamacita, qué buena estás.

PRIETA: Let go, baboso! (SHE *pulls his hair and goes. Others laugh.*)

GREÑAS: ¡Ay, jodido! How come everybody's always pulling my greña?

TAPÓN: Por pendejo.

TEODORO: Órale, compa', no te metas.

HUESOS: You couldn't handle Prieta anyway, Greñas.

TAPÓN: Simón, te chinga la Güera.

GREÑAS: Y a ti que te importa, Tapón? (GÜERA *brings the beers.*)

GÜERA: That'll be $7.20.

TAPÓN: ¿Siete bolas?

GÜERA: You didn't pay me for two rounds.

TAPÓN: What rounds?

GÜERA: Si no vas a pagar, no tragues,

TAPÓN: Qué pasó with the twenty I gave you?

GÜERA: You drank it up an hour ago.

TAPÓN: Pura madre, all we had was three beers.

TEODORO: Forget it, compadre, yo pago.

TAPÓN: No, chale, esta Güera se clavó mi feria. That money was for my kids.

GÜERA: Look, Tapón, don't start making pedo. I don't need it in my place, ¿sabes? This isn't the welfare department!

TEODORO: No, Güera, déjalo. He's had a little too much, nomás. Toma, keep the change.

GÜERA: Tell your compadre if he can't afford to pistear, to get out!

HUESOS: Órale, Güera. Tú eres un bato a toda madre, ¡ése! (GÜERA *goes as* PRIETA *brings the food.*)

PRIETA: Tortillas, carnitas, and tripas. Who ordered the tripe?

HUESOS: Don't look at me.

PRIETA: Come on, guys, ¿quién fue?

GREÑAS: Maybe it was Mundo.

PRIETA: Where's he at?

HUESOS: He's on the phone.

PRIETA: Tell him his tripas are here.

TAPÓN: Chale, his tripas are over there. En el toledo. Alguien echó las tripas. (FLACO *upchucks in the toilet.* SUGAR *enters from the rear.*)

SUGAR: Oye, chula Prieta, you got my order?

PRIETA: What did you order? Oh yeah, I remember. (PRIETA *goes.* SUGAR *hangs around.*)

GREÑAS: Who's Mundo talking to for so long?

HUESOS: Learn, ése, learn. You don't ask that.

SUGAR: He's talking to some vieja. Una gabacha.

HUESOS: Who asked you?

SUGAR: I heard him on the way to the escusado. Puro English. ¿Y saben qué? The toilet's messed up.

GREÑAS: Don't tell me.

TAPÓN: He's right! Full to the brim. Con pura . . .

GREÑAS: I told you, don't tell me.

TEODORO: Oye, compa', we're eating.

SUGAR: I had to use the vieja's.

HUESOS: (*Mocking him.*) ¡Ay, no se te vaya a caer el pelo! (PRIETA *comes back with* SUGAR*'s order.*)

PRIETA: Here's your huevos . . . con chorizo.

SUGAR: I'll eat at the bar. Caballeros. (SUGAR *strolls over to the bar and sits on a stool.*)

TEODORO: Oiga, compa', you didn't go back there with el gay caballero, did you?

TAPÓN: Who?

HUESOS: Sugar?

TAPÓN: Is he here?

HUESOS: I saw him heading back there after you, Tapón.

TAPÓN: Ya ni la joden.

HUESOS: Sugar's okay, for a joto.

TEODORO: Don't tell me you don't like it.

HUESOS: Well, ése, in this world, I figure e'erybody's a little queer, ¿me entiendes cómo?

GREÑAS: Not me, man.

TAPÓN: ¡Ni yo!

HUESOS: ¿Saben qué? I'm going to tell you batos something, but if you pass it on, I'll kick your ass.

GREÑAS: I don't wanna hear it.

HUESOS: Oreja. You know Barnes, el cepillo?

GREÑAS: Who?

HUESOS: Sam Barnes, el Deputy Sheriff.

TEODORO: Simón, the one con la crewcut.

HUESOS: That one. I heard he's jineteando a Sugar.

GREÑAS: Nel.

HUESOS: I swear, man. Mundo told me.

TEODORO: I heard the same thing in jail.

TAPÓN: How does Mundo know?

HUESOS: Because, dig this. He's giving it to Barnes' old lady.

GREÑAS: The Sheriff's ruca?

HUESOS: Me la rayo.

TEODORO: Is that who he's talking to?

HUESOS: Prob'ly. Barnes don't make it home that much.

TAPÓN: He's too busy arresting la raza.

GREÑAS: That's how he gets his kicks.

HUESOS: So while he's jailing la raza, Mundo's nailing his ruca en la casa.

TAPÓN: ¡Pos, qué viva la casa!

HUESOS: Chale, ése, que viva la cosa.

TEODORO: I'll remember that next time Barnes throws me in the bote.

GREÑAS: His wife's a pig too! (*Laughter.* MUNDO *turns, standing at the public phone.*)

HUESOS: Órale pues. Don't let Mundo catch you laughing.

TEODORO: ¿Y qué? I'm not sacred of him. I'm his pinche Tío. Where do you think he gets his savoire faire?

TAPÓN: Uy, yu, yui. Qué sangrón. (VERA *enters, looking for* FLACO. PRIETA *brings more food.*)

PRIETA: Okay, here's the last order. Cesos.

GREÑAS: ¿Cesos? You're eating brains?

HUESOS: Me arranco, carnal. Some batos go for the feet, I go for the brains.

GREÑAS: I go for something else.

PRIETA: ¿No van a querer nada más?

TAPÓN: (*Very drunk.*) Yo sí. Let these mensos have their gabachas secas. I'll take a greasy prieta anytime. ¡Véngase, mi India! (*Grabs her arm.*)

PRIETA: ¡Suéltame!

TAPÓN: Oh, come on, no te hagas, mi chula. Sit down! Have a cheve con tu papi.

GÜERA: (*Slamming a bat on the bar.*) ¡Tapón!

HUESOS: Ya pues, Tapón, ¡cálmala! (PRIETA *gets loose and flees.* FLACO *comes out of the toilet.*)

TAPÓN: Pinche raza. You try to do them a favor y mira qué pasa. They despise their own gente!

HUESOS: Take it easy, viejo. She's been working all night.

TAPÓN: Qué nuevas. We're all burros here. ¡Sin mecate!

VERA: (*Stopping* FLACO.) Flaco, you're not doing what I think you're doing, are you?

FLACO: (*Nauseous.*) What do you want from me, Vera?

VERA: I'm sorry I kicked you out. I want you to come home. (FLACO *turns.*) Flaco! (FLACO *runs back into the men's room.* VERA *leaves.*)

HUESOS: Where you going?

TAPÓN: To get more beer.

HUESOS: We're all right, ése.

TAPÓN: (*Going to the bar.*) No. Tonight todo el pinche mundo is going to drink y yo voy a pagar. ¡Güera, más bironga! Put it on my tab.

GÜERA: Go home, Tapón, before your wife kicks your ass for drinking your welfare check.

TAPÓN: (*To crowd laughter.*) What are you laughing at? Méndigos burros. Como dijo Amado Nervo, el gran poeta mexicano: "Desgraciada Raza Mexicana. Obedecer, no quieres. ¡Gobernar, no puedes!" (MUNDO *comes up to the table.* GÜERA *comes over also.*)

MUNDO: ¿Qué trae Tapón? ¿Se está destapando?

HUESOS: Tú sabes. He's feeling his huevos. Oh, sorry, Güera.

GÜERA: Don't scare yourself. Oye, ¿Mundo?

MUNDO: What's up, carnal?

GÜERA: I got a mensaje for you.

MUNDO: I know. Barnes came by, ¿verdad?

GÜERA: He's looking for you.

HUESOS: The deputy sheriff?

GÜERA: I don't know what about. I can guess.

MUNDO: No hay pedo. Everything's cool.

GÜERA: You sure?

MUNDO: Órale, ése. El Mundo's got it down, ¿qué no? Worry about the jefita.

GÜERA: What do I tell mi 'amá if Barnes plugs you full of holes?

TAPÓN: ¡Oye, Güera! (TAPÓN *is at the bar.* SHE *goes.* MUNDO *sits down to eat.*)

MUNDO: This my tripas?

HUESOS: Ése, what do you think Barnes is going to do?

MUNDO: Barnes is going to do what Barnes always does.

GREÑAS: What's that?

MUNDO: Barnes sucks. Let him come. I'm ready.

HUESOS: I'm with you. También Greñas.

MUNDO: Chale. I got to meet him alone.

HUESOS: Alone? I don't like it.

MUNDO: No te escames, Huesos. What is that you always say? El Mundo rifa?

HUESOS: Simón, el Mundo rules.

TEODORO: Until now. (*At the bar* TAPÓN *starts a fight.*)

TAPÓN: ¿Y tú qué tiznados me estás bobiando? I mean you, cabrón!

¿No te gusta? Pos vamos pa' fuera. ¡Ándale! ¡Vente! ¡Chingue su madre todo el pinche mundo! (HE *goes out with another man.* RAZA *heads for the door to watch.*)

RAZA: Fight! Fight! ¡Va a ver chingazos! Make room. ¡Déjalos!

GREÑAS: ¡En la madre, it's Tapón!

TEODORO: ¡¿Mi compadre?! (MUNDO *stays at the table eating. The rest of the cantina is by the door cheering on the fight. Suddenly the noise stops dead.*)

RAZA: ¡La placa!

¡Al alba, la jura!

The man!

It's Barnes.

The Sheriff.

Órale.

Everybody inside! (RAZA *starts coming back in.* GÜERA *comes to* MUNDO.)

GÜERA: It's Barnes! You sure you wanna see him? There's a back door.

HUESOS: Ése, Mundo, take my cuete.

MUNDO: I don't need it.

GREÑAS: Un filero at least!

MUNDO: Ya me están agüitando. (*The cantina settles quickly.* BARNES *enters.*)

GÜERA: Sheriff Barnes! How about a beer?

BARNES: No thanks, still working. (*Goes to* MUNDO.) Hello, Ray.

MUNDO: Reymundo, ése. They call me Mundo.

BARNES: I wonder if I could have a talk with you?

MUNDO: What about?

BARNES: It's a personal matter. Wanna take a little drive?

MUNDO: Simón. (*Gets up.*) Ésa, Güera, ¿sabes qué? Tell Prieta the tripitas are all right. Se aventó. (*To* BARNES.) Let's go, ése.

BARNES: After you.

MUNDO: Chale, after you. (THEY *go out. The cantina murmurs with excitement.*)

GREÑAS: Qué huevos.

HUESOS: Don't I tell you, ése? El Mundo don't take shit from nobody. He's got this world under control, jack!

Fade to black.

Segue: Sounds of Motown "War."

SCENE THREE

A country road. Night. BARNES *and* MUNDO *drive up in* SHERIFF's *car.*

BARNES: Okay, Ray, this is about as far as we go. (*Pause.*) Look at all them stars up there! You know where we are?

MUNDO: Looks like a field.

BARNES: Try this other side of the road.

MUNDO: That's your house.

BARNES: Yep. That's where I keep the little woman. You know my wife, Ella Mae, don't you?

MUNDO: We've met.

BARNES: Really, where?

MUNDO: Right here. The first time I dropped off your cut. You introduced us, remember? (*Gives him an envelope.*) Ahí te llevo.

BARNES: (*Distracted.*) Uh, yeah, right. I forgot. Just keep this business between us, huh? The only reason I let you carry on is because you keep all the other Mexican gangs from coming in. Like weed control.

MUNDO: Simón. I control the weed.

BARNES: Cool as a cucumber. You ever do time?

MUNDO: You tell me.

BARNES: I couldn't find anything on you. Found a couple of other Ray Matas in Lompoc and Folsom, but they're still behind bars. You still live with your mother.

MUNDO: Leave my jefita out of this.

BARNES: Don't get me wrong. I've known Lola since she had the bar. She sent her younger son off to college, but you were drafted. I got a hold of your service record. Quite a record.

MUNDO: Bullshit.

BARNES: Come on now. I know you served in Vietnam, '66 to '68. Charlie Company, 11th Brigade, American Division. Your immediate superior was Lt. William Calley. You took part in the My Lai Massacre . . . right?

MUNDO: I was just a grunt.

BARNES: You're a godamn hero, boy! LBJ should have given you a bronze star, not discharge you as a Section Eight crackpot.

MUNDO: Fuck LBJ. And Nixon. You, too.

BARNES: (*Angering.*) Just a minute, kid. What kind of jackass do you take me for?

MUNDO: Listen, burro . . .

BARNES: Just a minute.

MUNDO: You're the one who wanted to . . .

BARNES: Just a second!

MUNDO: Talk to me, man! I didn't . . .

BARNES: Hold it, GODAMMIT!

MUNDO: Okay. Now you sound more like a pig, see?

BARNES: Is that what you think I am? A pig?

MUNDO: Well, where are we, ése? On the moon? Ain't this still the San Joaquin Valley? Ain't that a field that some fat grower owns? Did the world stop all of a sudden or what? What the fuck do you think this is, "Chico and the Man?" You've been shitting me since we left town!

BARNES: I been trying . . .

MUNDO: You been cagando la estaca!

BARNES: What's that supposed to mean?

MUNDO: It means, ése, that I know why you brought me out here, you dig? El Mundo no es pendejo, marrano.

BARNES: You know I don't speak Spanish.

MUNDO: Why not? Sixty percent of the whole county does. Why don't you speak the language of most of the people in the county, carnal? You're a county Sheriff, ¿qué no?

BARNES: Actually, I'm a deputy. But I'm glad you asked. Would you believe I'm running for the job?

MUNDO: Shit.

BARNES: I'm serious. I'm a candidate for County Sheriff in November. Can I count on your support?

MUNDO: Toma. (*El violín, obscene Mexican gesture.*)

BARNES: What's that?

MUNDO: That's Spanish for this. (*The all-American finger.*)

BARNES: You're a very bitter young fellow. (MUNDO *and* BARNES *sit for a beat. Then a car is heard.*)

MUNDO: Órale. Here they come.

BARNES: Who?

MUNDO: Your friends, Sheriff. Two growers called Gudunritch and Roddenberry. Qué placas. I couldn't name 'em better myself.

BARNES: (*Stunned.*) Who gave you this information?

MUNDO: No te hagas pendejo. You know who . . . Somebody sweet as sugar. (*Two growers drive up in another car.*)

BARNES: (*Defensively.*) Take my advice. Keep your mouth shut and listen. Who in the fuck do you think you're dealing with?

MUNDO: G&R Farms. Me caen guangos. (MUNDO *and* BARNES *step out.*)

GUDUN: Deputy Barnes?

BARNES: Right here, Bob.

GUDUN: Roddenberry's with me.

BARNES: Jack.

RODD: Hey, Sam. This isn't him, is he?

BARNES: Gentlemen, this is the young fella you've heard so much about. Name's Mundo Mata.

GUDUN: Mundo Mata? Doesn't that mean the world kills?

MUNDO: Chale, puto. It means the world plants.

GUDUN: Look here, uh, gentlemen, why don't you sit in the back here, and we'll, uh, talk. There's obviously more room in my towncar.

BARNES: Get in.

MUNDO: You get in. I'm staying out here.

RODD: Hell, let's all get out. C'mon, Bob. Get your corporate ass into the wide open spaces. (*Corporate* GUDUNRITCH *and local grower* RODDENBERRY *step out.*)

BARNES: All right. We're all friends here, right? I should warn you guys that Mr. Mata is a very sharp young fella. We had a real int'rasting conversation while we were waiting—ain't that right, son?

MUNDO: That's right, mother.

BARNES: See what I mean?

GUDUN: Great. Well, in that case, there's not much sense in casual amenities. We'll proceed right to the point. Okay, Jack?

RODD: Shoot.

GUDUN: (*At* MUNDO.) Bang. (*Nobody else laughs.*) Mr. Mata, we've been led to believe that our area is about to become the theater of operations for a calculated, highly organized, publically financed drive by subversive, left-wing interests with an eye toward controlling the agricultural labor pool as it exists in our area of the state.

RODD: Oh, fuck, Bob. Get to the point.

GUDUN: I'm trying.

RODD: Shit. César Chávez is coming, okay?

GUDUN: That's the point.

RODD: The United Farm Workers Union is planning to open an office in your town.

GUDUN: Burlap is going to be the central organizing headquarters for the entire county.

RODD: They're going to petition every godamn ranch for union elections come this summer.

GUDUN: Naturally, we have no plans to comply.

RODD: Hell no! This is a red chili-belly Communist crusade to take over the whole blasted state. Mexicans have never asked for elections, why now? . . . Because Chávez says so? We could frigging lose California.

GUDUN: No, Jack. Even if they win, there's no law that says we must abide by election results. Our lobbyists in Sacramento have fixed that.

RODD: How about the Grape Boycott—did they fix that yet? They need expense accounts just to take a crap.

GUDUN: I told you to consider the Teamsters.

RODD: The Teamsters are losing elections all over the frigging state, Bob. What the hell's the use of calling in the Mafia if they can't even win a goddamned dishonest election?

GUDUN: Well, then, what's left?

RODD: Him! What the hell else are we doing out here in the middle of the night?

GUDUN: Mr. Mota . . .

MUNDO: Mah-ta, ése. Mota is something else.

GUDUN: You don't say.

MUNDO: Simón. Watcha. (*Pulls out a joint.*)

GUDUN: What's that?

MUNDO: Un leño of some of the most beautiful mota these fields have ever grown. Lemme lay it on you.

GUDUN: A joint. He gave me a joint. . . .

BARNES: Marijuana!

MUNDO: Killer Green from San Joaquin. (*Pause. All look at each other.*)

RODD: Well, what the hell you all waiting for? Gimme that shit. (*Takes the joint and lights it. Sucks it in, holds his breath.*) Want some, Sheriff?

BARNES: What the hell, why not? Me and my wife, we do this once in a while in, uh, bed. It shore puts the spark back on your plugs. (*Tokes up.*) Know what I mean?

RODD: (*Exhaling.*) Oh, yes.

GUDUN: Which part of México are you from, Mr. Mota?

MUNDO: Burlap, Califas, México, buey.

RODD: (*Laughs.*) Wanna hear something funny? Me too. Yep. Old Jack Roddenberry was born in Burlap, California. It was a different town then lemme tell ya. Shit. The whole town's a wreck. Hardly any white familes left. Nothing but wetbacks coming and . . . well . . .

MUNDO: What's that, ése?

RODD: Forget it. (*Pause.*) You're Lola Torres' boy, aren't you?

MUNDO: I'm nobody's boy.

RODD: I used to do business with your stepfather. Torres was the best damn labor contractor I ever had till he croaked.

MUNDO: You're still getting your wetbacks, aren't you?

RODD: Lola's good at running the labor camp, I'll grant her that. A woman contractor? Naw.

GUDUN: (*Cutting in.*) Gentlemen, why don't we come to some kind of agreement here, so that we can all get home to our respective families, hm? Mr. Mota, I am serving as the legal representative for a number of growers who shall remain nameless. We want to hire you.

MUNDO: To do what, pick grapes?

RODD: To stop Chávez!

GUDUN: By any means necessary.

MUNDO: (*Pause.*) You mean like Malcolm X?

GUDUN: Why should Malcolm, Martin, and the dead Kennedys hog all the glory? Are you interested?

MUNDO: Well, Bob-oso. Not for chump change. For that movida you're talking at least . . . thirty G's, up front, with a back end of . . . a mil.

GUDUN: That could be arranged.

RODD: You're outa your frigging mind! We're not asking you to snuff Chávez, okay! All we want is for you to screw up the election drive in any way you know how. Get in there and spy, bribe whoever you

got to, threaten the hell out of whoever gets in your way. Piss on the
goddamn ballots if you have to, but make them lose the godamn
elections! Can you do that?

MUNDO: For how much?

RODD: We'll pay you a hundred a week . . .

MUNDO: How much?

GUDUN: Two hundred a week . . .

MUNDO: How much?

RODD: Three hundred a week and that's it.

MUNDO: Fuck you.

GUDUN: How much do you want?

MUNDO: I want a thousand a week from each grower in the deal.

RODD: Are you crazy?

GUDUN: That's ten thousand a week, in round figures.

RODD: Shove it.

MUNDO: Look, man, what the hell you been so greedy about? If the
union gets in, you sonavubitches are going to pay through the nose.
All I'm asking is a thousand a week from you, and you, and everyone of your bloodsucking friends. What the hell is that? Shit! Ten
grand a week!

RODD: We'll pay you two.

MUNDO: Five!

GUDUN: What are you prepared to do for this money?

MUNDO: Man, in my town, I can do anything.

RODD: You're on. (*Sticks out his hand.*) Pay him.

GUDDUN: Five thousand a week for how long?

RODD: As long as it takes.

GUDUN: We'll expect weekly reports. The Sheriff here will take care
of paying you off . . .

BARNES: Do you have to put it that way?

GUDUN: Sheriff, come on. It will be cash, of course.

MUNDO: Of course.

GUDUN: Here's five hundred to start. We weren't prepared to go any
higher. (*Gives him money.*) Next week we'll balance if off. And if
you're ever caught . . . we don't even know you ever existed. Do I
make myself clear?

MUNDO: As clear as Watergate, ése. I've never see your ugly face in
my whole life.

GUDUN: (*Slowly, deliberately.*) Fuck You.

MUNDO: In your mouth.

RODD: Come on, Bob, let's get the hell out of here.

GUDUN: My pleasure. (GUDUNRITCH *and* RODDENBERRY *get into their car.*)

BARNES: Jack, Bob? I'll see you. (*The growers peal off without another word.*) Those bastards. Come on, son, I'll drop you off in town. (MUNDO *and* BARNES *get back into the* SHERIFF'*s car and drive back to town in silence.* THEY *pull into town.*) Where you wanna be dropped off?

MUNDO: Wherever, man.

BARNES: You didn't say nothing on the way back. (*Pause.*) That's okay. I understand. Listen, about my wife . . . (*A man staggers across the path of the car.*) Oh, Christ! What the hell is he . . . ! (HE *hits him.*) Shit, I hit him! Did you see that? He just walked right into the street!

MUNDO: (*Jumps out the car.*) It's Flaco.

BARNES: Who?

MUNDO: A friend of mine.

BARNES: I'll call an ambulance.

MUNDO: Wait a minute, ése. Hold on. Look, éste, he's all right.

BARNES: Are you sure? He looks kinda bad to me.

MUNDO: He's always this way, man. I know him. He's a . . . drunk. He lives right upstairs above the old drugstore. Ése, Flaco, you okay, carnal?

FLACO: Mundo?

MUNDO: ¿Quihúbo, ése? ¿Qué pasó pues?

FLACO: Tú sabes.

MUNDO: He's going to be fine. You better leave him to me. It's better if nobody else saw us together tonight, you know what I mean?

BARNES: Oh. Right, sure, good thinking.

MUNDO: I'll see you in a week.

BARNES: Right. A week. Where shall I meet you?

MUNDO: Just drop the bread off at the bar, man. With my sister.

BARNES: Gotcha. (*Pause.*) Which dyke's your sister? The brown one?

MUNDO: La Güera, man, the light one.

BARNES: Well, I'll be, you learn something new every day, don't you? Buenas noches.

MUNDO: Yeah. Fuck off. (BARNES *drives off.*) Pinche Flaco. What
    you doing out in the streets so late, ése?
FLACO: No la chingues. I was looking for you, Mundo. Ya no aguan-
    to, ése. I need some scag.
MUNDO: Qué bato.
FLACO: Did you collect for the last fix?
MUNDO: ¡Chale! Don't start with that pinche rollo again. I'd never do
    that to you, carnal. You've got a beautiful wife and kid, man. I don't
    ever want to hear you pimping Vera to me again, ¿me entiendes
    cómo?
FLACO: Simón.
MUNDO: Come on, I'll take you home and fix you up.
FLACO: Ése, I got no bread.
MUNDO: Man, who you with? Yo soy tu carnal, El Mundo. Y con el
    Mundo money is no fucking object, homes.

Black.

Transition: Sounds of Hitsville USA: Pusher Man.

SCENE FOUR

*Vera's apartment above the old drugstore. Afternoon. Bedroom—
interior/exterior.* MUNDO *is lying in bed with* VERA.

MUNDO: I love the smell of mota in the afternoon . . . it reminds me of
    . . . old times. I still feel the same about you, chula. Since that sum-
    mer cuando te watché en la packing shed, sorting tomates. You were
    always mine.
VERA: I can't believe I did this.
MUNDO: Face it, Vera, your old man's a hype. Anda prendido de a
    madres. Flaco's my camarada. We were chavalos together. He
    wants me to be his curandero. I want him to see what he's doing to
    himself! What's the problema?
VERA: I love him.
MUNDO: (*Pause.*) What about me . . . and my kid? (GÜERITO, *7,
    enters the house.*)
GÜERITO: ¡'Amá, 'amá!
VERA: (*Sitting up.*) Oh, my God! There's Güerito!
MUNDO: He's home already?

VERA: What time is it? He musta already got out of school. Chihuahua, why did you have to do this to me? And in the middle of the day?

GÜERITO: (*Outside the door.*) Hey, 'amá? Where are you?

VERA: Uh. Sí, ¿mi'jito? (SHE *comes out of the room tightening her bathrobe.*)

GÜERITO: The old drugstore downstairs is open! Who's moving in a new store?

VERA: I don't think so.

GÜERITO: The man said it's a union. What's a union? (*Sniffs.*) What's that funny smell?

VERA: I'm burning some incense. Go play with your friends, mi'jito.

GÜERITO: I'm hungry.

VERA: I'll fix something for you to eat in a little while. Tell you what, why don't you go to the tienda del chino and get some milk and pan dulce? That's a perty good idea. Tell him to put it on the bill.

GÜERITO: Can I get a Sugar Daddy?

VERA: Get what you want.

GÜERITO: Cigarettes?

VERA: (*Getting irritated.*) No! Yes, but for me not you. Menthols.

GÜERITO: I need a note.

VERA: What for?

GÜERITO: The chino won't sell 'em to me.

VERA: Tell him I said so.

GÜERITO: He won't believe me.

VERA: Güerito, ¡no me hagas enojar! Now get going!

GÜERITO: All right. I'm going! (HE *goes.*)

VERA: (*Turns to bedroom.*) Okay, man, now it's your turn. Get going before he gets back.

MUNDO: (*Still dressing himself.*) ¿Por qué?

VERA: Put on your shoes.

MUNDO: ¿Qué traes, ésa? Everything's cool. It was a beautiful afternoon.

VERA: Hurry up, will you?

MUNDO: That's not what you said in bed.

VERA: You're spoiling it! Please leave.

MUNDO: Eres una ruca a toda madre, Vera, and I hate to see a good ruca go to waste. Relax. I'm only here to bring a little love back into your life, mi vida. For old time's sake. What's wrong with that?

VERA: I'm a married ruca, that's what. My parents live in town over at the labor camp! I have a seven-year-old son, and he's coming right back—that's fucking what!

MUNDO: Why're you getting mad? ¿Por qué te enojas?

VERA: Because I'm ashamed.

MUNDO: Chale. (HE *holds her tenderly.*) Your body don't lie, loca. You need me.

VERA: (*Pushing him away.*) Cómo eres, cabrón, you know that? What do you want from me? Flaco needs me.

MUNDO: Flaco can't love you, ésa. Not like I can. I'll be back tonight.

VERA: Don't be stupid! I start work tomorrow.

MUNDO: (*Bristling.*) ¿Sabes qué? Don't ever call me stupid. I never went to college like my pinche kid brother, but I've never had to bust my ass in the fields neither. How long are you going to stay beautiful working in the packing sheds? It's dog eat dog, mi vida.

VERA: Get the hell out of here!

MUNDO: Think about it. (*Starts to go.*)

VERA: Mundo. (HE *stops.*) Please don't come back.

MUNDO: You don't mean that. (MUNDO *stashes a couple of bills on the bed as he exits.* HE *meets* GÜERITO *coming back empty handed.*)

GÜERITO: Hi. Mundo!

MUNDO: Ése, Güerito, how you doing?

GÜERITO: Okay.

MUNDO: (*Slipping* GÜERITO *a coin.*) A toda madre. Ahí te watcho. (HE *goes.*)

GÜERITO: What was he doing here?

VERA: Looking for your father. What you doing back so soon?

GÜERITO: I ran.

VERA: Did you get some cigarettes?

GÜERITO: No. I told you he was going to ask for a note. Beside he said no more credit until the bill's paid. It's up to $200. He told me in front of e'rybody in the store.

VERA: I'll make you some beans.

GÜERITO: I don't want no pinche beans.

VERA: Don't talk like that.

GÜERITO: Well, I don't.

VERA: Then don't eat! (SHE *notices and picks up the money* MUNDO *left on the bed.*)

GÜERITO: How come we never got any money?

VERA: (*Softening.*) We're poor, okay? There's no paycheck if there's no work. It'll be better next week. I promise.

GÜERITO: Mundo always has money. Why didn't you ask him for some?

VERA: What's that supposed to mean?

GÜERITO: Nothing.

VERA: ¡Entonces, cállate! Go out and play.

GÜERITO: Was Mundo here all afternoon?

VERA: He came to fix the plumbing.

GÜERITO: What plumbing?

VERA: (*Confused, mad, half-crying.*) The plumbing, the plumbing in the kitchen, don't you know what plumbing is? (SHE *exits into the bathroom.*)

GÜERITO: Yeah, plumbing. I bet!

Blackout.

SCENE FIVE

Scene: A meeting is underway in the sparsely furnished office in the old drugstore. A United Farmworkers flag hangs on the wall. CHUCK WHITTAKER *is talking to* SUGAR, TEODORO, TAPÓN *and* BOTELLA.

WHITTAKER: Compañeros, three years ago, César Chávez led the Delano Grape Strike to victory. Our huelga brought the growers to their knees with the National Grape Boycott and won the first ever union contracts for farm workers in U.S. history.

TAPÓN: ¡Viva Chávez!

FARMWORKERS: ¡Qué Viva! (*Applause.*)

WHITTAKER: Unfortunately, they've expired. When it came time to renew those contracts, the same growers stabbed us—you—in the back! Sin consultar los trabajadores, they threw out our union and signed with the Teamsters.

BOTELLA: Pos, mira que arrastrados, ¡tú!

TAPÓN: ¡Abajo los Teamsters!

FARMWORKERS: ¡ABAJO! (FLACO *enters, strung out, being pushed by* VERA.)

WHITTAKER: Now every damn grower in the state is doing the same without consulting the workers. You know what Agribusiness wants, don't you? No more union wages, no more drinking water, no more portable toilets in the field. Yes, back to child labor and feudal exploitation.

SUGAR: ¡Abajo los rancheros!

FARMWORKERS: ¡ABAJO!

BOTELLA: (*To* VERA.) Vera, mi'ja, mira, siéntate aquí. (VERA *sits down beside* BOTELLA. GÜERITO *runs in and joins them.*)

WHITTAKER: Brothers and sisters, if we don't stop them now by fighting for union elections, ranch by ranch and county by county, as the harvest moves north, we'll lose everything we've ever fought for. The future of our families, our children, our union depends on it. Are you ready to put on a fight? ¿Sí o no? ¿Se puede? (¡SÍ SE PUEDE!) Now you're talking. (*Handing out forms and buttons.*) Okay, let's get out and hit those labor camps after work. We want every man, woman and child over sixteen registered to vote. Be sure they sign the membership forms.

TAPÓN: Oye, Chuck, ¿y mi botón qué?

SUGAR: Me too. I want a union button. I love the little red one with the thunderbird.

WHITTAKER: Wear them so they'll know who you are.

TEODORO: Oye, compa', you wanna go out with me to Rottenberry's rancho?

TAPÓN: Are you taking Azúcar?

TEODORO: N'ombre, my diabetes is acting up.

SUGAR: I heard that. Flaco and I will take the Gudunritch ranch. Right, ése? (FLACO *sneaks out the back.*) I guess not. (*Exits.*)

WHITTAKER: You guys better get going.

TAPÓN: Vámonos. (HE *and* TEODORO *start to go.*) I'll be back for dinner, vieja. Bye, mi'ja.

VERA: Bye, Papá.

BOTELLA: Oye, oye, and what about the plumbing?

TAPÓN: Habla con el Chuck. I'm organizing. (*Exits.*)

WHITTAKER: What plumbing?

BOTELLA: At the Torres Labor Camp. Where we live. You know the place, at the edge of town? The pipes are rotten, and the water stinks like . . . well, you know . . . like puros farts. I'm afraid to cook for my kids.

WHITTAKER: Have you tried talking to the owner?

BOTELLA: (*Scoffing.*) Doña Lola?! Cállate, the woman is a scorpion. She used to work at Torres Bar as a cantinera, before she married him. Then he dropped dead. Now she's the contratista! And she still lives in that rat hole. (*The phone rings.* WHITTAKER *answers, as* VERA *and* BOTELLA *talk.*)

WHITTAKER: Excuse me. (*Picks up.*) Farmworkers. Oh, hi, Dolores. Yeah. Tell César the Eagle has landed.

VERA: (*To* BOTELLA.) You, too, huh, 'amá?

BOTELLA: Me, too, what? Joining la unión? ¿Y por qué no? We viejas work in the fields too.

VERA: I mean the plumbing.

WHITTAKER: (*Talking on the phone.*) Burlap's a company town, Dolores, practically owned by G&R Farms, but what's new, right? Can you send me any more people?

VERA: I'm having the same problem upstairs.

BOTELLA: Pos luego. Doña Lola owns this rotten building, too.

WHITTAKER: (*On phone.*) Who? Salvador? Right on! When's he getting here? He left this morning? All right. Then he oughta be here anytime now.

BOTELLA: Torres left Doña Lola everything. He didn't leave his son Flaco nothing, ni un méndigo centavo. I don't know why you married him. Yes, I do. How's my Güerito? (SHE *hugs her grandson.*)

GÜERITO: Fine, Grandma. Can I have a huelga button?

BOTELLA: (*Removing her button.*) Say Viva Chávez first. (GÜERITO *says it.*) Louder. (GÜERITO *repeats it.*) ¡Más louder! (GÜERITO *shouts it.*) ¡'Ora sí! (BOTELLA *pins the button on* GÜERITO *as* MUNDO *walks in with* HUESOS.)

WHITTAKER: Hold the phone. Wait a minute. (*To* MUNDO.) Come in. Be right with you. Hey, Dolores, I've got people in the office, okay? Listen. Don't forget the check for the rent. Right. Hasta mañana. (*Hangs up.*) Hello there. I'm Chuck Whittaker. Can I help you?

MUNDO: Where's everybody at, ése?

WHITTAKER: Depends. Who you looking for?

MUNDO: (*Looking at* VERA.) All the people, bato. Where's all the workers, tú sabes.

WHITTAKER: You mean the organizers? Well, we're a little under staffed right now, but the ones we got are hitting the ranches. You from around here?

MUNDO: (*To* HUESOS.) Este bato, man.

WHITTAKER: I'm sorry. I've only been here a week.

HUESOS: He's been here all his life.

MUNDO: (*To* VERA *and* BOTELLA.) What's this, the ladies auxiliary? What you doing here, ésa?

BOTELLA: You leave my daughter alone, Mundo! (BOTELLA *rushes out with* VERA.)

WHITTAKER: Hey, wait a minute. Your name is Mundo? Are you Mundo Mata?

MUNDO: You got it.

WHITTAKER: I know your brother. Salvador.

MUNDO: Oh yeah? How do you know my kid brother?

WHITTAKER: We met in Delano. Listen, you wanna sit down and talk?

MUNDO: What about?

WHITTAKER: (*Pause.*) The elections.

MUNDO: I don't vote, ése. That pinche Nixon's a crook.

WHITTAKER: Sorry. I'm talking about the coming elections for a farmworkers union.

MUNDO: Oye, Huesos, do we look like farmworkers, ése?

WHITTAKER: You don't work in the fields?

HUESOS: We don't work, if we can help it.

MUNDO: What do you get out of this, ése?

WHITTAKER: Me?

MUNDO: Simón, everybody's got a movida.

WHITTAKER: I'm working for a cause I believe in.

MUNDO: The cause of my people, carnal?

WHITTAKER: The cause of the farmworker.

MUNDO: But you're a gabacho, right?

WHITTAKER: (*Pause.*) Yeah. I'm a gabacho.

MUNDO: Órale. Así me gusta. Pull out all the pelos from the start. What do you want?

WHITTAKER: I want you to help us.

MUNDO: Who's us?

WHITTAKER: The union.

MUNDO: What union? You see a union here, Huesos? Something tells me this union's having trouble getting the raza in here, ¿te das cuenta? Maybe they don't speak the right language.

WHITTAKER: ¿Quieres hablar en español?

MUNDO: Chale, I can speak English.

WHITTAKER: Okay, then I'll talk as plain as I can. I know that you're a heavy in this town.

MUNDO: Heavy? Who told you that?

WHITTAKER: Sal. Your brother.

MUNDO: Ése, I haven't seen my carnalillo since I got back from 'Nam.

WHITTAKER: He says you're a natural born leader.

MUNDO: He said that? Puro pedo. What do you care?

WHITTAKER: We both work for the same cause.

MUNDO: We'll see. (*Walking.*) Mind if I look around?

WHITTAKER: There's nothing back there but mattresses on the floor.

HUESOS: You got any *Playboy*'s? (MUNDO *and* HUESOS *exit into the next room.* BULLET *enters, a ball of youthful energy carrying a duffle bag and his guitar.*)

BULLET: Say, Chuck!

WHITTAKER: Sal! You're just in time. They told me you were coming. Welcome to Burlap, buddy.

BULLET: This is the old drugstore. So this is it, huh? How's it going?

WHITTAKER: It's going. Everybody's still out at the labor camps. That's all your stuff?

BULLET: That's it.

WHITTAKER: Some of us are sleeping in the back there. Pick out a mattress. Make yourself at home. (BULLET *picks up his stuff.* HE *turns toward the back room.*)

MUNDO: (*At the door.*) Ése, Bullet!

BULLET: Oh, no!

MUNDO: ¿Qué pues, nuez?

BULLET: Mundo? (*The brothers embrace with joyful surprise.*)

MUNDO: Pinche bato, what are you doing here?

BULLET: Pos ¿qué? La unión.

MUNDO: Naa. You, with Chávez?

BULLET: For almost two years now.

MUNDO: (*Concealing his let down.*) ¿Y qué pasó con la university y el track y todo ese pedo?

BULLET: This is more important,

MUNDO: ¿Ya te watchó la jefita?

BULLET: No, I just got into town. Chuck's the only one who knew I was coming. I thought I'd surprise you all.

MUNDO: Watcha, Huesos. ¿Te acuerdas de mi carnal? El famoso Bullet de Washington High, Salvador Mata. ¡El tiro!

HUESOS: Right on.

MUNDO: You know why they called him Bullet? Because he was so fast. You know why he was so fast? Because he used to run from me.

HUESOS: Who used to win?

MUNDO: ¿Pos quién?

HUESOS: El Mundo.

MUNDO: Chale, baboso, el Bullet.

WHITTAKER: Maybe you can talk your brother into signing up, Sal. (*Phone rings.*) Excuse me.

MUNDO: Pinche carnal. The only one to finish high school and go to college, y watcha dónde anda? Back in Burlap in the old drugstore.

BULLET: It's time it served for something. It's been useless for years.

MUNDO: Chale, carnal. It's holding up the apartments upstairs. There's a lotta raza up there.

BULLET: I know, that's why I'm here.

MUNDO: (*Curious.*) Órale pues, capea un application. Un menú, lo que sea. I'll sign up. Huesos, a firmar, ése.

HUESOS: No shit?

MUNDO: Sign, man. (*Goes to sign.*) We might as well give the bato two members. He's not going to get anybody else in town.

WHITTAKER: (*On the phone.*) Okay. Hold the phone. (*To the room.*) Sal, can you watch the office? I've got a house meeting.

BULLET: No sweat.

WHITTAKER: Great. (*Into phone.*) I'm on my way. (*Hangs up.*) Mundo, it was great to meet you and your friend. Enjoy your reunion. See you, Sal. (WHITTAKER *leaves.* MUNDO *signals* HUESOS *to follow him.*)

MUNDO: (*Harsher.*) How long you been taking orders from gabachos, ése?

BULLET: What orders?

MUNDO: From that bato. Se la tira de muy chingón.

BULLET: He's just doing his job. He's in charge of organizing our campaign here.

MUNDO: How can a gabacho organize campesinos, man? Especially la raza around here. Most of them are still wet, de aquí pa' abajo.

BULLET: Habla español.

MUNDO: No shit? Well, maybe with a good tan y más greña he can pass as one of us. Si no lo agarran a chingazos.

BULLET: It won't be anything new. He's a Migrant Minister. They beat him up in Coachella.

MUNDO: Hubo, un desmadre, ¿eh?

BULLET: The Teamsters and their goons. Man, those pinches rancheros have tried everything to stop us. But nothing will. Not violence or blood or death. Or money.

MUNDO: Money?

BULLET: They always try to bribe a few people. Those who are pendejos enough to accept it. They've probably bribed somebody around here already.

MUNDO: Chale. Here?

BULLET: Simón. When the growers start paying feria, the vendidos come out like pinacates. You can always tell who they are.

MUNDO: Oh yeah? Well, you tell me who they are, carnal, y yo les doy en la madre.

BULLET: What for? They always trip themselves up. ¿Sabes por qué? Because they're stupid. You can't go against the union, man. This thing is big! Millions of people are involved. Man, con la unión we've dug into the very guts of this country. I spent a year in New York. Simón, New York, on the boycott. This thing involves the whole country. Shit, the whole world. This is a revolutionary movement.

MUNDO: What are you talking about, cabrón? You sound like a pinche communist.

BULLET: That's the cagada of the growers.

MUNDO: What cagada?

BULLET: Anticommunist cagada.

MUNDO: You mean you're not a draft dodger?

BULLET: I'm a conscientious objector. I don't believe in war and I renounce all kinds of violence. That's why I joined César. He's America's Mohandas Gandhi, man.

MUNDO: He's mojandas, all right. Mojado Gandhi.

BULLET: Same old Mundo. It's like nothing's changed, but everything's different.

MUNDO: Qué loco, ¿no?

BULLET: Life is full of contradictions, man.

MUNDO: What's that—rubbers?

BULLET: What?

MUNDO: Nada. (*Laughs.*) Bueno pues, talonéale. Let's go see the jefita.

BULLET: No puedo.

MUNDO: ¿Cómo que no? What about all this sí se puede shit?

BULLET: I mean until Chuck gets back. I got to keep the oficina open.

MUNDO: For what, the cucarachas? Pura madre. (*Grabs him.*) I'm taking you home, carnal. Right now!

BULLET: Mundo! (MUNDO *drags him out.*)

Blackout.

SCENE SIX

Torres labor camp. Interior/exterior. A compound of dingy shacks, gathered around a long house. DOÑA LOLA *rolls in, sitting in her wheelchair, completely dressed in black. Deathly intense.*

DOÑA LOLA: Pos mira nomás. Qué milagro. So you finally decided to come see your madre, eh? Bendito sea Dios. I was expecting to see you from my coffin. Is it really you? (MUNDO *escorts* BULLET *into the light from the shadows.*)

BULLET: (*Nervous.*) Sí, 'amá, ¿cómo está?

DOÑA LOLA: ¿Pos cómo? Can't you see? Me está llevando la chingada. I'm falling apart piece by piece. These old legs, ya no me sirven. The doctors want to cut them off, fíjate. It's good you came while I'm still in one piece. Have you eaten?

BULLET: I'm not hungry.

DOÑA LOLA: There's meat in the refrigerator. ¿No quieres?

BULLET: I don't eat meat anymore, 'amá. But thanks.

DOÑA LOLA: Reymundo, bring your brother a beer. And one for you too. Están bien heladas.

MUNDO: Órale, jefa. (*Goes for the beer.*)

DOÑA LOLA: So you don't eat carne no more, eh? ¿Qué chirriados tragas entonces?

BULLET: Grains mostly. Rice, corn, beans.

DOÑA LOLA: (*Laughing.*) N'ombre, is this why I sent you to college? So you could eat like a pobre desgraciado? Didn't your padre teach you anything? Reading the Bible never kept him from eating. Skinny hypocrite! He took you from me when you were only eight years old. Did he think he could divorce me from my own son? ¡Qué pendejo! (SHE *coughs, hacking terribly.* MUNDO *brings two bottles of beer.*)

MUNDO: Easy, jefa.

DOÑA LOLA: Narciso Mata was always a baboso. He never would have crossed the border, if I hadn't pushed him under the wire. I was pregnant too, with Mundo, carrying Güera in my arms.

BULLET: Do we have to talk about my dad? He doesn't even know I'm here.

DOÑA LOLA: He was never too smart. Why do you think he spent five years in prison? If it hadn't been for Torres, we would have starved to death. En paz descanse. (*Crosses herself.*)

MUNDO: Ask the carnal why he's here, 'amá.

DOÑA LOLA: Oyes, didn't you come back to see me?

BULLET: Sure. But I'm working with César Chávez.

DOÑA LOLA: ¿¡Chávez!?

BULLET: Organizing union elections. Here in Burlap.

DOÑA LOLA: (*Tragically.*) ¡Me lleva la triste tiznada! Do you want to kill me, Salvador? Don't you know what kind of man Chávez is? He's a living santo! The only saints you can trust are the dead ones. ¿Qué no sabes nada? Look at your father!

BULLET: Are we back to him again?

DOÑA LOLA: Coming back from prison, all full of Jesus. Cursing me for working at Torres Bar. Who was he to judge me? He never told you why he went to prison, did he?

BULLET: I know. He was caught smuggling mojados.

DOÑA LOLA: No, mi'jito. He fell asleep at the wheel, driving back from the border. In the rain, a speeding train hit his truck at a railroad crossing. ¡Y ZAS! Heads, arms, bodies flew everywhere. Thirteen men, women and children. All killed.

BULLET: (*Shocked.*) What? He said he went up for manslaughter.

DOÑA LOLA: El que nace pa' Cristo del cielo le cae la cruz. (*The phone rings.*) ¿Halo? ¿Quién es? Who? Un momento. (*Calls at door.*) ¿Botella? ¡BOTELLA!

BOTELLA: (*O.S.*) Sí, ¿señora?

DOÑA LOLA: You're wanted on the teléfono. (*Turns back.*) The neighbor. I let her use the phone. (BOTELLA *knocks*.) Come in, mujer, pasa.

BOTELLA: (*Out of breath*.) Gracias. I was just coming from downtown. (*Sees* MUNDO *with chagrin*.) Oiga, Doña Lola, now that I'm here, could I talk to you about the sewer pipes?

DOÑA LOLA: No me chingues, mujer. Answer the phone.

BOTELLA: Con su permiso. (*Picks up the phone*.) ¿Halo? Juan! Where are you? ¿Qué te pasa? WHAT! WHERE? WHEN? Oh, my God, viejito! Don't move, mi amor! I'm coming! (*Drops phone*.)

DOÑA LOLA: ¿Qué te pasa?

BOTELLA: (*Choking up*.) Tapón! He was just beaten up at one of the ranchos. They're taking him to the hospital! I gotta go to him!

BULLET: (*Snapping to action*.) I'll go with you. Where is he?

BOTELLA: (*Running out*.) The bar!

MUNDO: ¡Vámonos! (*Stops*.) You gonna be all right, jefa?

DOÑA LOLA: Pos luego, ¡vete! (MUNDO *exits*.) What do you all care if I live or die? (*Picks up phone*.) Halo, Güera, are you there? What's going on? (*Listens, laughs*.) ¡Otro pendejo!

Fade to black.

SCENE SEVEN

La Divina Garza. A bloodied TAPÓN *is at a table, attended by* WHITTAKER *and* TEODORO. *Shock and anger in the crowd, including* SUGAR, FLACO, HUESOS *and* GREÑAS. PRIETA *is behind the bar.*

TAPÓN: Por un botón nomás. Por un pinche botoncito me golpearon, ¿no les digo? After twelve years of working for the desgraciado, ¡y mira cómo me repaga! ¡Me agarraron entre tres!

WHITTAKER: Take it easy, Tapón. Just tell us how it happened.

TAPÓN: They attacked us walking into Roddenberry's rancho! For wearing a little huelga button, nomás ¡fíjense! ¡Uno me dio con un garrote!

TEODORO: I saw them do it. They hit him on the head!

WHITTAKER: Can you identify who did it?

TEODORO: ¡Pos luego! I saw them this close! It was tres pelados . . . in ski masks.

TAPÓN: We were just going to talk to the workers, when they stopped us. Uno me dijo: "¡Oye, tú! The patrón don't like huelga buttons. Take it off!" Y yo le dije, "You take it off, buey." ¡Y que me planta el guamaso! Three of them got me on the ground. ¡Desgraciados! I give thanks to Diosito Santo my vieja wasn't with me! They woulda had her on the ground también! (BOTELLA *runs in, and screams at the sight of bloody* TAPÓN.)

BOTELLA: ¡AYYY, Tapón! ¡Viejito! Are you all right? Dios mío, look what they did to you! (SHE *is followed by* BULLET *and* MUNDO.)

TAPÓN: ¡Ya pues! Ya, no es nada, vieja. I'm okay.

WHITTAKER: We better take you to the hospital, Tapón.

TAPÓN: ¡No! ¡Estoy bien! ¡Estoy bien les digo!

BULLET: Who did this, who beat him up?

HUESOS: Three guys in ski masks at Roddenberry's.

GREÑAS: Le dieron en la madre con un two-by-four.

SUGAR: ¡Ay! I missed all the fun at Gudunritch's.

BOTELLA: ¡Pero les va a pesar! They'll pay for this!

TAPÓN: ¡Seguro! They can't do this to us no more, ¿verdad, vieja?

BOTELLA: Para eso 'sta la unión aquí. ¡Pa darle guerra a los pinche rancheros!

MUNDO: Ése, Tapón, you say it was at Roddenberry's? Órale. Then let's go take care of 'em! Those pinche rancheros want pedo, let's give it to them! (*The crowd agrees.*) Huesos, get the cuete. Flaco, Greñas, all of you, your bats, sus fileros, ¡lo que sea! Vamos a darles en la madre a esos hijos de la . . .

WHITTAKER: Just a second! Just a second!

BULLET: That's not the way to do it, Mundo!

MUNDO: ¿Cómo chingados que no? Look at the carnal!

BULLET: We can't do it with violence!

MUNDO: ¿Qué traes, buey?

BULLET: If we go into that ranch with guns and bats, the growers will hit back with shotguns. And the law will be on their side!

MUNDO: Chale, ¿qué law? There's no law! Nomás esto, watcha! (*Pulls out filero.* VERA *runs in with* GÜERITO. THEY *run to* TAPÓN.)

VERA: ¡Papá! What happened? Who did this to you?)

SUGAR: Three goons con baseball bats.

HUESOS: In ski masks. Nobody saw faces. Right?

FLACO and GREÑAS: ¡Simón!

SUGAR: How do you know? Were you there? (HUESOS *and* GREÑAS *look at each other.* FLACO *looks anguished.*)

HUESOS, GREÑAS, FLACO: (*Ad libs.*) ¡Órale! Come on! ¡No la chingues!

BULLET: ¡Hermanos, hermanas! We are here to organize a union election. We don't need to fight them any other way. We'll only be playing into the growers hands! Every time there's violence, el campesino comes out losing!

MUNDO: Then what do we have to lose?

BULLET: ¡Es táctica, compañeros! I know you're angry about Tapón! Me too! But there's another way to teach those cabrones rancheros a lesson! ¡Con calma! ¡Con organización! ¡Con fuerza! ¡Ellos son pocos, nosotros somos muchos!

MUNDO: ¡Simón, pa' joderlos más pronto!

BULLET: That's right, pero con elecciones. ¡No con violencia!

MUNDO: Bueno, ése, you been gone a long time, ¿sabes? Maybe you forgot what your pueblo's like, man. Vamos a ver lo que dice el Tapón. He's the one que jodieron!

CROWD: ¡Es cierto! Simón. ¡Qué hable el Tapón! (TAPÓN *holds his head up, bloody but proud.*)

TAPÓN: Pos, yo creo que el respeto al derecho ajeno es la paz.

MUNDO: (*Slapping his fist.*) Simón, ¡paz, paz, paz!

BOTELLA: Ya estuvo con esos rancheros. We've been pushed around enough! We don't got to be afraid of them no more! ¡Tenemos derechos. Tenemos nuestra unión! (*Cheers in the crowd.* TAPÓN *Gets pumped up and makes a speech.*)

TAPÓN: Y vale más que vayan aprendiendo todos. This union is for the pobres, los de abajo! ¡Ahora sí soy Chavista! ¡Yo no tengo pelos en la lengua pa' decirle a todo el mundo! Por eso yo digo, que . . . (*Picking up* GÜERITO.) Qué hay . . . ¡AY! . . . qué chingazo me dieron . . . (HE *sits down woozily.*)

GÜERITO: Are you okay, Grandpa? Does it hurt?

TAPÓN: ¡Chale! I did it for the elecciones. ¡Es táctica y vamos a ganar! ¿Verdad? (*Crowd agrees.*)

BOTELLA: ¡Viva la Huelga! (VIVA.) ¡Viva la Causa! (VIVA.) ¡Abajo los rancheros! (ABAJO.)

WHITTAKER: All right! Let's take this meeting to the union office and organize.

BULLET: ¡Órale, organícense, Raza!

SUGAR: (*To* VERA.) ¡Vámonos! I don't wanna miss this. Don't forget to bring Flaco. For your own sake.

VERA: Where is he? (SUGAR *nods toward* FLACO. TAPÓN *and* BOTELLA *exit with* GÜERITO. SUGAR *follows the crowd.* GÜERA *appears behind the bar.* SHE *talks to* PRIETA.)

GÜERA: My mom got me on the phone. Where's e'rybody going?

PRIETA: (*Tongue in cheek.*) To organize.

VERA: (*Stopping* FLACO.) I was looking for you. You had me worried. Where were you, Flaco?

FLACO: Out. I was with Mundo. Right? (VERA *glances over at* MUNDO *with hatred.*)

VERA: Why can't you stay the fuck out of our lives? (SHE *exits with* FLACO. *All exit except for* BULLET, WHITTAKER, MUNDO *and* HUESOS. *The phone rings.* PRIETA *answers.*)

WHITTAKER: I'm glad you're here.

BULLET: Looks like I got here just in time.

WHITTAKER: You telling me. I got a feeling things are going to start cracking perty damn soon.

MUNDO: Ése, Bullet? (BULLET *turns.*) Welcome home, carnal.

GÜERA: Aren't you going to say hello to your big sister?

BULLET: Oh my God, sorry, Güera! (*Gives her an abrazo.*)

GÜERA: My mom was just telling me you're back. How about a beer?

WHITTAKER: Sal, you coming?

BULLET: I got a meeting right now. You know how it is. Later, okay? I promise!

GÜERA: (*Shrugs coldly.*) That's cool. The beer's on ice.

WHITTAKER: (HE *goes out talking to* BULLET.) Okay, let's go. Strategy for tomorrow: Let's get a leaflet out on the goon squad and hit the ranches at sunrise. (PRIETA *hangs up.*)

GÜERA: Hey, Mundo. Barnes was here this afternoon. He left this for you. (*Holds up envelope.*)

MUNDO: What is it, carnal?

GÜERA: I don't know. And I don't wanna know. (MUNDO *grabs the envelope and walks with* HUESOS *and* GREÑAS. PRIETA *drops a coin in the jukebox.*)

PRIETA: What's Mundo up to?

GÜERA: What's Mundo usually up to?

PRIETA: ¡Chingaderas! You know that married gabachona he's been seeing? She just called again. She said to tell him: Sam knows. (GÜERA *tenderly strokes* PRIETA's *arm with her fingertips.*) GÜERA: I don't know what I'd do without you, Prieta. My family's so fucked up. You're the only one in my life that's normal.

PRIETA: (*Embracing her.*) I love you too. (THEY *slow dance to the music. Fats Domino's "Blueberry Hill."*)

Fade to black.

ACT TWO

SCENE ONE

Torres Labor Camp. Exterior day. Two weeks later. A picketline of farmworkers march into the compound, led by BOTELLA *and* TAPÓN, BULLET, WHITTAKER. THEY *sing.*

FARMWORKERS: (*Chorus.*)
    El picket sign, el picket sign
    lo llevo por todo el día
    el picket sign, el picket sign
    conmigo toda la vida
BULLET: Desde Texas a California
    campesinos están luchando
    los rancheros a llore y llore
    de huelga ya están bien pandos (*Chorus.*)
TAPÓN: Me dicen que soy muy necio
    gritón y alboratapueblos
    pero Juárez fue mi tío
    y Zapata fue mi suegro. (*Chorus.*)
BOTELLA: Hay muchos que no comprenden
    aunque uno les da consejos
    la huelga es un bien pa' todos
    pero se hacen bien pendejos. (*Chorus.*)

Cheers and vivas. DOÑA LOLA *emerges from her long house on her wheelchair, with* MUNDO *pushing her. The crowd quiets down.*

DOÑA LOLA: Bueno, bueno. ¿Qué se traen? What is this, a parade of locos?
BULLET: (*Kidding.*) We're here to serenade you, 'amá.
DOÑA LOLA: For what, Mother's Day? You're too late. Sing me a serenata when I'm dead. What are you all doing here?

102

WHITTAKER: Well, Mrs. Torres, we're here to try and resolve a little problem between you and the Juan Pérez family next door. That eviction notice you gave them this morning? We got a judge to look at it.

DOÑA LOLA: (*To* BOTELLA.) ¿Ya fueron a chillar allá?

BOTELLA: (*Emotionally.*) Sí, Señora Lola! We made un complain' con la unión. I came to talk to you about the plumbling two weeks ago. That was the night Tapón, I mean, Juan got that garrotazo. I told you I couldn' even clean his wounds because the water was so dirty. ¡Fuchi que cochinada! You said you'd fix it. Nada. I remind you again. You said you were raising the rent to pay for it. I told you we weren't gonna pay any more rent without improvements. So this morning you evicted us!

DOÑA LOLA: So . . . ¿y qué?

TAPÓN: (*Holding his temper.*) After all these years, Doña Lola. ¡Esto no es justo! It's not fair. ¿Verdad, compa'? (DOÑA LOLA *spots* TEODORO *in the crowd.* HE *retreats to his cabin.*)

DOÑA LOLA: Teodoro! Are you with these condenados?

TEODORO: I don't have anything to do with this, hermanita. They're crazy. I'm happy here!

TAPÓN: Pos luego. She lets you stay here for free. Órale, Doña Lola, this camp was always a little rasquachón, but Torres never let it get this bad.

DOÑA LOLA: Benjamín Torres is dead! I'm in charge here.

BULLET: Then why don't you just fix up the place like I asked you, jefa? It's the simplest solution.

MUNDO: (*Stepping forward.*) The simplest solution is for all of you to get the fuck off my mother's land! This labor camp is private property.

WHITTAKER: Hey, Mundo, come on now. There's no need to get belligerent. We just want to talk.

DOÑA LOLA: Who are you?

WHITTAKER: Chuck Whittaker, Migrant Ministry, ma'm. Like your son Sal, I'm working with the farmworkers.

DOÑA LOLA: Can't Chávez find nobody but Hippies and Holy Joes to work for him? He must be paying you plenty.

WHITTAKER: Five dollars a week plus room and board.

DOÑA LOLA: (*Laughs.*) He's worse than a contratista! Is that what he's paying you, Salvador? ¡Bendito sea Dios!

BULLET: We're not doing it for the money, jefa.

DOÑA LOLA: I know. It's for La Causa . . . de pendejos. (*Laughs.*)

BULLET: I'm sorry you feel that way. Can we talk about this eviction business?

MUNDO: (*To* BULLET.) You don't turn against your own familia, carnal, no te hagas pendejo. If you wanted to talk, why didn't you come by yourself? Afraid to face your jefita alone, ése?

BULLET: I was here yesterday. And the day before. Didn't you tell him, Mom? You wouldn't talk about it.

DOÑA LOLA: Why should I? Do you think I'm rich? What lies did Narciso tell you about me?

BULLET: This isn't about our family.

MUNDO: You better straighten out real fast, carnal. Leave the jefa alone, or I'll have to get your pump in working order, ¿me oyes?

TAPÓN: Órale, pues, Mundo, no te pongas belligerent. We've lived here for years, hombre. Calmantes montes. Queremos negotiate.

DOÑA LOLA: (*Fiercely.*) Negotiate? I've been housing you and your vieja since the day you arrived sopping wet in the truck from Mexicali, Tapón. Ingratos, there's nothing to negotiate! ¡Lárgense!

BOTELLA: (*Defiantly.*) Oh, NO! We're not getting out! You hear that, Doña Lola? We got rights here! ¿Verdad que tenemos derechos, Chuck?

WHITTAKER: We have a restraining order from the court, blocking your eviction notice, ma'm.

MUNDO: You heard what the jefa said, get off our property, gaba! (HE *pushes* WHITTAKER.)

BULLET: Órale, Mundo, ¡no! (*The famworkers close in around* WHITTAKER, *as* MUNDO *is joined by* HUESOS, GREÑAS *and* FLACO. *There is a minor scuffle.*)

TAPÓN: ¡Epa, epa, epa!

BOTELLA: ¡Abusón!

HUESOS: ¡Trucha, trucha!

GREÑAS: ¡Chíngalo!

WHITTAKER: (*On the floor.*) Nonviolence, nonviolence!

SUGAR: Hey, hey, hey, man! Don't kick him!

BULLET: (*To MUNDO.*) What are you doing?

MUNDO: What I'm doing? What the fuck are you doing?

HUESOS: ¡Aguas! ¡Ahí viene la chota! (DEPUTY SHERIFF SAM BARNES *arrives with short burps from his siren.*)

BARNES: (*Getting out of his car.*) Saludos, amigos. What's going on here?

MUNDO: Eviction! Do your duty, Barnes.

BULLET: No, we have a restraining order. Chuck?

SUGAR: (*Intimately.*) Mundo was just kicking the shit out of him, Samson. Honest.

BARNES: (*Getting away.*) Where's Lola? There she is! Hey, there, Lola, long time no see. What's the problem?

DOÑA LOLA: These people are trespassing on my private property, Sammy. Get them off.

BARNES: (*Turning officiously.*) All right, everybody back, out to the road. Off the lady's property.

TAPÓN: Órale, don't push! We live right there!

BOTELLA: And we're not leaving! Ya basta! Let them drag us out! (THEY *retreat to their cabin.*)

WHITTAKER: (*Showing documents.*) Here's the restraining order, Sheriff. It blocks the eviction, pending further investigation by the County Health Department. (BARNES *studies the document judiciously.*)

BARNES: Yep. Sorry, Lola, as an officer of the law I'm not legally authorized to evict anybody. Yet. (*Farmworkers cheer.*) But I'm not going to allow any trespassing into this here labor camp by anybody other than blood kin to these tenants. So out you go! Let's go! (*Pushing* GREÑAS.)

GREÑAS: ¡Órale, marrano!

HUESOS: Us too? We're with Mundo.

MUNDO: Do as he says, ése. Wait outside.

SUGAR: Don't push, Samson. (SAM *pushes.*) Don't push!

WHITTAKER: (*Taking charge.*) Spread out! Line up along the road!

DOÑA LOLA: (*Laughing.*) ¡Váyanse! ¡Váyanse mucho a la jodida! (*The pickets retreat.* BARNES *approaches* MUNDO.)

BARNES: I need to talk to you, pal.

MUNDO: Not here, baboso. Meet me tonight. At the usual place. At midnight. (BARNES *glances at* SUGAR *walking out.*)

BARNES: That's past my bedtime. How about earlier? (BARNES *talks to* MUNDO *before* HE *extis.* DOÑA LOLA *stares at* BULLET.)

DOÑA LOLA: Who are you, Salvador? No te conozco. Are you following Chávez or your pinche padre? You remind me of Narciso, preaching a line of bullshit to the poor. How are you going to save all of them? There's too many of them, coming across the border desperate for work, and millions more where they came from. Things are never going to change.

BULLET: A journey of a thousand miles begins with one step, 'amá. You can start by fixing the plumbing.

DOÑA LOLA: At least here they have plumbing. ¡Chúntaros roñosos! Do they have to run down to the river barefoot to get water like in Mexico?

BULLET: (*Humoring her.*) Ay, Mamá. It wouldn't be so hard to do, would it? How much could it cost? They themselves could do the work.

DOÑA LOLA: Do you know what Torres used to call our tenants? He called them la cosecha, the harvest, because while they picked fruit during the day, he picked their pockets at the cantina every night. (*Laughs with pain.*)

BULLET: We need to talk, 'amá. Your tenants are all union members. They want to call a rent strike.

DOÑA LOLA: Tell them to go to hell! When I first got here, we lived in a chicken coop for six months. Look at me now, do I live in a mansion?

BULLET: You have a choice. They don't.

DOÑA LOLA: (*Fiercely.*) I rented the old drugstore to the union for your pinche office. What more do you want? Why are you chingando conmigo?! Mundo!

MUNDO: Right here, jefa. Want me to kick his ass out?

DOÑA LOLA: (*Painfully.*) No, hombre, I need my pills! (*Gasping for air.*) Necesito mis pastillas. ¡Ándale!

MUNDO: (*To* BULLET.) Be gone when I get back, ése.

BULLET: I'm staying right here, Ray. (MUNDO *wheels* DOÑA LOLA *into her house.* WHITTAKER *returns.*)

WHITTAKER: Look, Sal, maybe this wasn't such a hot idea. I told you not to get involved.

BULLET: I'm involved, man!

WHITTAKER: Of course, you are. But it's distracting both of us from the field elections.

BULLET: I can fix this. I only need to talk to Ray.

WHITTAKER: Ray? Who's Ray?

BULLET: Mundo. Reymundo. That's his full name. King of the World.
It never bothered me as a kid, because all big brothers act that way.
I just never got to know him. Except as Ray.
WHITTAKER: How did he get from Ray to Mundo?
BULLET: Vietnam. (*Pause.*) The day he returned I thought his eyes
looked like gaping wounds. It was like Ray had been killed in
action, and only Mundo survived. (*Pause.*) Ray's still in there
though. Somewhere. I just have to find a way to pull him out.
WHITTAKER: Be careful he doesn't pull you in. You're getting really
personally involved here. How can I help?
BULLET: Take the pickets back to the office.
WHITTAKER: Are you sure?
BULLET: Grass roots organizing begins at home, right? (MUNDO
emerges from LOLA*'s house.* WHITTAKER *leaves* reluctantly.)
WHITTAKER: I'll pray for you, brother.
MUNDO: Why are you picking on the jefita, ése? She's not a pinche
grower.
BULLET: No, she only supplies their cheap labor.
MUNDO: There's always going to be wetbacks. You think people in the
supermarkets give a fuck where their eats come from? You might as
well stop drugs and prostitution. It's dog eat dog.
BULLET: Come on, Ray.
MUNDO: Cut this Ray shit. Yo soy El Mundo, ése, de Burlap, Califas,
¿me entiendes como?
BULLET: Can we go in and talk to the jefa?
MUNDO: Chale. Didn't you see her? She's dying, bato. Ya mero se va
a descontar—you know what I mean?
BULLET: You're not serious.
MUNDO: Mira, ése, you been in this town for two weeks. How many
times have you been over to see her?
BULLET: I've been really busy.
MUNDO: Doing what? Planning to give her a heart attack? You didn't
come back home, man. You're still some place else, over in New
York, or wherever your pinche huelga exists! No estás aquí, carnal.
Not in my world, anyway. Get the fuck out of here.
BULLET: (*Bristling.*) What if I refuse?
MUNDO: I'll kick your brown ass, little brother. (*Pushes* BULLET.)
Now move! Out! ¡Píntate!

BULLET: (*Resisting.*) Don't push. Stop, Mundo! NO! (THEY *scuffle.*
DOÑA LOLA *rolls of her house.* TAPÓN *and* BOTELLA *emerge
from their own shack. So does* TEODORO *from his.*)
DOÑA LOLA: Reymundo! Salvador! Stop this dog fight! (MUNDO
and BULLET *stop.*) Have you no shame? This is none of your busi-
ness, Botella.
BOTELLA: We're making it our business.
TAPÓN: ¡Simón que yes! We live here. ¿Pos qué?
TEODORO: You're the boss, Lola. Put your foot down!
DOÑA LOLA: Let your brother go, Mundo.
TEODORO: No se peleen, muchachos. ¡Son hermanos!
MUNDO: (*Releasing him.*) Take off, Bullet! (BULLET *stares at*
MUNDO *and* DOÑA LOLA *for a beat, looking hurt.*)
BULLET: Home Sweet Home. I'm not going away, you know. You're
either part of the solution or part of the problem. You can't stop the
world from changing, 'amá. See you, Ray. (BULLET *leaves.*
TAPÓN *and* BOTELLA *exit.* DOÑA LOLA *looks at* MUNDO.)
DOÑA LOLA: Salvador is as stubborn as Narciso and twice the fool.
He really believes he can change the world. But promise me,
Mundo. No matter what happens, don't ever hurt your brother. He's
your blood. We're not dogs to spill each other's blood. Swear it to
me.
MUNDO: What for?
DOÑA LOLA: For all that you love in this world!
MUNDO: (*Kisses her forehead.*) You got it. Jefa.

Fade to black.

SCENE TWO

The Union office. Same evening. BULLET *is sitting with* WHIT-
TAKER *blowing off steam from the day.* WHITTAKER *is working at
his desk.*

BULLET: I went to live with my dad after the divorce. Ray and Güera
stayed with Mom, and I didn't live with them again until I started
high school. That's when my dad remarried, so I came back to
Burlap. I fucking hated it, man. Then my mom married Torres, the
labor contractor.

WHITTAKER: (*Tongue in cheek.*) Stop it, you're breaking my heart.

BULLET: That's how she ended up with the labor camp. Mundo supplies the tenants from the border.

WHITTAKER: Did you tell César about this?

BULLET: Word for word. He said: I know Doña Lola. She helped me out in the early days. She'll help you. You're her son.

WHITTAKER: Well, the tree never falls too far from the apple. Especially the rotten ones.

BULLET: I'd forgotten what life is like here in the Valley, man. You can't go home again.

WHITTAKER: Not unless you take Highway 99. Listen, César is going to be here in two weeks. Are you going to help me plan this rally? Fill out this request form to use Burlap Park.

BULLET: I forgot: an organizer has no private life. (*Lights change. VERA enters in work clothes, looking distressed with a couple of young campesinas. SHE goes right to CHUCK's desk.*)

VERA: (*Angry.*) Why me, Chuck? First you got my parents to go on rent strike, and now I'm fired! Is it my turn now?

WHITTAKER: What happened?

VERA: We were on our lunch break! I was just standing there, talking to these girls at the packing shed, when the foreman comes up to us and says we were fired. Just like that! They got no godamn right to fire us! Right?

WHITTAKER: I hope you were talking union.

VERA: I was just showing them your leaflet. I found it on the ground.

WHITTAKER: Riiight.

BULLET: Chuck, let me talk to her.

WHITTAKER: Right on. You talk to Sister Vera here, and I'll help these other sisters.

VERA: (*Pause.*) Well, aren't you going to protest or anything? I've worked there for nine years. I need my job! I've got a kid! (CHUCK *talks with the two women.* BULLET *grabs a pad and pencil.*)

BULLET: Why don't you come work with us . . . at least through the election campaign? Five dollars a week plus room and board.

VERA: I don't think so. I need a real job.

BULLET: You've got a real job, Vera—here and now—trying to get your old job back. Can you type?

VERA: A little. Not since high school.

BULLET: Welcome to the University of Hard Knocks.

VERA: (*Pause.*) I saw how you stood up to Mundo at the labor camp. I didn't know you were his brother.

BULLET: I used to be. Your husband's my stepbrother, too.

VERA: Flaco? I mean, that's his nickname. He's Benny Torres, the son of Benjamín Torres. But you know that. (*Pause.*) He looks bad, doesn't he?

BULLET: Honestly? I hardly recognized him.

VERA: He's all strung out on chiva, no thanks to Mundo. I'm just waiting for the day Flaco odees and wakes up dead.

BULLET: There's a methadone treatment center in Bakersfield. I'll see if they can take Benny. Okay?

VERA: Just get him the hell away from Mundo. (MUNDO *enters alone.*)

MUNDO: I just came over to tell you batos that the jefita is evicting you from the old drugstore. You had your chance, Bullet, but you fucked up. Take all your communist bullshit and clear out!

BULLET: Who do you think you are, Ray. The King of the world?

MUNDO: (*To* VERA.) I heard you were fired, ésa. You want your job back? Come with me to the packing shed. I'll get you a better job.

VERA: I've already got a job. Organizing.

MUNDO: (*Reaching for her.*) Come on! Come with me.

VERA: (*Recoiling.*) Mira, cabrón, don't even touch me, ¿sabes? I don't need any help from you. You're like a vampire.

MUNDO: What have you been teaching her, carnal? A little organizing on the side?

BULLET: That's a sexist pig insult to Vera, brother.

MUNDO: (*To* VERA.) Are you fucking him? (VERA *tries to slap him.* MUNDO *blocks her.* WHITTAKER *intercedes.*)

WHITTAKER: All right, Mundo! That's quite enough. We've got sisters present here. I'm going to have to ask you to leave. (MUNDO's *glare forces the young campesinas to hurry out.* HE *then looks up at a photo of César Chávez.*)

MUNDO: (*Pause.*) This guy César Chávez, he's really brown like a Mexican indio, you know? He reminds me of a chief. Like in one of those western movies with cowboys and indians, where the big chief bites the dust in battle, and all the brave warriors run for the hills. ¿Me entienden cómo? Hay los watcho. (MUNDO *saunters out.*)

WHITTAKER: What was that, some kind of veiled threat? It wasn't a very thick veil.

BULLET: He's bluffing.

VERA: He wasn't always this bad. He's gotten worser. Like a caged animal.

BULLET: He's still fighting a war he can't win. He just doesn't know it yet.

Fade to black.

SCENE THREE

MUNDO*'s car. MUNDO on speed drives with HUESOS and GREÑAS to meet at the country road.*

MUNDO: ¡Órale, trucha! Something's up with this puto Barnes, and you're my back up. If he makes any pedo about his vieja, I can deal with it. If he tries to muscle me about the growers, eso es otra cosa! That's where you come in. (*Pulls over.*)

GREÑAS: ¡Lo chingamos!

MUNDO: Not until you get my signal.

HUESOS: (*Incredulously.*) To snuff him?

MUNDO: ¿Qué traes? He's our business partner. (*Getting out.*) Mad-dog him for all you're worth, but don't waste him. ¿Me oyen?

GREÑAS: Can't we rough him up a little, siquiera?

MUNDO: Chale. Stand lookout in both directions till you hear this. Then come running. (*Blows on a silent whistle. HUESOS covers his ears, as GREÑAS react with pain.*)

GREÑAS: Ah, ca-brón, what the hell was that?

HUESOS: Dog whistle—from Vietnam.

MUNDO: Órale, here comes Barnes. Get lost. (HUESOS *and* GREÑAS *back off, as BARNES drives up and gets out.*)

BARNES: Hey there, Mundo, waiting all alone?

MUNDO: All by my lonesome.

BARNES: Any sign of life? At my ranch house, I mean. The Little Lady went shopping in Fresno this morning. (*Getting out.*) You didn't see her come in, did you?

MUNDO: Was I supposed to?

BARNES: What do you mean by that?

MUNDO: If you want me to keep an eye on your old lady, you'll have to pay me, Barnes. For professional services rendered.

BARNES: Don't make me laugh.

MUNDO: You called this meeting. What do you want?

BARNES: (*Stressed.*) The growers want some action.

MUNDO: What kind of action?

BARNES: Some stop-the-frigging-elections kind of action! Your little ski mask escapades are for amateurs. Stop fucking around and get down to business!

MUNDO: You don't tell me what to do, puto.

BARNES: They want you to start a union. Not a real union, just a phony front. You can call it the Independent Farm Workers of Burlap or some such shit and work openly against Chávez.

MUNDO: Fuck you.

BARNES: After today at Lola's labor camp, what's the difference?

MUNDO: I'm not starting a fucking phony union, okay?

BARNES: What are you going to do?

MUNDO: I'm going to deploy my men as I see fit.

BARNES: Deploy? What is this, cholo wargames?

MUNDO: (*Grabbing him.*) What the fuck do you know about war? The National Guard?

BARNES: (*Caught.*) Hold on there! Time out! Get your paws offa me, Mundo. I'm not kidding. (MUNDO *gets a clinch on* BARNES *and puts a knife to his throat.*)

MUNDO: War is pulling out all the stoppers, puto. Is that what you want? (BARNES *frees himself.*)

BARNES: The growers are on my ass! Look, I sold them on you. You said you could stop Chávez. I want to be Sheriff of this frigging county. My goose neck is cooked if you don't start earning the big bucks they're paying you.

MUNDO: What do you want, your cut?

BARNES: Fucking A. Ella tells me you're carrying a wad that could choke a horse.

MUNDO: (*Suspiciously.*) Ella told you that? Chale.

BARNES: (*With deep fury.*) Come on, Mundo. You've been schtupping my wife for six months.

MUNDO: And you've been in the closet—watching.

BARNES: What do you know?

MUNDO: El Mundo no es pendejo. I know what you and your old lady want. It's all coming together. It's the same thing Gudunritch & Roddenberry want.

BARNES: What's that?

MUNDO: Mis huevos. You want me to kill Chávez.

BARNES: (*Taken aback.*) Could you? I mean, would you? César is marching into town in two weeks. Can you be ready by then?

MUNDO: Money talks, and bullshit walks, Barnes. Tell your friends to deposit thirty thousand in cold hard cash in the refrigerator at the bar. Then we'll talk. (*Blows whistle.*)

BARNES: Are you serious? (HUESOS *and* GREÑAS *rush in, and stand ready, mad-dogging* BARNES.)

MUNDO: As serious as a heart attack, ése. Let Chávez come. I'll turn him into a national hero.

Black.

SCENE FOUR

La Divina Garza. Night. The place is virtually empty. GÜERA *and* PRIETA *are at the bar.* HUESOS *and* GREÑAS *are sitting in a booth.* MUNDO *walks in alone.*

HUESOS: ¡Ese Mundo!

GREÑAS: Over here, man.

HUESOS: Scoot over, ése. Dale campo a bato. I'll get you a beer, carnal. Prieta!

MUNDO: (*Sarcasm.*) Man, the place is really jumping tonight, eh?

HUESOS: There's a rally in the park.

GREÑAS: Simón, Chávez is coming.

MUNDO: (*Cryptically.*) Well, he won't stay for long.

HUESOS: I don't know. You should see the park! Está hirviendo de raza. There must be—what?

GREÑAS: About a thousand.

HUESOS: Campesinos, carnal. Viejos, viejitas, men, women, mocosos. Ése, it feels like the 16 de septiembre!

GREÑAS: This town has really turned on since the huelga came. And the rucas. You seen all the Berkeley gabachas coming and going?

MUNDO: Free love, ése. Organizers.

GREÑAS: I'm going to organize me one, man!

HUESOS: Órale, can we have a bironga here? (PRIETA *comes with a beer for* MUNDO.)

PRIETA: Did you hear about the union office, Mundo?

MUNDO: Hear what?

PRIETA: Somebody broke in anoche, and tore the place up.

MUNDO: No, really? That's too bad.

PRIETA: They started a fire también. ¿Pero sabes qué? It looks like they put it out before it went too far. There was water all over the floor.

HUESOS: That's crazy. Why would they start a fire, then put it out?

PRIETA: Maybe they thought about all the raza that lives upstairs.

GREÑAS: ¿Verdad?

HUESOS: (*Looks at* MUNDO.) I din't think about that.

GREÑAS: Hey, maybe the arsonists are the pinche Teamsters. What do think, Mundo?

MUNDO: I think if I find anybody chingando con mi pueblo, I'll kill 'em. (PRIETA *goes,* GÜERA *calls from the bar.*)

GÜERA: Mundo, you want a beer?

MUNDO: I got one. (HE *goes to the bar.*)

GÜERA: Have another one. How's 'amá?

MUNDO: Not too good.

GÜERA: Has she asked for me?

MUNDO: Tonight. She's fading fast, loca. Maybe you should go see her, eh? No seas gacha.

GÜERA: Who's taking care of her? Teodoro?

MUNDO: Todo crudo.

GÜERA: Why don't you put her in the hospital, man?

MUNDO: Why don't you, man? You know the jefa, cuando no quiere, no quiere. Stubborn.

TAPÓN: ¡Arriba la huelga!

HUESOS: (*Turns.*) Tapón.

TAPÓN: ¿Quihúbo pues, pela'o? ¿Qué te haz hecho? I haven't see you around.

GREÑAS: We've been in town.

TAPÓN: ¿Verdad? It's me that's been going out. ¡A todo los ranchos! Mírame, ando todo enbotonado. Watcha la aguilita en la espalda! (HE *has a huelga eagle on the back of his Levi jacket.*) Qué a toda madre, ¿no? Pa' que sepan los desgraciados. I even saw el patrón y le dije a su cara. I told it to his face: ¡Viva César Chávez, cabrón! I'm organizing here now and the election nos va caer guango. You should have seen his face! Se quedó con el hocico colgando. Have you ever worked for Roddenberry, Mundo?

MUNDO: Never.

TAPÓN: I've been with that bolio for twelve years, and he don't even know my name. But he will. When we win, I wanna be on the ranch committee that negotiates el contrato. Me lo voy hechar al plato. Oye, Sugar?

SUGAR: Olegario.

TAPÓN: ¿Cómo?

SUGAR: My real name is Olegario Gaona, Tapón.

TAPÓN: Oh. Pos, my real name is Juan entonces. Tell Mundo here how I told off Roddenberry. ¿Verdad que le eché a su cara?

SUGAR: Te aventaste, Juan. Entonces.

TAPÓN: ¿No que no?

SUGAR: Ése, Mundo, you think I can talk to you for a second? Excuse us, okay, Tapón? Shall we go out to the back?

MUNDO: Aquí mero.

SUGAR: What's a matter? Afraid of what the batos will think.

MUNDO: No te hagas pendejo.

SUGAR: I've a message for you. From Ella.

MUNDO: Ella who?

SUGAR: Now you're acting pendejo. Ella Barnes. The Deputy Sheriff's wife, okay? She says to tell you certain friends of yours are using you as a patsy.

MUNDO: What kind of patsy?

SUGAR: Sabrá diosito. But it's been five weeks since a certain deal was made, and so far the Chavistas are mopping up the town. Not to speak of the county. She's worried about you.

MUNDO: I don't know what the fuck you're talking about, ésa.

SUGAR: Don't ésa me, cabrón. There's worse things than being a marica.

MUNDO: Like what?

SUGAR: Like selling out to the growers? Which side are you on, Mundo? Your friends would like to know. And they don't mean beating up farmworkers. Or burning a couple of lousy union applications and then putting out the fire, carnal. So far the only bato you got convinced is Huesos, and he only goes out to the fields to plant mota.

TAPÓN: ¿Pos mira quién entró? (BULLET *comes into the bar.*)

BULLET: Quihúbole, raza.

TAPÓN: ¡Viva la huelga! (¡VIVA!) ¡Viva César Chávez! (¡VIVA!) ¡Una canción! ¡Échate una canción!

BULLET: En la junta, raza. At the rally. Right now we need a couple of volunteers. Como saben todos, César is going to be here any minute, and the park is full of campesinos from all over the county. There's a lot of new faces, and it's impossible to tell our friends from our enemigos. No hay pedo. Ninety-nine percent están con la unión, verdad. (*Cheers in agreement.*) But we've heard a rumor that some cabrones might be gunning for César. (*Everybody freezes.*)

HUESOS: Ése, is something going on I don't know about?

MUNDO: ¿Qué traes? Shut your trap!

BULLET: (*Unfreezing.*) Simón, es cosa seria. So lo que necesitamos son más guardias. More guards to surround the whole park, and it has to be faces we know. Like you, Tapón, Olegario, Huesos, Greñas. Mundo, ¿qué tal?

MUNDO: De aquéllas, carnal.

BULLET: So what I'm asking is for you to finish your cervezas, and come with us right now, and we'll get it together, ¿'ta bien? (SIMÓN) After the junta we'll all come back and celebrate a bit more, ¿qué dicen? (¡ÓRALE!) (*The workers drink up and start getting ready to leave.*)

BULLET: (*Walking over.*) How you been, carnal?

MUNDO: I've been with the jefita.

BULLET: Órale, how is mother?

MUNDO: What the fuck do you care?

BULLET: I'll go see her tomorrow.

MUNDO: Tomorrow may never come, ése.

TAPÓN: (*At the door.*) ¡Ahí viene Chávez!

RAZA: César is coming!

He's driving into town!

Let's go to the park!

¡Guardias, no se desparramen!

Where is he?

I want to meet him!

BULLET: Those that are coming with me let's go! (*The workers go out with* BULLET.)

RAZA: ¡Organícense, raza!

control, control.

¡Con calma se hacen las cosas!

¡Viva Chávez!

¡QUÉ VIVA!

¡Viva La Causa!

¡QUÉ VIVA!

¡Viva la Virgen de Guadalupe!

¡QUÉ VIVA!

(GREÑAS *and* HUESOS *hold back.*)

HUESOS: What do we do, ése?

MUNDO: (*With deadly irony.*) ¿Pos qué? Go see that nobody snuffs Chávez.

HUESOS: (*Nervous.*) Chávez! I'd rather stay y pistiamos juntos. Just like the old days.

MUNDO: The old days are gone, ése.

HUESOS: Who says?

MUNDO: ¡Píntense! (HUESOS *and* GREÑAS *exit.* MUNDO *stays behind at a table.* GÜERA *comes over and sits down.* SHE *pulls out a box.*)

GÜERA: Carnal, there's thirty thousand in cold hard cash in my refrigerator. What do you want me to do with it?

MUNDO: Hold on to it.

GÜERA: I don't know where it's coming from, but I'm getting nervous just stashing it.

MUNDO: (*Eye to eye.*) You know where it's coming from. (MUNDO *slyly checks his gun.* TEODORO *comes rushing into the place.*)

TEODORO: ¡Me lleva la chingada, hombre! Where you been?

MUNDO: (*Leaving.*) Órale, Teodoro. Have a bironga.

TEODORO: (*Holding him back.*) ¡No, qué bironga! I been looking for you, hombre. I was in that park por una hora. What a crowd, nomás vieras!

MUNDO: (*Anxious.*) ¿Qué pues? What's up?

TEODORO: Pos muy malas noticias. My sister, tu madre, she got worse after you left. I called an ambulancia. They said she had a stroke. You better go to the county hospital, si no la quieres ver ya tendida, pobrecita mi sister.

MUNDO: (*Stunned.*) ¿No te dije? I told you.

GÜERA: She ain't going to die.

MUNDO: Fuck that shit. (*Instantly changing plans.*) You better come with me. Come on! Tío, you go over to the park and find Bullet.

TEODORO: What Bullet?

MUNDO: Salvador. Tell him to come to the hospital right now. Y si no quiere venir, drag him there, you understand?

TEODORO: Pos, a ver, let's see if I find him.

MUNDO: Let's go, Güera.

GÜERA: (*Hugging* PRIETA.) Al rato vuelvo, Prieta. (GÜERA *and* MUNDO *leave.* TEODORO *starts to follow them, stops, looks back at* MUNDO'*s half-full glass of beer. Returns and drinks it down. The phone rings.* PRIETA *answers.*)

PRIETA: Hello? Who? (*Turns.*) Miss Mata just left. You want to leave her a message? Yes, I'm family! (*Pause.*) Oh no! I'll tell her.

TEODORO: ¿Quién era?

PRIETA: The doctor at the hospital. Doña Lola's dead.

TEODORO: ¡Bendito sea Dios! I knew it. Now what? What's going to happen to Mundo? What's going to happen to me!

Black.

SCENE FIVE

VERA'*s upstairs apartment. Night.* MUNDO *and* VERA *are in the bedroom.* GÜERITO *is at the door.* MUNDO *is sitting in* LOLA'*s wheelchair.*

GÜERITO: Heh, 'amá, come on! We're going to be late.

VERA: Okay, okay, I'm coming. Listen, Mundo, I've got to go.

MUNDO: You going to leave me alone, ésa?

GÜERITO: Hurry up!

VERA: I've got to go to a meeting

MUNDO: (*Scoffs.*) Another pinche huelga meeting?

VERA: I want you out of this house by the time we get back. I'm not kidding! Flaco's getting out of rehab and he's coming home tomorrow. You can't keep staying here.

GÜERITO: Ma! We're going to miss the Teatro Campesino!

VERA: Güerito, go ahead! I'll meet you there!

GÜERITO: You sure?

VERA: Yeah, vete. (GÜERITO *splits.*) Listen, Mundo, I really don't want to hurt your feelings. I'm sorry your mother's dead, but it's been two weeks already. All you've been doing is drinking and feeling sorry for yourself. People at the labor camp are still on rent strike! They want to know what you're gonna do. Your mother's place is empty, except for your tío and he's been drinking, too. Why don't you go home, huh?

MUNDO: You need bread?

VERA: No, man, I don't want your money.

MUNDO: (*Gets money out.*) Toma. Go to Fresno or something. Buy something for you and our chabalo.

VERA: Two hundred dollars?

MUNDO: Three hundred, four hundred, how much do you want? Ándale, it's right here. Take it.

VERA: How much is that?

MUNDO: Enough.

VERA: For what?

MUNDO: You tell me.

VERA: (*Pause.*) Tell you what? That we take the money and run off together? You're crazy if that's what you're thinking. Where did you get this money anyway?

MUNDO: What do you care? Take it.

VERA: I don't want your drug money. I'm trying to make some kind of life for my son here.

MUNDO: He's MY SON, TOO!

VERA: (*Tears.*) I told you I was pregnant before you were drafted, Mundo. You had your chance to claim your son. Flaco was willing to marry me. You got no right to screw up my whole life. ¡Chinga tu madre! (*Stops.*) I take that back. I'm sorry, Mundo. I gotta go. (SHE *exits.*)

MUNDO: Esta ruca. (MUNDO *rises from the wheelchair and walks down to the street.*)

HUESOS: (*On the corner.*) ¿Ése? ¡Ése!

MUNDO: ¿Q-vo, Huesos? What's going on?

HUESOS: ¿Pos qué? ¡Otro pinche meeting! El gabacho está hable y hable y tu carnal 'stá cante y cante.

MUNDO: Bullet is singing, eh?

HUESOS: Simón. Rasque y rasque su guitarra.

MUNDO: Déjalo. He's grieving. Está de luto.

HUESOS: (*Pause.*) What are we gonna do, ése?

MUNDO: We're gonna go talk to my carnalito. I promised my jefa not to spill his blood, but I'm going to get his pump going in front of the whole pinche mundo!

HUESOS: All-riiight! (THEY *walk out.*)

Black.

SCENE SIX

The Union meeting. Night. The place is packed. Huelga flags in the audience. A microphone stands before a huge thunderbirds banner. BULLET is singing with a chorus.

BULLET:
>¡UNIDOS EN LA CAUSA! ¡NO NOS MOVERÁN!
>¡UNIDOS EN LA CAUSA! ¡NO NOS MOVERÁN!
>¡COMO UN ÁRBOL FIRME JUNTO AL RÍO
>NO NOS MOVERÁN!
>
>(MUNDO *and* HUESOS *come in at the back.* BULLET *nods at* MUNDO.)
>
>¡ABAJO LOS RANCHEROS! ¡NO NOS MOVERÁN!
>¡ABAJO LOS RANCHEROS! ¡NO NOS MOVERÁN!
>¡COMO UN ÁRBOL FIRME JUNTO AL RÍO
>NO NOS MOVERÁN!

TAPÓN: ¡Viva nuestra Unión! (VIVA)
>¡Viva César Chávez! (¡QUÉ VIVA!)
>¡Abajo con los Teamsters! (¡ABAJO!)

WHITTAKER: Y ahora, I want to introduce one of our newest organizadoras, que todos conocen, Vera Campos. (*Applause.*) This sister has been working extra hard for tomorrow's elections. Vera, come say a few words. (*Crowd cheers.*)

VERA: Gracias Chuck, Well, I really don't know what to say. I feel a lot of things, but it's hard to put it into words. I just want to say nomás that I think the union's going to help us all make a better life for ourselves here in this pueblo. And not just for us, but for our kids. Nosotras, las mujeres, tenemos que ser fuertes. We gotta be strong for our familias, but I'd like to thank Salvador for helping my husband Benny. I know now we're gonna make it. Por favor, tomorrow, everybody vote por la unión de César Chávez! ¡Qué viva la huelga! ¡Sí se puede!

WHITTAKER: Gracias Vera. Bueno, hermanos, this is it. I want you to go to your ranch committees and tell them to be ready at dawn to bring in a big election victory. Remember! We've got the workers. So we've got the votes! Somos la mayoría aplastante. ¡Viva la causa!

CAMPESINOS: ¡VIVA!

MUNDO: Just a minute, ése.

WHITTAKER: ¿Quién me habla?

MUNDO: I do, ése. And you can speak to me in your own language bato.

WHITTAKER: Which language is that?

BULLET: Mundo, this isn't the time.

MUNDO: Chale, carnal, chale, I'm making the time, tú sabes? This is my time, ése, my raza, my town, you dig? I'm a Chicano—simón— a Chicano farmworker, man. From right here! I just buried my jefita. In the old cemetery over there two weeks ago. Ain't that right, Bullet? Se nos acabó la Jefita, man. She's dead. Gone. Puf. Who knows where she is now.

WHITTAKER: Mundo, maybe we can sit down . . .

MUNDO: Cálmala, cálmala, ése, now, just let me rap, okay? You like to talk, bato. Shit. You been talking for seven weeks without stopping, carnal. Give a local loco a chance, ¿me entiendes cómo? Especially one that's related to your personal clown there. Now what I want to know, speaking as a farmworker y todo ese pedo, is what does Chávez have against the raza from el otro lado, you dig? What's he got against mojaditos?

WHITTAKER: Now, look, the Union is very clear on the whole question of undocumented workers!

MUNDO: Undocumented workers? Órale. Wait a minute. When did you start calling them that? I'm talking about what you used to call wetbacks, carnal! Mojados, alambristas, chúntaros, esquiroles muertos de hambre.

BULLET: We never called them that, Mundo!

MUNDO: Oh. The revolutionary brother speaks. A toda madre. Speak, carnal. Let's hear from a Chicano organizer for a change.

BULLET: (*Pause.*) The whole, US-Mexican border is an instrument in the exploitation of poor people on both sides of the border! The growers work in collusion with the US Border Patrol in order to . . .

MUNDO: Wait a minute, carnal. The growers work in what with the migra?

BULLET: Collusion.

MUNDO: No te entiendo. You're going to have to come down to earth, Sally. Not all of us had the chance to go to college and come back using palabrotas de gabacho. Maybe your friend there understands you, pero come on, we're raza here!

VERA: Are you saying the raza's stupid o, ¿qué?

MUNDO: Leave it to a vieja to twist my words around!

BOTELLA: Oh chattap! La raza es la raza! Here, there, anywhere. El campesino from here is no different than the campesino del otro lado. Same people.

VERA: We know what a sellout is, Mundo! Do you?

TAPÓN: ¡Vendido! ¡Es un vendido! ¡Lacayo de los patrones! ¡Lambiscón! ¡Coyote!

CAMPESINOS: (*Ad libs.*) ¡Sí! ¡Sí es! ¡Un sellout! ¡Sinvergüenza!

BOTELLA: He's a bloodsucker! Living off the poverty of his own people!

WHITTAKER: Hermanos, hermanos, un momento. Por favor. There's been enough name calling tonight. We're not afraid of whatever he has to say. If he's confused, let him ask questions.

TEODORO: ¡Es cierto! ¡Déjenlo hablar! ¡Nadie le tiene miedo! ¡Silencio! (*The hall quiets down.*)

WHITTAKER: Go ahead, Mundo.

MUNDO: Too much. That's just too much, man. You see that, Huesos? Did you see this gabacho, turn our raza off and on, just like that? Speak when the gabacho says to speak. Shut up when the gabacho says to shut up. Man, this bolillo has you controlados, qué no ven? What are we? The ass suckers of the white man all around the world?

TAPÓN: ¡Epa! ¡Cuidado con la lengua! ¡Hay mujeres y niños aquí! ¡Más respeto, Mundo!

BOTELLA: ¡Cállenle el hocico! ¡Está loco!

SUGAR: What about the money you've been taking from the growers?

MUNDO: What money?

SUGAR: They been paying him five thousand dollars a week!

TAPÓN: ¡En la madre! ¿Cinco mil dólares?

BOTELLA: ¿A la semana? ¿Para qué?

SUGAR: That's why he's here. He's trying to earn his money.

MUNDO: Where did you get your information, Sugar?

SUGAR: A little bird told me.

MUNDO: A little bird called Sheriff Barnes who's been giving it to you in the back, ésa? You wanna know where our raza's at, raza? ¡Aquí está! Es este joto standing right there! That's what the man has done to us! (SUGAR *loses it. HE leaps on* MUNDO *with fury.*)

SUGAR: Mira, hijo de tu chin . . . (*A scuffle erupts with others jumping in to a separate the two.*)

WHITTAKER: (*Stopping them.*) No! No! That's enough. Stop! ¡Párenle ahí! ¡Más orden, más orden! Sit down! ¡Siéntense todos! ¡No queremos violencia! (SUGAR *is escorted out, kicking and screaming.* WHITTAKER *follows.*)

MUNDO: Simón, no violence. Don't get violent. The man's dragging our guts through the street but don't get violent! Vamos a ver. How about you carnal? Are you nonviolent?

BULLET: You're blowing it, Ray. You can't bully me any more. I'm no longer intimidated by your bullshit. (*Face to face.*) You want to talk? Let's go talk. Just me and you. Like brothers. It's what Mom would want us to do.

MUNDO: (*Turning away.*) You know what this bato did, raza? About two weeks ago? Remember the night the whole town went ape shit because el Señor César Chávez came to the park?

TAPÓN: ¡N'ombre! ¡Otra vez la burra al maíz! Shut up or te charapeo!

BULLET: Let him finish.

MUNDO: Well, that night, down the street over here, in her labor camp, my jefita, his jefita, was having a stroke. Simón, se estaba muriendo. Do you know where this bato was? At the rally con César Chávez. He was being a bodyguard just in case, tú sabes? At the same time he was standing around, haciéndose muy chingón, watching out for snipers over there, la pinche muerte was stealing his jefita's life down the street over here!

BULLET: I didn't know.

MUNDO: Bullshit. I sent Tío after you.

TEODORO: I never found him!

BULLET: He never found me.

MUNDO: That's because you got yourself lost, carnal. And you're still lost. Pero, ¿sabes qué? I'm going to teach you some respect. You wanna know what violence is, cabrón? Violence is killing gooks. Old men, women, children. Everybody! It's raping twelve-year-old girls and blowing their brains out. And then setting fire to their hooches. You think you could do that, ése? (*There is a desperate silence.*) Órale pues, conscientious objector. Let's see qué tan non-violent eres, eh? I promised the jefita not to kill your ass. So if you want, tú me puedes plantar el primer chingazo, but I'm going to wipe the floor with your culo! (*Pushes him.*) ¡Ándale! Come on, carnal, hit me!

BULLET: No, Mundo.

MUNDO: Hit me! Hit me! ¡Hijo de la chingada! (HE *starts pushing* BULLET *and falls on his face on the floor. Long pause.* VERA *comes up and stares down at* MUNDO. SHE *leaves, followed by* GÜERITO, BOTELLA *and* TAPÓN. *Then* GREÑAS.)

WHITTAKER: Come on, Sal. This meeting is over. (BULLET *and* WHITTAKER *leave.* HUESOS *is the only one left;* MUNDO, *half-crying, lays there for a while then gets up, staggering.*)

HUESOS: Mundo? What now, carnal?

MUNDO: Get lost, ése. Leave me the fuck alone! (HUESOS *backs off and exits.* MUNDO *stands with his back to the audience, looking up at the thunderbird banner. HE exits. Lights fade as the red flickering flames of a growing offstage fire dance across the huelga eagle. We hear the distant sirens of fire engines.*)

Black.

SCENE SEVEN

La Divina Garza. TEODORO *drops a coin into the jukebox and turns to the batos standing at the bar.*

TEODORO: Bueno, mis chachos, that's it! Mundo se chingó a los rancheros, se chingó al Barnes, se chingó a su ruca, and today, la unión se chingó a Gudunritch and Roddenberry.

HUESOS: No la chingues. That was the plan.

GREÑAS: You mean Mundo wasn't against Chávez?

HUESOS: Contrólate, he wouldn't do that.

GREÑAS: What about what he said at that meeting? Regó a toda la huelga.

HUESOS: That was just to give más salsa to the elecciones. Shit, it's been too easy, man. Today la raza voted con fuerza! This place ain't going to be the same again.

TEODORO: Especially since Mundo burned down half the labor camp.

HUESOS: It wasn't Mundo! He helped to put out the fire. It was the rent strikers.

TEODORO: The rent strikers live there, baboso.

GREÑAS: What kind of bato would burn down his own jefita's chante?

TEODORO: ¡Está loco! He's my nephew but he's out of control. This time he almost killed people. (MUNDO *enters. All eyes turn toward the door. HE looks spent.*)

MUNDO: Where's Güera?

TEODORO: Back in her apartment—with Prieta. Knock before you enter. (MUNDO *disappears into a door behing the bar.*)

GREÑAS: What's up with Mundo? He looks like shit. Ya no se watcha tan killer diller.

HUESOS: He's just tired. He hasn't slept in days.

TEODORO: His jefita's death unplugged his ombligo. He's running low on batteries. (*Sudden backstage uproar:* MUNDO *comes rushing back out.*)

GÜERA: (*O.S.*) Mundo, godammit! Close the door!

PRIETA: (*O.S.*) Don't you know how to knock, bobo?

MUNDO: Órale, sorry! ¡No se agüiten!

TEODORO: I hate to say I told you so, pero I told you so. Sit down, sobrino. I'm tending bar. You look like you need a beer.

MUNDO: (*Ironic.*) Beer?

TEODORO: To put you to sleep. So you can rest.

MUNDO: That won't do it.

TEODORO: How about a whiskito? (*Beat.*) ¿Yesca? (*Beat.*) A little female goat?

MUNDO: Chale, Tío. I'm off the chiva for good. No more night sweats, choking in my sleep. I want you batos to be the first to know. I'm swearing off todas las drogas.

GREÑAS: (*Baffled.*) All the drugs?

MUNDO: ¡Todas! Bueno, except maybe a little mota once in a while. But that's it.

HUESOS: This almost sounds like one of those religious contortions.

TEODORO: Don't tell me. Did you see the light, Mundo? (BULLET *enters unseen by* MUNDO.)

MUNDO: Simón. The light of the camp fire. (*Turning.*) You got something on your mind, Bullet?

BULLET: Just a couple of questions . . . about the fire.

MUNDO: Pinche carnal. You sound like a pig. What's your first question? (THEY *sit off in a side booth.*)

BULLET: Does the labor camp have fire insurance?

MUNDO: You think I'm trying to collect?

BULLET: Why did you do it?

MUNDO: I wanted the fire to burn away all the shit. It got away, that's all, out of control. I heard women screaming and dogs barking. Suddenly I was there, back in the jungle, setting fire to the hooches. One second there, the next second back here. Like in a dream. But it was real. (*Pause.*) What's your second question?

BULLET: (*Intimately.*) What do you have against your brothers, Ray? When I was a kid, you were my hero, man. Benny felt the same way, but you turned him into Flaco.

MUNDO: (*Quietly intense.*) Benny's old man sent our old man to the joint for manslaughter, ése. Torres was driving the night of the train wreck. He was drunk, but after the accident, he ran away—like a skunk. So Narciso Mata took the rap because the truck was in his name, thanks to Benjamín Torres, you dig?

BULLET: So you're taking out your revenge on Torres by destroying Benny? Why did you work for him then?

MUNDO: Why not?

BULLET: That's no answer!

MUNDO: (*Despairing.*) The world's a rotten cesspool, carnal. ¿Qué no sabes? The pendejos are on the bottom. Only the strong survive.

BULLET: There's strength in numbers. (MUNDO *rises.*) You're in deep shit, Mundo! The families at labor camp want to bring criminal charges against you.

MUNDO: Is the plumbing that fucking important?

BULLET: It's more than that now. They want justice.

MUNDO: (*Switching gears.*) Okay. If that's how it is, you got it.

BULLET: Justice?

MUNDO: The plumbing. I'll fix the whole fucking place up. It'll look like Motel 6.

BULLET: How are you going to do this?

MUNDO: Trust me. El Mundo no es pendejo, carnal. You know, before I went to 'Nam, I had never been out of this valley. The biggest cities I ever saw in my life was Fresno and Bakersfield. No shit. I feel like hitting the road. Tengo ganas de estirar las patas.

TEODORO: ¿Estirar las patas? That means to die.

MUNDO: Chale, Tío, not me. Not yet. I got everything to live for. Estoy free and unattached.

GREÑAS: What about la Mrs. Barnes?

MUNDO: If she lets you, ése, you may enter with my permission.

GREÑAS: ¿Me das entrada?

MUNDO: Que se vaya a chapetear el mundo.

GREÑAS: You mean you?

MUNDO: No, carnal, I mean you.

HUESOS: What about me?

MUNDO: Todo el mundo, ¿qué no dije? I'm taking off, locos. To see the rest of the world.

TEODORO: What about your tío favorito?

MUNDO: You've got Güera here. She can feed you and keep you drunk todos los días. Con el last installment, I have como unos fifty grand más o menos. Not bad for seven weeks in the fields, ¿no crees?

BULLET: What about the union? You can't just walk away without dealing with it.

MUNDO: ¿Verdad que sí? Maybe I'll leave you unos 500 bolas, carnal, so you can buy a pair of pantalones for Chávez. (GÜERA *emerges from the back, followed shortly by* PRIETA.)

GÜERA: (*To* MUNDO.) Are you still here?

MUNDO: Not for long. I'm blowing this town. ¿On 'ta mi fiera, ésa? Capea.

GÜERA: You're not going to get away with it, Mundo.

MUNDO: Who's going to stop me—Bullet?

GÜERA: Your friends.

MUNDO: I don't got any. It's me against the world.

BULLET: Then it's you against your self, brother. (VERA, FLACO *and* GÜERITO *enter, followed by* TAPÓN *and* BOTELLA. *The whole familia.* MUNDO *is deeply moved by their appearance.*)

VERA: Look who's home.

MUNDO: (*Emotional.*) Flaco.

FLACO: (*Clean and strong.*) Give it up, carnal. Let all the shit go. We'll catch you. Ándale. (*There is a tense pause, as* MUNDO *stares at* FLACO. *Then the damn breaks.* MUNDO *breaks out sobbing, falling into* BULLET*'s arms.*)

Fade to black.

SCENE EIGHT

The park. Flood lights. CHUCK WHITTAKER *and* BULLET *are on stage.* WHITTAKER *is talking through a bullhorn. Excitement, noise, crowd.*

WHITTAKER: ¡Qué viva la huelga! (¡VIVA¡) ¡Qué viva la Causa! (¡VIVA!) Compañeros, the election has been won and victory is ours, but the struggle is far from over. We want to introduce a brother you all know. Es un bato muy conocido aquí en Burlap, el hermano de Salvador, ¡Mundo Mata! (HUESOS *and* GREÑAS *applaud.*)
MUNDO: (*Through the bullhorn.*) Estimado público, uh, éste... I'm not used to speaking into these madres... éste, I mean, I'm a little nervous, ¡tú sabes! (*People crack up.* HE *feels better.*) Saben qué, it feels de aquéllas, being up here. I never knew we had so much gente around during la pisca, you know? Simón, there's a lotta of us. You're beautiful, raza. (*People clap.*) Yo soy El Mundo. De aquí de Burlap. Soy un bato nomás, you know. Nothing special. But tonight, I feel special. ¿Saben por qué? Because I know we got the gabachos. (*Pause.*) I mean the growers... sorry ése... (*To* CHUCK.) We got them on the run. Mañana will be the beginning of a new world for our people here. Y los Rottenberries, los Gudunritches y los Sonavubitches are through! (*There are cheers in the crowd.* MUNDO *warms up to them.*) And let me say a thing about the Sam Barnes of the world. They can take their Sheriff's Department and shove it! Because we won't be pushed around anymore. We're not going to be bought out! Y ¿saben qué? I did take money from the growers, simón! Fifty thousand bolas. Right here. But I didn't do shit for it. I was going to leave town because I was medio escamado, but not anymore. Seeing you all here makes me feel a toda madre. I'm going to stay and fight! (*Applause.*) And you know what? I'm kicking back all this bread to the Union so it can help the rent strikers fix the plumbing! 'On 'ta el éste... ¿cómo

se llama? (*Someone says the name.*) Chuck, right. Hay te llevo, carnal. (*Hands him the money.*)

WHITTAKER: (*Holds up the money.*) Here it is! The rent strike is over! (*Cheers.*)

MUNDO: I just want to say one more thing. This is the first time in my life I ever believed in something besides myself. ¡Viva la Causa, y qué Viva César Chávez! Y ¡qué rife el Nuevo Mundo! (*Cheers start up again. Applause. Suddenly there are gunshots.* MUNDO *falls dying. Screams. Pandemonium.*)

Blackout.

EPILOGUE

MUNDO*'s body is elevated on the stage, a black huelga flag is draped over him and* VERA *is kneeling next to him, as are* FLACO, GÜERITO, GÜERA *and* PRIETA. *Mourners are softly humming "We Shall Overcome."*

BULLET: Some people are saying Mundo died for La Causa, and it's true. He did die for his people. But as his carnal, I want to say something that I think Mundo would have said if he was here instead of me. You see he never held back on anything. He always told the truth he felt in his heart, even if it hurt. And the truth is that Mundo was killed by Sam Barnes. Why did he kill Mundo? Some people are saying it was jealous rage. Others are saying the growers wanted it. Either way people are afraid to remember what Mundo was really like, so everybody pretends he was a hero and a martyr. Well, he was. But he was also his own worst enemy. A wounded soldier lost in a war without moral compass. What's this struggle about, as César Chávez says, if not to fight the hatred, violence and injustice in our own hearts? That was the struggle Mundo gave his life for. Good or bad, he was my brother, and I loved him. But I never knew that until the very end. (HE *joins the mourners, embracing* MUNDO*'s flag-covered body.*)

Fade to black.

The Shrunken
Head of
Pancho Villa

CHARACTERS

PEDRO, the jefito, an old Villista con huevos.
CRUZ, the madre, long-suffering but loving.
JOAQUIN, the young son, a bato loco and a Chicano.
LUPE, the daughter.
MINGO, the son, a Mexican American.
BELARMINO, the oldest son.
CHATO, the dim-witted boyfriend.
LA JURA, a police officer.

SCENE

The interior of an old house: a large, imposing two-story building sagging into total dilapidation. The front room with tall cracked windows; doors to a stairwell and the kitchen; and an adjoining room with a curtained doorway, once a study now also a bedroom. This front room, which is the center of the play's action, has been repainted with a true Mexican folk taste. Bright reds, yellows and blues try to obscure the shabby, broken-down "chingado" quality of it all.

NOTE ON STYLE

The play is not intended as a "realistic" interpretation of Chicano life. The symbolism emerging from the character of Belarmino influences the style of acting, scene design, make-up, etc. The play therefore contains realistic and surrealistic elements working together to achieve a transcendental expression of the social condition of La Raza in los Estados Unidos. The set, particularly, must be "real" for what it represents; but it must also contain a cartoon quality such as that found in the satirical sketches of José Clemente Orozco or the lithographs of José Guadalupe Posada. In short, it must reflect the psychological reality of the barrio.

PROLOGUE

(Narration accompanying a slideshow of historical photos.)
FRANCISCO VILLA, born 1878—died 1923.

Campesino, bandit, guerrilla, martyr, general, head of Northern Division of the Revolutionary Army, and finally an undying legend. He is born and christened Doroteo Arango in the town of Río Grande, state of Durango. In 1895, when he is 17, he is outlawed for killing an *hacendado,* a landowner—a member of the ruling class who had raped his sister. He is caught, but escapes and he takes the name of Francisco Villa. Thus, during the years between 1896 and 1909, the legend of Pancho Villa is born. The legend of the providential bandit: rob the rich to give to the poor. And the poor give him their faith.

The year 1910 brings the beginning of the Mexican Revolution. Pancho Villa enlists his band of men as a guerrilla force. Minor victories grow into major victories: San Andrés, Camargo, Juárez, Torreón, Zacatecas, Irapuato, Querétaro. The bandit force becomes a Revolutionary Army with horses, trains, cavalry, artillery and a mass of 50,000 men. The peasant outlaw evolves into one of the most brilliant military strategists of our century.

November 27, 1914: Pancho Villa and Emiliano Zapata meet in Mexico City. It is a triumph for the poor, the campesinos, the disinherited. Pancho Villa tries out the presidential chair, yet neither he nor Zapata are compromising types. They are not politicians.

1915: Against the recommendations of his advisors, Woodrow Wilson, President of the United States, recognizes the rival Carrancista government and permits Carranza to transport troops over American soil and thus outflank Villa's División del Norte at Agua Prieta. Villa is defeated. It is the beginning of the end.

1916: Villa retaliates with a raid on Columbus, New Mexico. He is declared an outlaw by the Carranza government, and Wilson sends General John J. Pershing into Mexican territory on a "punitive expedition" looking for Pancho Villa. Pershing fails, and Villa resumes his guerrilla warfare. His military strength, however, is flagging.

1919: Emiliano Zapata is murdered on April 10 in Chinameca.

July 28, 1920: Francisco Villa surrenders the remains of his army to the government. He settles in Canutillo, NM to live peacefully.

July 23, 1923: Pancho Villa is ambushed and he dies in the streets of Parral, Chihuahua. His body is dumped into an unmarked grave. Three years later it is disinterred and the corpse is decapitated. The head is never found. This is the story of a people who followed him beyond borders, beyond death.

ACT ONE

A sharp-stringed guitar plays "La Cucaracha." It is afternoon.
PEDRO, *the aged father of the family, is asleep on a broken-down
couch. He is on his back—his paunch sagging—and snoring loudly. He
has a long, drooping white moustache and toussled white hair. The guitar concludes "La Cucaracha" with a sharp, final note.* PEDRO, *as if
on cue, shouts violently!!*

PEDRO: (*In his sleep.*) ¡¡VIVA VILLA!!
BELARMINO: (*Screams from the curtained bedroom. It is the cry of a
full-grown man. He starts singing with vengeance.*) Aarrrrgh!
(*Sings.*) ¡La cucaracha! ¡La cucaracha!
ya no quiere caminar
porque le falta, porque no tiene
Marihuana que fumar!
CRUZ: (*Running from the kitchen.*) Dios mío, you see what you do,
hombre? You have wake up your own son! (BELARMINO *repeats
"La Cucaracha," getting louder and more viciously impatient.*
CRUZ, *distraught, runs into the curtained bedroom. From off.*)
Belarmino, Belarmino, my son, go to sleep. Go to sleep. A la rurru,
niño, duérmete ya. (BELARMINO *dozes off singing and is finally
silent.* CRUZ *emerges, sighing with relief.*) ¡Gracias a Dios! He's
asleep! (*To* PEDRO, *a harsh whisper.*) Be quiet, you old loco! You
know he always wakes up hungry. I got enough trouble catching
your son's lices so they don't eat us alive! You are crawling with
them already.
PEDRO: (*In his sleep.*) Señores, I am Francisco Villa! (*Scratches.*)
CRUZ: Sweet name of God.
PEDRO: ¡Pancho Villa!
CRUZ: Pedro!
PEDRO: I am Pancho Villa!
CRUZ: Yes with lices!
PEDRO: ¡Viva Villa!
CRUZ: Qué hombre. (*She goes to him.*)

PEDRO: VIVA PANCHO VEE-

CRUZ: (*Pulls his leg.*); PEDRO!

PEDRO: Yah! (*He wakes* up.) Uh!

CRUZ: Stop shouting, hombre.

PEDRO: Uh. (*He goes back to sleep, scratching his belly.*)

CRUZ: Viejo loco. Pancho Villa. I don' know what goes through that head he gots. (JOAQUÍN *rushes in and stops, panting against the door. His shirt is torn.*) ¡Joaquín! What happen to you?

JOAQUÍN: Nothing.

CRUZ: What did you do?

JOAQUÍN. Nothing.

CRUZ: What happen to your shirt?

JOAQUÍN: Nothing!

CRUZ: Don' you know nothing but nothing?

JOAQUÍN: (*Pause.*) I beat up some bato.

CRUZ: Another fight, my son?

JOAQUÍN: I never start it. Dumb gabacho. He come up to me and says "Heh, Pancho!"

PEDRO: (*In his sleep.*) Uh?

CRUZ: You hit him for that?

JOAQUÍN: Well, how would you like it, man? I wasn' looking for no trouble. I even take Pancho Villa at first, which was bad enough, but then he call me a lousy Pancho, and I hit the stupid bato in the mouth.

CRUZ: ¡Dios mío! (*Pause.*) What is wrong with you hombre? Don' you think? You on patrol!

JOAQUÍN: Parole.

CRUZ: Sí. (*Sighs.*) And mañana it will be the jail again, no? How come you this way, hijo? Your brother Mingo, he never fight so much.

JOAQUÍN: He was pus-pus.

CRUZ: (*Miserable.*) Don' you know nothing else? Your brother he's coming from the war today with muchos medals, Joaquín. That is not so pus-pus. If he fight, he do it in the right place. Only you turn out so lousy.

JOAQUÍN: (*Fiercely.*) I ain' lousy, ma!

CRUZ: (*Pause.*) You goin' to hit me in the mouth too, my son? (JOAQUÍN, *starts to go.*) What you doin'?

JOAQUÍN: Splittin'!

CRUZ: Joaquín!

JOAQUÍN: (*He stops.*) Stop bugging me, jefita!

CRUZ: (*With deep concern.*) What trouble you so much, hijo?

JOAQUÍN: The gabachos.

LUPE: (*Comes in from the kitchen.*) Mamá, the beans are ready! You wan' me to bring 'em?

CRUZ: No, Lupe, Belarmino is asleep.

LUPE: What happened to our favorite jailbird?

JOAQUÍN: Shut up!

LUPE: Been out duking again, huh? Rotten pachuco.

CRUZ: Guadalupe, don' say that.

LUPE: It's true. He barely got outta jail yesterday, and now look at him. He don' even care that Mingo's coming home from the war. I bet he's just jealous.

JOAQUÍN: Of what?

LUPE: His medals.

JOAQUÍN: Screw his medals!

CRUZ: Joaquín! Don' you even feel glad your brother's come home alive and safe?

JOAQUÍN: Simón, it makes me feel real patriotic.

LUPE: Liar! Just wait till Mingo gets here. He'll cool your bird. Lousy hoodlum.

JOAQUÍN: Lousy, huh? Well, how about this? (*He grabs* LUPE *and pretends to set a louse loose in her hair.*) Ha! Who's lousy now, man?

LUPE: Ayy, Mamá! Mamá!

CRUZ: Haven' you do enough already, muchacho?

JOAQUÍN: I was only joking.

CRUZ: But Belarmino . . .

JOAQUÍN: I was only joking, man! I don' got no piojos.

LUPE: That's what you think.

JOAQUÍN: Shut up!

LUPE: You lousy Mexican!

CRUZ: Stop it, señorita. Din't I tell you to go water the beans?

LUPE: No!

CRUZ: Go water the beans. (*Pause.*) Ándale. Go, Guadalupe. (LUPE *exits.*)

JOAQUÍN: And stay out!

CRUZ: You stop too, Joaquín. Wha's wrong with you, anyway? Are you as loco as your padre?

JOAQUÍN: Loco?

CRUZ: Making noise! This morning your poor brother he eat 50 plates of beans and 100 tortillas. This afternoon I find 30 lice on him—do you hear, hombre? 30! My poor Belarmino, some of this days if he don' eat us out of the house, his lices they will do it. (*She turns and notices* JOAQUÍN *scratching his head.*) Joaquín, what you doing?

JOAQUÍN: (*Stops.*) What? (*Lowers his hand.*)

CRUZ: You was scratching your head! Blessed be the Señor! Come here, sit down.

JOAQUÍN: (*Guiltily.*) What?

CRUZ: (*Inspecting his head.*) Dios mío, this all we need.

JOAQUÍN: (*Angry.*) What?

CRUZ: For you to catch the lices, muchacho.

JOAQUÍN: (*Tries to rise.*) Lices!

CRUZ: Don' move. (JOAQUÍN *remains still.*) Joaquín! I think I find one! No . . . sí . . . sí! It is one. It gots little legs!

JOAQUÍN: (*Jumps up.*) Let's see.

CRUZ: Put him up to the light, my son. (*Pause.*) It is . . . one lice, no?

JOAQUÍN: A louse.

CRUZ: What is that?

JOAQUÍN: One lice.

CRUZ: May the Señor help us all! (BELARMINO *grunts.*) Ay. Now he's waking up again. I better fix his frijolitos. (*Exits to kitchen.*)

JOAQUÍN: Me too, huh, señora? My pipes are rumbling.

PEDRO: Sí, mi general. I hear the rumbling. The gringos got cannons y aeroplanos, pero no se apure . . . mi general! ¿Qué pasó con su cabeza? ¡Muchachos, abusados! ¡Alguien se robó la cabeza de Pancho Villa! Ayyy.

JOAQUÍN: (*Shaking him.*) Pa! ¡'Apá!

PEDRO: (*Awaking.*) Uh? What?

JOAQUÍN: You have a nightmare.

PEDRO: How you know?

JOAQUÍN: You shout. Something about Pancho Villa and his head. I don' know. It was in Spanish.

PEDRO: Huh. (*Sits up.*) Where's your madre?

JOAQUÍN: In the kitchen.

PEDRO: Frying beans no doubt, eh? Only I never get to try 'em. The loco in the room over there always eat 'em first. Curse the day all my sons was born starving in the land of the gringos! (HE *finds an empty wine bottle under the couch.*) Ah, here it is. No, hombre, my little bottle is dead. Oye, my son, you got enough maybe for one . . . bueno, you know, eh?

JOAQUÍN: Nel, I'm sorry, jefito.

PEDRO: No, don't start wis your "I'm sorrys." Don' you find work yet?

JOAQUÍN: Work?

PEDRO: Field work.

JOAQUÍN: You mean like farm labor?

PEDRO: Man's work!

JOAQUÍN: Cool it, ése, I just get here. They work me enough in the can. I pull off more than a year wisout pay.

PEDRO: Bueno, it's your own fault. For your itchy fingers . . . stealing tires.

JOAQUÍN: What tires?

PEDRO: Pos what ones? They din' catch you red-handed?

JOAQUÍN: Simón, but it wasn' tires. They arrest me for a suspect together with nine other batos. Then there at the station the placa gives us all matches, and the one wis the short one was guilty. They catch me red-handed! But I din't swipe no tires.

PEDRO: No, eh? Well, I hope maybe you learn something.

JOAQUÍN: No sweat, jefito. I learn to play the guitar.

PEDRO: Tha's all?

JOAQUÍN: Nel, I sing too. Honest. Loan me your guitar, I show you.

PEDRO: No, Joaquín, I don' like to loan that guitar. I have too many year with it, since the Revolución! Qué caray, what happen if you break it. Ees too old.

JOAQUÍN: What about when I fix it that time?

PEDRO: When?

JOAQUÍN: When you smash it on Mingo's head.

PEDRO: Oh, sí. But the baboso he talk back to me, tha's how come. Bueno, qué caray, go bring it, pues—I want to see if you really know how to play it.

JOAQUÍN: Órale. (HE *goes into the side room and comes out with an old guitar.*)

PEDRO: What you play? ¿Corridos, rancheras?

JOAQUÍN: Rhythm and Blues.

PEDRO: (*Pause.*) What about "Siete Leguas"?

JOAQUÍN: What about it?

PEDRO: You see, you don' know nothing.

JOAQUÍN: What's "Siete Leguas"?

PEDRO: "Seven Leguas"! How you say leguas in . . .

JOAQUÍN: Uh, leagews.

PEDRO: What?

JOAQUÍN: Lea-gews.

PEDRO: That's right. "Siete Leguas. " The song of the horse of Pancho Villa. The horse he mos' estimated. (*Solemnly.*) He ride that horse until the day he die.

JOAQUÍN: The general?

PEDRO: No, the horse. After that Pancho Villa buy a Chivi. Maybe it was a Ford? No, it was a Chivi. 1923! That was the year they kill him, you know. A revolutionary giant like he was.

JOAQUÍN: Aah, he wasn' a giant.

PEDRO: Oh, caray, you don' know, my son! Francisco Villa was a man to respect. A man to fear! A man con muchos . . . ummmhh (*Whispering.*) huevos. He rob from the rich to give to the poor—like us. That's why the poor follow him. Any time he could rise 50,000 men by snapping his fingers. You should have see what he do to the gringos.

JOAQUÍN: The gabachos?

PEDRO: No, the gringos. In them times they was only call gringos. Not gabachos. Pancho Villa have 'em running all over México.

JOAQUÍN: What was they doing in México?

PEDRO: Chasing him! But they never catch him. He was too smart, eh? Too much cabeza. He ride on Siete Leguas and stay in the mountains. Then he ride his men around the back, and they kill gringos until they get tired! Sometimes they even get more tire' than picking potatoes, but they go back to the mountains to rest.

JOAQUÍN: (*Impressed.*) Hey, man, tha's too much.

PEDRO: I myself ride with him, you know. See this scar? (*Points to his neck.*) From a bullet. And listen to this: ¡VIVA VILLAAA!

CRUZ: (*In the kitchen.*) ¡Pedro, hombre! You wake your son!

PEDRO: (*Shouts back.*) Oh, you and that crazy loco! (*To* JOAQUÍN.) Huh, that stinking madre of yours! All she live for is to feed that bean belly! He has curse my life.

JOAQUÍN: What about Pancho Villa? When he got the Chivi? I bet he run down a lotta gabachos, huh? Squashed 'em!

PEDRO: (*With exaggeration.*) ¡Oh sí! He . . . (*Pause.*) The Chivi? No, hombre, when he get the Chivi, then they get him. Right in Chihuahua too, in Parral. He was just driving down the street one day, not bothering nobody, when they shoot him down and kill him. (*Mournful pause.*) So . . . they bury him, and then in the night three years later, somebody come and—ZAS! They cut off his head.

JOAQUÍN: His *head?*

PEDRO: Chattap! (*Whispering.*) You want Belarmino to hear?
JOAQUÍN: How come they cut off his head? Who done it?
PEDRO: Pos, who you think?
JOAQUÍN: ¡Los gabachos!
PEDRO: (*Nods.*) Maybe they still even got it, too. To this day nobody has find it.
JOAQUÍN: Híjole, how gacho, man. (*Pause.*) How did that song goes?
PEDRO: "Siete Leguas"?
JOAQUÍN: Simón.
PEDRO: (*Sings.*) "Siete Leguas, el caballo que Villa más estimabaaa."
BELARMINO: (*In his room.*) ¡Ay, yai, yai, yai!
PEDRO: Oh-oh, now we do it.
CRUZ: (*Entering.*) What have you do, hombre?
PEDRO: Nothing. (BELARMINO *yells and howls, sings "La Cucaracha."*)
CRUZ: No, eh? (*Shouting back.*) Lupe, bring the tortillas!
PEDRO: We eat now?
CRUZ: You wait!
PEDRO: I don' want to wait! (BELARMINO *yells.*)
CRUZ: Lupe, bring the beans too! (SHE *goes into the bedroom.*)
PEDRO: I don' got to wait! I wan' to eat—EAT! ¡Quiero tragar! (LUPE *comes out of the kitchen with beans and tortillas.* JOAQUÍN *grabs a tortilla with a laugh.*)
LUPE: You pig!
PEDRO: (*Turns around.*) Pig?
LUPE: I meant Joaquín. (*She goes into the bedroom quickly.*)
PEDRO: ¡Sinvergüenzas! Who's the boss here, pues? Who buys the eats!
CRUZ: (*Inside the room.*) ¡El Welfare!
PEDRO: And before that?
CRUZ: Your son, Mingo.
PEDRO: Mingo? (*Throws his arms out in a helpless gesture.*) So this is what I get, eh? In 1927 I come here all the way from Zacatecas. For what? CHICKENSQUAT? Everybody talks back, that . . . that loco in there eats before his padre does, and Mingo . . . Mingo . . . where's Mingo?
JOAQUÍN: (*Eating the rolled up tortilla.*) Not home from the war yet. (MINGO *walks into the room through the front door. He is in a soldier's uniform and carries a sack with his stuff in it.*)
MINGO: Somebody say war?

LUPE: (*Peeking out of* BELARMINO'*s room.*) Mamá, Mingo's home!

CRUZ: (*Coming out with the bowl of beans.*) My son! (SHE *embraces him and cries.*)

PEDRO: Bueno, bueno, lemme see him. He's my son, too!

MINGO: Hello, Pa. (*Offers his hand.*)

PEDRO: ¿Halo qué? Give me one abrazo, I'm your padre! (HE *hugs him.*) Tha's it—strong like a man. Look, vieja, see how much medals he gots?

LUPE: Hi, Mingo, remember me?

MINGO: Sure. ¡María!

LUPE: María!

MINGO: (*Pause.*) ¿Rosita?

LUPE: ¡Lupe!

MINGO: Oh, yeah, Lupe.

PEDRO: And over here you got your brother Joaquín.

MINGO: Hi, punk. Shake.

JOAQUÍN: Órale. (*They shake hands.*)

CRUZ: Well, my son, sit down. Rest. You must be tired.

MINGO: Not at all, Mom.

CRUZ: ¿Tienes hambre?

MINGO: What's for dinner?

CRUZ: Papas con huevos.

MINGO: What else?

LUPE: Huevos con papas.

MINGO: Is that all?

JOAQUÍN: Papas a huevo.

MINGO: No, thanks. I had a steak in town.

CRUZ: Oh. Well, thank God, you have come home safe and sound. (SHE *takes him to the couch.*) Look, sit down over here. Tell us about . . . (SHE *sees the wine bottle.*) Pedro hombre, this dirty bottle!

MINGO: Still at it, huh, Pa?

PEDRO: No, only from time to time, hijo. For the cough. (HE *coughs.*)

LUPE: Tell us of the war, Mingo.

CRUZ: What's wrong with you, woman? Your brother he want to forget such things. It already pass, gracias a Dios.

PEDRO: Huh, it pass? You mean we don' suppose to know where the muchacho was? War is war! If the sons fight today, we fight yesterday. Mira, when I was with Pancho Villa, we kill more Americanos than . . .

MINGO: ¿Americanos? Americans!

BELARMINO: (*In his room.*) ARRRRRGGHH!

MINGO: (*Alarmed.*) What the hell's that?

CRUZ: ¡Belarmino! Lupe, please give him the beans that was left. I had forgot he didn' finish eating.

MINGO: Mom, who's Belarmino?

CRUZ: (*Surprised.*) Pos . . . you know, hijo. You don' remember?

PEDRO: Of course, he remember! Caray, how he's going to forgot that animal? Don' let him bother you, my son. Come here, tell me your plans. What you going to do now?

MINGO: Well, 'apá, I been thinking. (*Long pause.*)

PEDRO: He's been thinking, qué bueno. What you been thinking, hijo?

MINGO: I been thinking I wanna help the family!

CRUZ: ¡Ay, m'ijito! (SHE *embraces him.* PEDRO *shakes his hand.*)

MINGO: As a matter of fact, I got a surprise for you. I bet you didn't expect me till tonight, right? Well, you know how come I'm home early? I bought a new car!

JOAQUÍN: A new car!

CRUZ: A new car!

LUPE: (*Reentering.*) A new car! (BELARMINO *grunts three times, mimicking the sound of the words, "A new car."*)

CRUZ: ¡Dios mío!

LUPE: We didn't even hear you drive up!

MINGO: Natch. She's as quiet as a fly in the beans. Mom, sis, hold on to your frijole bowl. There she is! (*Points out the window.*) A new Chevrolet!

LUPE: A Chevi! ¡Mamá, un Chevi!

CRUZ: Blessed be the name of the Señor. That one is ours, Mingo?

MINGO: All ours, only forty more payments to go. (*Everyone looks out the window except* PEDRO.) What's wrong, Pa? Ain't you going to look?

PEDRO: For what? They going to come for it in two months.

MINGO: Not this baby. I'm gonna keep up all my payments.

PEDRO: Tha's what I used to say. I never make it.

MINGO: I know, but I ain't you. (*Pause.*) I mean, it wasn' necessary, Dad. Give me one good reason why you didn't keep good credit. Just one!

PEDRO: (BELARMINO *grunts hungrily in his room.*) There it is.

CRUZ: Guadalupe, go. (LUPE *exits to room.*)

MINGO: (*Pause. Everybody dejected.*) You know what's wrong with you people? You're all defeated! Just look at this place! Well, it ain't gonna get me down. I learned some skills in the Marines, and I'm gonna use 'em in the best place I know to get ahead!

PEDRO: Where?

MINGO: The fields.

JOAQUÍN: At farm labor? (*Laughs.*) You going to be a farm laborer?

MINGO: Listen, you cholo.

CRUZ: Cállate el hocico, baboso.

MINGO: What's he ever done but land in jail, Mom? What you ever done? (JOAQUÍN *blows a raspberry in his face.*)

CRUZ: Joaquín, es-stop it.

MINGO: You drop-out. You high school drop-out!

CRUZ: Mingo, please.

MINGO: You know what you're gonna end up like? Like the old man— a stinking wino!

PEDRO: WHAT!

MINGO: (*Embarrassed pause.*) Aw, come on, Dad. I din' mean nothing bad. Look, let's face it, okay? You're just a wino, right? Like I'm a Marine. What's wrong with that? There's a million of 'em. Today I was even going to buy you a bottle of Old Crow.

PEDRO: Whiskey?

MINGO: Damn right. $6.50 a quart. It's better than that 35 cent stuff you been drinking. From now on it's nothing but the best for us. Only, we gotta be realistic. Plan everything. Okay, Tomahawk, you'll be working with me. You got a job now?

JOAQUÍN: Chale.

MINGO: You mean Dad's the only one working?

PEDRO: (*Pause.*) Eh . . . no, I don' work neither, Mingo.

MINGO: Then how do you support yourselves?

JOAQUÍN: How come you don' tell him, Pa? The jefitos are on welfare, ése.

MINGO: Welfare? WELFARE! (HE *turns away, sick.*)

CRUZ: We always been poor, my son.

MINGO: (*Determined.*) That's true, Mom. But now things are gonna be different. I'm here now, and we're going to be rich—middle class! I didn't come out the war without learning nothing.

JOAQUÍN: Then how come you going back to the fields? Nobody get rich in that jale.

MINGO: No, huh? (HE *embraces* CRUZ *and* PEDRO.) Well, thanks to this old man and old lady, who were smart enough to cross the border, we live in the land of opportunity. The land I risk my life for. The land where you can start at the bottom, even in the fields, and become a rich man before you can say . . .

BELARMINO: ARRRGGGHHH! (LUPE *comes running with her blouse torn on one side.*)

LUPE: Ay! Mamá! He ate all the beans then he try to bite me!

CRUZ: Por Dios. The poor man.

LUPE: The poor man? He's a pig. Look at the hole he made.

CRUZ: All right pues, I see it.

LUPE: And he give me his piojos.

CRUZ: No matter. Go bring more tortillas!

MINGO: Wait a minute, wait a minute! Mom, for the last time, who's in there?

CRUZ: Your older brother, hijo. Belarmino.

MINGO: Brother? I don't remember no other brother. What's wrong with him? How come he shouts?

PEDRO: Ay, pos 'tá loco el baboso.

CRUZ: (*Surprised.*) He's sick . . . but you should know. You used to play with him when you was little.

MINGO: Ma, don' lie to me. Are we so poor we gotta take in braceros? Or maybe it's a wetback you're hiding?

JOAQUÍN: (*A whisper to* PEDRO.) Or maybe he's suffering from shell-shock?

MINGO: I ain't suffering from nothing, man!

JOAQUÍN: Take it easy, carnal, cool it.

MINGO: Well, Ma, is that guy a wetback?

CRUZ: No, he's your brother.

MINGO: Brother, huh? We'll soon find out! (HE *charges into the bedroom.*)

BELARMINO: (*After a pause.*) ARRRRRRRGGGGHH.

MINGO: (*Running out.*) ARRRRGGGGHH! He ain't got a body. He's just a . . . HEAD!

Curtain.

ACT TWO

Three months later. The walls of the house are moderately speckled with red cockroaches of various sizes. LUPE *is standing behind* PEDRO, *who is asleep on a chair, delousing him. On an old sofa in the corner, a white lace veil covers* BELARMINO—*like a child. The radio is blaring out frantic mariachi music, "La Negra."* LUPE *finds something in* PEDRO's *hair.*

LUPE: (*Gasps.*) Lousy cucaracha!

CRUZ: (*Shouting from the kitchen.*) Negra, shut off the noises, diablo! (*Pause.*) ¡Negra! Belarmino is sleeping!

LUPE: Mamá, stop calling me negra.

CRUZ: Shut off the noises, sonavavichi!

LUPE: (*Shuts off radio.*) Okay, pues, I did, man! (BELARMINO *grunts from under the veil.*) What you want? (BELARMINO *grunts louder.*) No, no more radio. Didn't you hear mi 'amá? Go to sleep! (BELARMINO *grunts again.*) Ay, that stupid cabeza! (*She removes the veil and* BELARMINO *is seen for the first time: he is the head of a man about 30–35 years old. That is all. He has no body. He has long hair and a large moustache. His black eyes are deep and expressive. The head is otherwise only distinguished by its tremendous size. A full eighteen inches in diameter.*)

BELARMINO: (*Singing.*) "¡La Cucaracha!"

LUPE: Shut up! (BELARMINO *laughs idiotically.*) Idiot, because of you I'm like a slave in this house. Joaquín and Mingo and e'rybody goes to town but they never let me go. I gotta be here—ready to stuff you with frijoles. Like a maid, like a negra.

CHATO: (*At the front door.*) Hi, negra.

LUPE: (*Covering* BELARMINO.) What did you call me?

CHATO: N—othing.

BELARMINO: ¡Cállate el hocico!

CHATO: Why!

145

LUPE: Mi papá, he's asleep.

CHATO: Oh! Heh, tha's Belarmino behind there, huh?

LUPE: Where at?

CHATO: Under that velo. (*Points to veil.*)

LUPE: No! My brother's a man, how can he fit in there?

CHATO: You know. (HE *laughs.*)

LUPE: Look, Chato, if you come to make fun of us, you better cut it out, man. Belo's sick, he don'—(BELARMINO *grunts.*) Okay, okay, hombre. In a minute. Here, have a cockroach. (SHE *takes a cockroach off the wall and gives it to him.*)

CHATO: (*Open mouthed.*) How come he eats cockroaches?

LUPE: Because he's hungry, dumbbell.

CHATO: I'm not a dumbbell!

LUPE: Oh, no, *you're* real smart. Only you don't even know how to read or write. You think we didn't go to the second grade together? Menso.

CRUZ: (*In the kitchen.*) ¿Guadalupe?

LUPE: Sí, mamá? (SHE *makes a sign to* CHATO *not to say anything.*)

CRUZ: Who you talking to?

LUPE: Belarmino, Mamá. I'm cleaning his cucarachas.

CRUZ: Okay pues, don' let him eat 'em.

CHATO: (*Looking under the veil.*) En la madre, what a big head.

LUPE: (*Turning, whispering furiously.*) What you doing? Let him alone! Nobody tell you to come in. Get out!

CHATO: How come?

LUPE: Because.

CHATO: Huy, huy qué touchy. Come on, ésa. Don' play hard-to-get.

LUPE: (*Menacing the fly-spray pump.*) Look, stupid, I'll hit you.

CHATO: Okay, don't get mad. I come over to see Mingo. He don' pay me yet.

LUPE: Liar. He said he paid you two days ago.

CHATO: What days ago? I been searching for a week for him. He haven't pay me nothing. I go to the rancho, he ain't there. I come over here—same story. This whole thing is beginning to smell. (BELARMINO *farts loudly.*) ¡Sacos! De potatoes. Heh, wha's wrong with this ruco?

LUPE: None of your business. Pig!

CHATO: Din' he just learn to talk too?

LUPE: No!

CHATO: Joaquín says he sings "La Cucaracha."

LUPE: He's crazy, man.

BELARMINO: (*Singing.*) ¡LA CUCARACHA, LA CUCARACHA!

CHATO: ¿No, qué no? That cat do okay.

LUPE: Oh, how you know? I'm sick and tired of this freak. Feeding him beans, taking out his louses. Listening to that stupid little song. That's all he knows. He don' talk. If he wants to eat, he still shouts or grunts like he's doing it all my life. I almost can't stand it no more!

CHATO: (*Putting his arm around her.*) Okay pues, mi honey. Don't cry. Some of these days I'm going to take you away from all this.

LUPE: What? All this?

CHATO: This poverty, this cucarachas, this . . . this . . .

LUPE: This what?

CHATO: You know . . . Belarmino. I don' say nothing, but . . . well, there's the Raza, no? El chisme. People talk.

LUPE: (*Sobering.*) What they say?

CHATO: Well, you know . . . dicen que tu carnal es una cabeza.

LUPE: Una what?

CHATO: Cabeza.

LUPE: Sorry, guy. I don' speak Spanish.

CHATO: Una HEAD! (PEDRO *wakes, goes back to sleep with a grunt.*) Tha's what they say. No arms, no legs, no nothing. Just a head. (*Laughs.*)

LUPE: You black negro! You dirty Mexican! (*She attacks* CHATO.)

CHATO: Órale, hold it there! (HE *grabs her.*)

LUPE: Let me go, Chato.

CHATO: Who's a dirty Mexican!

LUPE: You, and ugly too. And more blacker than an Indian.

CHATO: Uy, yu, yuy, and you like cream, uh. I'm dark because I work in the fields all day in the sun. I get burn! But look here. (*Shows her his armpit.*) See? Almost tan.

LUPE: You're loco.

CHATO: Chure, loco about you, mi vida. Don' make me suffer. I don' care if Belarmino's a cabeza.

LUPE: Chato, mi papá'll wake up.

CHATO: So what? Te digo que te quiero, que te amo, que te adoro.

LUPE: My mother's in the kitchen.

CHATO: Tú eres mi sol, mi luna, mi cielo . . .

LUPE: Chatito, por favor.

CHATO: Mis tamales, mis tortillas, mis frijoles . . .

CRUZ: (*Entering from the kitchen.*) GUADALUPE!

LUPE: (*Matter-of-factly.*) Mi mamá.

CHATO: (*Turns.*) Buenas tardes. (HE *runs out.*)

CRUZ: Sí, buenas tardes, you shameless goddammit! (*Turns.*) ¡Pedro!

PEDRO: (*In his sleep.*) ¿Sí, mi general?

CRUZ: Pedro, hombre, wake up.

PEDRO: ¡Viva Villa!

CRUZ: You old loco.

PEDRO: Viva Pancho Vi—(CRUZ *pulls his leg.*) Yah! Uh? ¿Qué pasó?

CRUZ: ¡Chato!

PEDRO: (*Jumps up.*) Chato? (*Pause.*) ¿Chato who?

CRUZ: He was after Lupe, hombre.

PEDRO: (*Heads for kitchen.*) Where's he at?

CRUZ: (*Pulling him back.*) He went that way! Go, hombre! Serve for something!

PEDRO: Where's my rifle! WHERE'S MY GUN?

LUPE: (*Throws herself upon him.*) ¡No, Papá!

PEDRO: You chattap! WHERE'S MY GUN, WOMEN!

CRUZ: (*Pause.*) You don' got a gun, Pedro. (*Silence.*)

LUPE: I din' do—

PEDRO: CHATTAP! Dios mío, how lousy. (HE *grabs his wine bottle beside the chair.*) You see? This is what I get for coming to the land of the gringos. No respect! I should have stay in Zacatecas. (HE *heads for the door.*)

CRUZ: Pedro, where you going?

PEDRO: Where I feel like it, sabes? To look for work.

CRUZ: At sundown?

PEDRO: La night shift, mujer! Maybe I go back to Zacatecas.

CRUZ: Oh sí, hitchi-hiking.

PEDRO: ¡Cállate si no quieres que te plante un guamaso! ¡Vieja desgraciada! (MINGO *enters dressed in new khaki work clothes, complete with new hat and boots.* HE *carries a clipboard with papers and a money box.*)

MINGO: Home sweet home! E'erybody yelling as usual? What was Super-Mex running for?

CRUZ: Who?

MINGO: Chato. He come flying outta here like the immigration was after him.

CRUZ: He was after Lupe.

MINGO: (*To* PEDRO.) Where were you, man?

CRUZ: Your padre was asleep.

MINGO: (*Deliberately.*) Oh.

PEDRO: (*Sensing disrespect.*) Oh, what?

MINGO: Oh, nothing . . . Dad.

PEDRO: Some of this days, cabrón, you going to say "oh, something else." Then we see who's boss around here. (*To* LUPE). I take care of you later, señorita. (HE *exits.*)

CRUZ: Dios mío, that old loco. Now he won' be home until it is so late. Then he gots to cross the tracks in the dark. (*To* LUPE.) You see? You see what you do?

LUPE: I din' do nothing! Chato grabbed me!

MINGO: What you mean he grabbed you? Just took a little grab, huh?

LUPE: No, he was telling me about Belo. The whole neighborhood's talking about him! They say he don' got no arms or legs or nothing. That he's a . . .

CRUZ: What?

LUPE: You know what. (*Uncomfortable pause.*)

CRUZ: No, I don' know. My son is sick! How can they say such things?

MINGO: Forget 'em, Ma. They do it from envy.

LUPE: Envy, of Belo?

MINGO: Of me! Since they always pass the time drunk or begging on welfare, they can't stand a man who betters himself. But they ain't seen nothing yet. Mom, sit down over here. I got something to tell you. You too, negra.

LUPE: Don' call me negra, Mingo.

MINGO: Can't you take a joke?

LUPE: No!

MINGO: Sit down. (SHE *sits.*) Okay, now. Ma, remember that place where we picked prunes for so many years? On Merde Road? (CRUZ *nods.*) Well, it's called Merde Boulevard now. They cut down the orchard and built new houses on the land. They got a big sign up: Prune Blossom Acres. And right under it: No Down Payment To Vets. You know what it means, Ma? I'm a vet and we're gonna get a new house!

LUPE: A new house! Mamá, a new house!

MINGO: (*Laughs.*) I thought that'd grab you. Well, Mom, what do you say? Shall we move outta this dump? (CRUZ *is silent,* SHE *stands.*) Heh, what's wrong?

CRUZ: This ain't a dump, Mingo. It is the house of your padre.

MINGO: Padre, madre, so what? I'm talking about Prune Blossom Acres. America's at out doorsteps. All we have to do is take one step.

CRUZ: What about Belarmino?

MINGO: Somebody can carry him, what else? Put him in a shoebox.

LUPE: He don't fit in a shoebox.

MINGO: Not a real shoebox, stupid. A cardboard box. We can put holes in it so he can breathe. That ain't no problem.

CRUZ: I know, Mingo, but . . . it is not the same. In this barrio they don' care.

MINGO: I care!

CRUZ: And the gringos?

MINGO: Whatta you mean, gringos?

CRUZ: Who else lives in new houses?

MINGO: Americans, Ma. American citizens like me and y . . . (*Pause.*) Aw, whatta you trying to do? Get me defeated too? You wanna spend the rest of your life in this stinking barrio? What about all the gossiping beanbellies? You know they're laughing at this head.

CRUZ: This what?

MINGO: (*Pause.*) Shorty.

LUPE: That's not what I heard.

MINGO: You shut up, sister.

CRUZ: His name ain't Chorti, Mingo.

MINGO: For pete's sake, Ma, I'm trying to help out here! He's my brother, so I call him Shorty. What's wrong with that? He's short. The important thing's the lies people are telling about us, about Shorty, about me. I don't owe them peons nothing.

JOAQUÍN: (*Standing in the doorway.*) Simón, just pay Chato what you owe him. Come on in, ése, don' be chicken.

MINGO: And what do I owe him?

JOAQUÍN: His pay.

CHATO: Buenas tardes. (HE *hides behind* JOAQUÍN.)

CRUZ: You say that before, sinvergüenza! (CHATO *runs out again.*) You dare to come in after he try to steal our respect!

CHATO: (*Reentering.*) Aw, I din't come to steal nothing. I come because you robbing me!

CRUZ: What?

CHATO: Well, maybe not you, but Mingo. Tell you right off the bat, Doña Cruz, this bato's nothing but a crooked contractor!

MINGO: Crooked?

LUPE: ¿Mingo?

CRUZ: My son?

BELARMINO: AAARRRRGH!

CRUZ: (*To* BELARMINO.) Ay no, my son, not you. You ain't crooked.

MINGO: What the hell you trying to say, Chato?

JOAQUÍN: What you think, you din't hear him? He says the big war hero's a thief just like e'rybody else! So you was going to get rich working in the fields, uh? Free country and all that chet! Simón, I believe it now. Anybody can get rich if he's a crooked farm labor contractor. Only this time it's no dice, ése. Chato's my friend. Pay him.

MINGO: I already paid him! If you don't believe me, look here in my paybook. Here's everybody that received their wages. See . . . what's signed here? (HE *shows* CHATO.)

CHATO: I don' know, ees in Spanish.

MINGO: Spanish? It's your name, stupid. Chato Reyes. You sign it yourself.

JOAQUÍN: Nel, carnal, we got you there. Chato don' know how to read or write.

MINGO: (*Pause.*) Of course he don't know—that's how come his "X" is here instead of his name. See? (HE *shows the "X".*) Okay, Chato, if you want to prove that this ain' your "X" or that I haven't paid you, you got to take me to court, right? But just to show you I ain't crooked, I'm gonna pay you again. Sit down. (CHATO *and* MINGO *sit down.*) All right, how many days do you work?

CHATO: Four.

MINGO: Four days, at ten hours each, is 40 hours. 40 hours at 85 cents an hour is . . . $34, right?

CHATO: Sí, muchas gracias.

MINGO: One moment, social security.

CHATO: But I don't got a card.

MINGO: You an American citizen?

CHATO: Simón.

MINGO: Good. You can still pay. That's $15, plus a dollar fine for not having a card. That leaves $18, right?

CHATO: Simón, gracias.

MINGO: Hold it, income tax. 50% of 18 is 9. That leaves you $9, correct?

CHATO: Órale, gra . . .

MINGO: The lunches. Five tacos at 40 cents each, one chili pepper at 15 cents and a large-size cola at 35 cents . . . that's $2.50 a day. $2.50 for four days are . . .

CHATO: Heh, cut it out!

MINGO: What's wrong, a mistake?

CHATO: Simón, that ain't right! I don't pay for mordidas.

MINGO: (Standing up.) ¡Mordidas! What you referring to?

CHATO: Pos what? The tacos. They have bites.

CRUZ: Bites?

CHATO: Mordidotas.

LUPE: Oh-Oh, I know who done 'em.

CRUZ: You shut up, woman. (To MINGO smiling.) I don't know who could have do it, my son. I put 'em in new every day.

MINGO: Well, (HE sits.) one cent discount for each taco for the bites are . . . 39 cents five times. $1.95, plus the chili pepper, the Coke., etc . . . $2.45 a day. For four days that's $9.80. You had 9 dollars; you owe me 80 cents.

CHATO: OWE?

MINGO: There's the proof. Pay me. (CHATO looks at the paper.)

JOAQUÍN: Lemme see that, ése. (HE takes the paper.)

MINGO: (Taking the paper from JOAQUÍN.) How about it, Chato? You pay me or what you gonna do?

BELARMINO: AARRRRRRRRGGGGGHHHHHHH!

CRUZ: ¡Ay, mi'jo! (SHE goes to quiet BELARMINO.)

CHATO: I see you! (HE runs toward the door.) And ees true what I say! You stupid, chet contractor! T'ief!

MINGO: Thief! You come here and say that, you little . . .

CHATO: ¡Ay! (HE runs out.)

BELARMINIO: AARRRRRGGGGGHHH!

CRUZ: Mingo, please, don' make so much fuss.

MINGO: Fuss? What you talking, señora? Din' you hear what . . .

CHATO: (*Peeking in again.*) I forget to say somet'ing. Stay wis you stinking head! (HE *ducks out quickly.*)

CRUZ: Stinking head? ¡Pos mira que jijo de . . .! (*At the door shouting.*) ¡Arrastrado! ¡Analfabeto! ¡MUERTO DE HAMBRE!

MINGO: Mom!

CRUZ: YOU GODAMMIT!

MINGO: Okay, Ma, that's enough! (HE *pulls her back.*)

CRUZ: He call your brother a stinking head. (BELARMINO *farts sonorously.* JOAQUÍN *leaves.*)

LUPE: ¡Ay! It's true! (*Everybody moves away from* BELARMINO *except* CRUZ.) It's true. He's disgusting.

CRUZ: And what you think you are, estúpida? Don' think I forget what you do with Chato, eh? Go make tortillas.

LUPE: For what? Belarmino eat 'em all?

CRUZ: No matter, go do it.

LUPE: He eats all the lunches.

MINGO: Lunches?

CRUZ: Don' talk back, I tell you. Go make tortillas!

LUPE: Oh no! I'm not a tortilla factory.

CRUZ: Pos, mira que . . . (CRUZ *starts to hit* LUPE.)

MINGO: Wait a minute, WAIT A MINUTE, MA! What's this about the lunches?

LUPE: It's Belarmino, Mingo. We make 200 tacos for the lunches tomorrow and he already eat 150! He never gets full. That's why Chato's tacos have bites, because mi 'amá give 'em to Belo.

MINGO: You give 'em to him, Ma? The tacos we sell to the men?

CRUZ: He was a little hungry, my son.

MINGO: A little hungry! What about all the beans he's already eating? You seen the bills at the store lately? He's eating more and more every week.

LUPE: And that's not all. He's also crawling wis more and more lices! And he eats cucarachas, and he stinks! I can't stand him no more. He's just a stupid . . . HEAD!

CRUZ: (*Pause.* SHE *slaps* LUPE.) Your brother is not a head.

MINGO: I oughta knock your stupid lips off.

LUPE: (*Anger, disgust.*) Go to hell. I'll never use 'em! Give 'em to Belo so he can eat *more!* I rather get married so I can suffer in my own house, even if it's with the ugliest, most stupidest man in the world.

It can't be worser than this. One of these days Belarmino's gonna grunt or yell for his frijoles, and I won't be here to stuff his throat. You going to see! (SHE *goes out crying.*)

JOAQUÍN: (*Reenters.*) Ma? This a piojo?

MINGO: ¿Piojo? A louse!

JOAQUÍN: One lice.

CRUZ: This ain't a piojo, my son. Ees one little . . . cucaracha, ¿qué no?

BELARMINO: ARRRRGGGHHH!

CRUZ: Ay! (SHE *removes* BELARMINO's *veil.*) ¡Dios mío!

MINGO: What the hell's on his face?

JOAQUÍN: Cucarachas! (BELARMINO's *face is covered with cock-roaches of various sizes.*)

BELARMINO: (*Smiling, singing.*)

¡LA CUCARACHA, LA CUCARACHA!

YA NO PUEDE CAMINAR PORQUE LE FALTA,

PORQUE NO TIENE

¡MARIHUANA QUE FUMAR!

ACT THREE

SCENE ONE

Later that same night. BELARMINO *is on top of an old table, asleep.* JOAQUÍN *staggers in drunk, singing, smoking a hand-rolled cigarette.*

JOAQUÍN: (*Singing.*)
I'm gonna sing this corrido
and I'm feeling very sad
cause the great Francisco Villa
some bato cut off his head.

La cucaracha, la cucaracha
she don' wanna go no more
you give her pesos and marijuana
Cuca open up her door! (*Sees* BELARMINO, *moves toward him.*)

When they murder Pancho Villa
his body they lay to rest
but his head somebody take it
all the way to the U.S.

La cockaroacha, la cockaroacha
she don' wanna caminar
porque le falta, porque no tiene
she's a dirty little whore!
(*Pause.*) Heh, Belo? You awake, ése? Come on, man. Get your butt
up! Oh yeah . . . you don't got one, huh? (*Laughs.*) So what? Get
up! (*Pulls his hair.*)
BELARMINO: (*Roars.*) ¡LA CUCARACHAAA!
JOAQUÍN: Tha's all you know, huh stupid! (*Mocks him.*) "¡Cucaracha!"
(*Pause.*) Oh, a real one, eh? They even coming outa your nose, ése.

155

Look at her . . . she's a dirty little whore. A putita. (*Holds out the small cockroach with his fingers in front of* BELARMINO's *eyes.*) ¡Puuuteee-ta! (*Laughs, throws it down, squashes it.*) Well, what you looking so stupid about? It was only a stinking cockaroach. Dumb Mexican . . . not you, ése, this stupid cucaracha I squash. They love to be step on. (*Laughs.*) You know what happen tonight, man? I been all over the barrio running away from batos. Simón, all my friends and camaradas. Like a big chingón I get 'em at work with Mingo, and he chisel 'em. Now I'm the patsy and they wanna knife me. Even Chato. He's telling e'ybody you're a head, ése. (*Laughs.*) With no guts.

BELARMINO: (*As if disembowled.*) ARRRGGGGHHHH!

JOAQUÍN: (*Whispering.*) Heh, MAN, CUT IT OUT! Shhh, the jefita's gonna hear. Okay, you ask for it! (HE *covers* BELARMINO *with his coat.*) Shhh. (BELARMINO *yells, muffled.* JOAQUÍN *laughs.*) Come on, ése, be a sport. You wan' me to throw you out the window? (BELARMINO *stops shouting.* JOAQUÍN *gives him a tug.*) Heh? (*No response.* JOAQUÍN *peeks under the coat.*) You awright?

BELARMINO: Simón.

JOAQUÍN: (*Covers him quickly.*) Dumb head. (*Pause.*) Heh, he say something. He's learning to talk! (*Uncovers him again.*)

BELARMINO: ¡Cabrón!

JOAQUÍN: Spanish.

BELARMINO: (*Grunts.*) Uh, ¡toque! ¡Toque, cigarro!

JOAQUÍN: What, you want a toke? (HE *holds out the cigarette.* BELARMINO *puffs on it eagerly.*) No, man don't just puff on it. You gotta inhale it. See, like this. (JOAQUÍN *inhales.*) Take in a little air wis it.

BELARMINO: (*Grunts.*) Uh-uh, ¡toque! (JOAQUÍN *holds out the cigarette again.* BELARMINO *puffs noisily, then sniffs vociferously.*)

JOAQUÍN: How do you like it, bueno?

BELARMINO: (*Holding his breath.*) Bueno.

JOAQUÍN: (*Laughs.*) Chet, man, you just as bad as me. A lousy head!

BELARMINO: ARRRGGGGHHH! (JOAQUÍN *covers him with his coat.*)

CRUZ: (*Runs in the front door.*) ¡Joaquín!

JOAQUÍN: Hi, Jefita.

CRUZ: What you doing? Where's Chorty?

JOAQUÍN: (BELARMINO *grunts under the coat.*) He went out to take
   a piss.

CRUZ: Wha's that?

JOAQUÍN: What? Oh, that—my coat. (BELARMINO *grunts.*)

CRUZ: Válgame Dios, do you got Belarmino in there, Joaquín?

JOAQUÍN: Nel, there's nobody under here. (*Lifts coat.*) See? No body!
   (HE *laughs.*)

CRUZ: ¡Belarmino! (SHE *goes to him.* BELARMINO *grunts, moans,
   breathes hard.*) He shrink . . .

JOAQUÍN: (*Moving away from* BELARMINO.) Don' let him fool you,
   jefita. Maybe you think the bato grunts and tha's it, but he talks.
   (CRUZ *looks at him.*) No chet, I mean no lie. He do it. And it's not
   only "La Cucaracha." He swing in pure words, huh, ése? Simón, he
   just barely talk to me. Go on, ask him something.

CRUZ: (*Emotionally.*) Mi'jito . . . my Chorti, ees true? You can talk at
   last? Ees me, your madre. Speak to me! (BELARMINO *grunts.*) Ay,
   Dios, he can talk inglés.

JOAQUÍN: That was a grunt. Come on, Belo. Talk right. (BELARMI-
   NO *laughs idiotically.*) Nel, ése, don' act stupid. This is the jefita.
   She want to hear you talk. (BELARMINO *grunts and makes idiot-
   ic noises.*) Come on, man!

BELARMINO: ARRRGGGGH!

CRUZ: Tha's enough, Joaquín. You scare him. I don' know how you can
   make fun of your poor brother.

JOAQUÍN: But he can talk, señora. He's faking.

CRUZ: Tha's enough! Din' I tell you not to bother him? I have enough
   to worry with your sister. She run out like crazy this afternoon, and
   haven' come back. Maybe she want to elope with Chato?

JOAQUÍN: Pos, so what? Chato's a good bato.

CRUZ: A good bato. An ignorant who let the contractors rob him!

JOAQUÍN: Simón, and who's the contractor? Mingo!

CRUZ: Shut up, liar! Thief!

JOAQUÍN: T'ief?

CRUZ: Since you was born you have give me nothing but trouble.
   Going out in the streets at night, coming late, landing in jail. I don'
   got no more hope in you. Or in Lupe. The only one who haven'
   come out bad is my poor Chorti who's only hungry all the time.
   Why don' you rob something for your brother to eat, eh? Serve for

something. (*Weeps.*) Válgame Dios, nobody care about my poor sick Belarmino. Only his madre. (SHE *starts to go out.*)

BELARMINO: Mamá.

CRUZ: (*Without turning.*) No, don' call me, Joaquín.

JOAQUÍN: But I din' . . .

CRUZ: No, I tell you, comprende, sanavavichi! I got to be out in the street. Maybe with the help of the Virgen, your sister come back. (*Exits.*)

BELARMINO: Pobre viejita.

JOAQUÍN: Pobre nothing! If you care so much, how come you keep your mouth shut when it count?

BELARMINO: (*Brusquely, furiously.*) ¡No seas torpe! Si todo el mundo se da cuenta que puedo hablar, van a saber quién soy. O mejor dicho, quién fui. Me vienen a mochar la lengua o ¡toda la maceta de una vez! ¿Qué no sabes que estamos en territorio enemigo?

JOAQUÍN: Órale pues, cool it, ése! You don't gotta make a speech. (*Pause.*) Man, what a trip! You know what? I think I been smoking too much. You din' really say all that, right? Simón, it's all in my head.

BELARMINO: Pos, quién sabe lo que dices, vale.

JOAQUÍN: What?

BELARMINO: Que no hable inglés. El totache. Háblame in espanish.

JOAQUÍN: Sorry, man, I don' speak it. No hablo español.

BELARMINO: Méndigos pochos. (*Pause.*) Mira, chavo . . . ah, you . . . mexicano, ¿no?

JOAQUÍN: Who, me? Nel, man, I'm Chicano.

BELARMINO: No seas pendejo.

JOAQUÍN: Who, you calling a pendejo?!

BELARMINO: You, tú, tú Mexican! ¡Pendejo! Mira, espérate . . . ahhh, you Mexican, me Mexican . . . ahhh, this one familia Mexican, eh? ¡Mingo, no! Mingo es gringo. ¿Comprendes?

JOAQUÍN: Heh, yeah, now you talking my language!

BELARMINO: Mingo ees gabacho, ¿eh?

JOAQUÍN: Simón, and a t'ief.

BELARMINO: Okay maguey. Now . . . you don' puedes atinar quién soy?

JOAQUÍN: Wait a minute man . . . Slower, I can't do what?

BELARMINO: Atinar.

JOAQUÍN: Atinar . . . that's *guess.* I can't guess what?

BELARMINO: Quién soy.

JOAQUÍN: Who you are. (*Pause.*) Who?

BELARMINO: Pos guess. You have hear . . . el Pueblo de Parral?

JOAQUÍN: Parral?

BELARMINO: ¡Chihuahua!

JOAQUÍN: Oh, simón. Tha's the town where they kill Pancho Villa and they cut off his . . . (*Pause.*) HEAD.

BELARMINO: Exactamente.

JOAQUÍN: Did you ever have a horse?

BELARMINO: Siete Leguas.

JOAQUÍN: And a Chivi?

BELARMINO: One Dodge.

JOAQUÍN: 1923?

BELARMINO: Simón—yes.

JOAQUÍN: (*Pause.*) I don' believe it. You? The head of Pancho . . .

BELARMINO: Belarmino, please! (*Secretively.*) Muchos carefuls. I only trust you. Ees one secret político ¿comprendes?

JOAQUÍN: (*Shocked.*) Simón, I don't tell nobody. (*Pause.*) Only the jefita. MAAA! (HE *runs out the front door.*)

BELARMINO: OYE! (*Alone.*) ¡Chi . . . huahua! ¡Qué feo no tener cuerpo, verdad de Dios! (PEDRO *is heard in the kitchen, yelling and singing drunkenly.* BELARMINO *feigns sleep.* PEDRO *enters with a wine bottle, and cartridge belts criss-crossed on his chest.*)

PEDRO: (*Sings.*)

¡Adiós torres de Chihuahua,

adiós torres de Canteraaa!

Ya vino Francisco Villaaa,

pa' quitarles la frontera.

ya llegó Francisco Villa

a devolver la fronteraaa!

(*Shouts.*) Ay, yai, yai, YAI! I'm home, cabrones. Your padre is home, come out! Come out from your holes! I am home!! (*Pause.*) Where's e'rybody at? (HE *goes to* BELARMINO.) Oye, Wake up, loco! (HE *pulls* BELARMINO's *hair.*)

BELARMINO: (*Opening his eyes.*) ARRRRGGH! ¡LA CUCA-RACHAA!

PEDRO: (*Furiously, in case of insult.*) What?

BELARMINO: Cucaracha.

PEDRO: (*Pause.*) You know "Siete Leguas"? (*Sings.*) "Siete Leguas el caballo que Villa más . . ."

BELARMINO: AY, YAI, YAI!

PEDRO: Heh, you do that pretty good, cabrón. (CRUZ *runs in the front door.* JOAQUÍN *follows her.*)

CRUZ: Pedro, what are you doing?

PEDRO: I am talking to my son.

CRUZ: Talking? (SHE *glances at* JOAQUÍN.)

JOAQUÍN: Din' I tell you? He can talk, huh Pa? (BELARMINO *grunts and spits at* JOAQUÍN.) Órale, carnal, take it easy. You can trust the jefitos . . . (BELARMINO *spits, hits* JOAQUÍN's *shirt.*) ¡Un pollo! (HE *exits upstairs.*)

CRUZ: It ees true, Pedro, my son talks?

PEDRO: Who? This animal? No, wha's wrong wis you, not even with a gallon of vino. (BELARMINO *laughs idiotically.*) You see? How can this idiota talk? He don' know nothing.

CRUZ: He is still your son, Pedro.

PEDRO: Pos, who knows, ¿verdad? A man almost forty years old which he don' even know his own padre? That is no son. You got this one for you, woman.

CRUZ: Tha's not true, Pedro. He look like you.

PEDRO: Oh yes, the face!

CRUZ: And the hair, the eyes, the mustaches.

PEDRO: CHICKENSQUAT! Those are things a madre notice. A padre he wants a son with a strong back. And arms and legs to help him work! You cheat me, woman. Caray, I will never forget the day Belarmino was born. 1928 and my first son! They run to the field to get me, and when I arrive . . . there you was with the niño in your arms . . . his big eyes looking out, his mouth open . . . with ears, a nose, and mucho hair, everything his madre want. Then I open the blanket: NOTHING. Nothing for his padre! Dios mío, what a lousy son!

CRUZ: (*Hurt.*) Yes, lousy, but it hurt me to have him.

PEDRO: Pos, I give him to you then. For your pains. I give 'em all to you. Joaquín, Mingo, Lupe, and the head, for good measure. (JOAQUÍN *enters with guitar.*) Anyway, I'm going across the border. My carrilleras and my 30–30 is all I take. Wis that I come, wis that I go.

JOAQUÍN: And your guitar, jefito?

PEDRO: You keep it, hijo. Of all my sons, I like you the most, because you're the only one who understand the Revolución. Maybe this guitarrita serve to remind you of your padre . . . when he's dead.

CRUZ: You're crazy, viejo.

PEDRO: Well, you will see. I going back to Zacatecas, to my tierra, to die.

CRUZ: (*Relieved.*) Okay, pues, go die! I don' care. Right now I'm worry about my Lupe. (SHE *wraps her shawl around her neck.*)

PEDRO: Where you going, to the street again like a crazy loca?

CRUZ: I'm going over to Señora Reyes house. Maybe Chato come back. I don' even know what to think, Dios mío. (*Exits.*)

PEDRO: Stinking vieja.

JOAQUÍN: Heh, Pa, can I go to México with you?

PEDRO: For what? You din' come from over theres, you was born heres.

JOAQUÍN: So what, maybe I gotta get outta town? I mean the U.S.

PEDRO: Can you ride a horse?

JOAQUÍN: No, pero . . .

PEDRO: Or eat chili peppers?

JOAQUÍN: No, but . . .

PEDRO: Ah! And tortillas, my son. How to know a good woman by her tortillas. You got to know. One don' buy burro just because she gots long eyelashes.

JOAQUÍN: Okay pues, but you know what? I find the head of Pancho Villa.

PEDRO: (*Pause.*) When?

JOAQUÍN: Today . . . tonight!

PEDRO: You crazy. How you going to find the head of the general? Pos mira . . . go say it up in the sierra, ¡qué! Where they believe you.

JOAQUÍN: You wanna see it?

PEDRO: (*Pause.*) ¿El general?

JOAQUÍN: Pancho Villa himself.

PEDRO: You sure ees him? How you know? He don' be in bad shape?

JOAQUÍN: He's like new.

PEDRO: (*Lowers his head emotionally.*) I don' believe it . . . after so many years? Just imagine, to rescue the general's head from the hands of the gringos, then to take it back to México con honor! In a big train like the old days! Qué caray, maybe even the Revolución break out again! Maybe they give us a rancho—in Zacatecas. ¡Ay, yai, yai! Think we better be careful, my son. (*Pause.*) Oye, you hide it good? If we lose that head again . . . !

JOAQUÍN: Nel, he's here in the house.

PEDRO: Who know about it?

JOAQUÍN: Nobody, just me and you, and the general.

PEDRO: General? He's dead.

JOAQUÍN: He ain' dead.

PEDRO: What you mean, hombre? They kill him.

JOAQUÍN: Not all of him.

PEDRO: Yes, all of him!

JOAQUÍN: Nel, he lives. Pancho Villa lives!

PEDRO: (*Pause.*) You chure?

JOAQUÍN: Simón, and there he is! (*Points to* BELARMINO.)

PEDRO: (*Scandalized.*) ¡Belarmino! ¡Pos, qué jijos . . .! What you thinking, baboso? Laughing at your padre?

JOAQUÍN: No, jefito! He prove it to you himself. Just give him a chance! (*Goes to* BELARMINO.) Heh, general. ¿General Villa?

PEDRO: (*Pulls his hair.*) Wake up, bruto.

BELARMINO: AARRRAAGGHH!

JOAQUÍN: Uh, general, here's one of your Villistas . . . my jefito. You know him already, tell him something, okay? Just a word or two.

BELARMINO: (*Smiles.*) UHHH.

JOAQUÍN: He's warming up.

PEDRO: For what, more frijoles? No, Joaquín, this go beyond a joke. I never going to forgive you this.

JOAQUÍN: But he's Pancho Villa, 'Apá. He tell me.

PEDRO: What I care what this animal tell you? How he's going to be the great Centauro del Norte? Pancho Villa was a giant, a legend, a big hombre!

JOAQUÍN: Simón, and this is a big hombre's head.

PEDRO: CHICKENSQUAT! Not in one thousand years can you compare this chompetita to the head of my general! Men like Pancho Villa ain't born no more, just lousies like this one. And cowards! T'iefs! Useless cabrones! Tha's all I got for sons.

MINGO: (*Standing in the front.*) And we're only chips off the old block, no Pa? (PEDRO *turns toward* MINGO *who* is *dressed in casual bowling clothes. HE also carries a bowling bag.*)

PEDRO: Pos, you tell me. What block you talking about?

MINGO: Skip it. What was the yelling about?

PEDRO: This pachuco . . . lying to his padre.

JOAQUÍN: I din' lie, jefito.

PEDRO: Chatap! Pos, this one . . . still at it, hombre? (*To* MINGO.) What you think he was saying, my son? That Belarmino is my General Villa! Mira . . . lousy goddamit. (*To* JOAQUÍN.) Why don' you be smart like your brother here. He don' go around wis stupid babosadas. He is a serious hombre con respeto y dinero.

JOAQUÍN: Órale, cool it pues.

PEDRO: Culo . . . ¿¡a quién le dices culo!? I still haven' die, cabrón. I still the boss in this house.

JOAQUÍN: Okay, okay. Keep your house. (*Gets the guitar and heads for the door.*)

PEDRO: Oye, oye, and my guitarra?

JOAQUÍN: You give me it. Want it back?

PEDRO: No, for what I want that junk?

JOAQUÍN: Here. (*Gives him the guitar.*) I get a new one. Órale, carnal, hand over 75 bolas.

MINGO: Bolas?

JOAQUÍN: Bones, maracas, bills, ése.

MINGO: Seventy-five dollars? What the hell for?

JOAQUÍN: My cut, ése! I get the workers, you screw 'em, we split the take.

MINGO: You're crazy.

JOAQUÍN: Simón, real loco. But I ain't stupid. All the batos in the barrio go to work for you because I ask 'em.

MINGO: So what? I paid you 50 cents a head for that truckload you round up and that was it.

JOAQUÍN: Nel, ése, you din' tell me you was going to burn 'em. Like Chato! Social security, income tax . . . that's a lotta chet, mano. You got itchy fingers too, qué! You pocket them coins yourself.

MINGO: (*Calm.*) Can you prove it?

JOAQUÍN: I see you do it!

MINGO: Then call the cops. Go on! Who you think the law's gonna believe, me or you?

JOAQUÍN: (*Pause.*) Eh, jefe, you loan me your guitar?

PEDRO: Now you wan' it back, eh? Bueno, take it. (JOAQUÍN *grabs the guitar and lifts it to smash it on* MINGO'*s head.*) FOR YOU TO PLAY IT!! (JOAQUÍN *stops.*)

JOAQUÍN: Don' you see he's cheating us?

PEDRO: I don' see nothing!

JOAQUÍN: The general see it!

PEDRO: ¡No qué general ni nada! (JOAQUÍN *leaves with the guitar.*) Useless! Huh, as if all people don' be crooked. No hombre, we all looking to see what we scratch up. (*Drinks from his bottle. It is empty.*) Chihuahua, it is finish. Bueno, no matter? Tha's how come we got money—for necessaries. Of all my sons I like you the most—porque tienes inteligencia, hijo, te juro por los cielos. Ándale, my son, let loose one pesito to go for more. But this time we get a big one, eh?

MINGO: No, señor.

PEDRO: Bueno, a small one, pues.

MINGO: No! Don' you understand? There's no money for booze.

PEDRO: Mira, mira, don't play the crooked contractor wis me, eh? I ain' Joaquín. All I ask is for 35 centavitos.

MINGO: I don't give a damn. That money ain't gonna support your habit. I want this family to be decent and that's how it's gonna be.

PEDRO: Oh sí ¿eh? Well, who are you to decide everything? I'm your padre.

MINGO: You're nothing. If it wasn' for me, we'd still be in the gutter, like usual. Confess it. You could never handle Shorty's hunger. You had to drag us all to the fields together with mi 'amá. And for what? We still ended up owing the store just to feed the head! That head's a pushover for me. From now on, I'm in charge here and you can do what you damn well please.

PEDRO: (*Pause.*) Pos, I think I damn well please to give you some chingazos well-planted, ¿sabes?

MINGO: If you can. Don' forget I was a Marine.

PEDRO: And I was a Villista!

MINGO: You want me to give you a judo chop?

PEDRO: (HE *runs to the door.*) ¡Joaquín! ¡Joaquín! Bring me my guitarra!

MINGO: The guitar? You going to play or fight?

PEDRO: I going to smash it on your head, pendejo!

MINGO: What's the matter, old man? Not so good with your fists anymore? Been picking fruit too long? Come on, gimme a try! This hand only broke a Chink's red neck once. WHACK! Come on, wetback, get a taste of an American fighting man overseas! Come, farm laborer! Greaser! Spic! Nigger! (*Pause.*) ¡GRINGO!

PEDRO: (*The dam breaks.*) ¡VIVA VILLAAAAA! (PEDRO *leaps on* MINGO *and they wrestle.* MINGO *quickly subdues him, giving him a couple of efficient judo chops. He pins him down and sits on him.*)

MINGO: All right, green-carder, you give up?

PEDRO: Cabrón.

MINGO: What?

PEDRO: ¡Cabrón!

MINGO: That's what I thought you said.

PEDRO: ¡Joaquín!

MINGO: Hee ain't coming back, man. You think he wants that guitar smashed? Besides, you ran him out. You better give up. What you say? No hard feelings? Look, I'll even get up. (HE *rises.*) Come on, Pete, be a sport. Don't be a bad loser. (*Nudges him with his foot.*) Come on, I don't like to see you sprawled out like that.

PEDRO: Get away, cabrón! Get away!

MINGO: Okay, stay down. I don't give a damn. (*Exists.*)

PEDRO: Now I don't got any sons . . . except Belarmino. He was the first. I like him the most. Besides, he always remind me of Pancho Villa. (HE *gets up and removes his cartridge belts.*) Eh, my son? You see this carrilleras? They're from the Revolución. They don' got any bullets, but I give 'em to you, eh? (HE *places the belts around* BELARMINO.) Now you look like the general. You remember Pancho Villa? There was a man, a giant . . . he rob the rich to give to the poor. You should have see him when we take Zacatecas. (HE *begins to walk around the room imagining the scene he describes.*) All the trains, the smoke, the people climbing all over like lices. (*Laughs.*) Caray, there was nothing like the trains. (*Train whistle in the distance.*) They would gather at the crossings. (*Under his voice: "Marcha de Zacatecas."*) Here comes Pancho Villa, they would say. ¡Ahí viene Pancho Villa! And mi general he would come to the back of the car. ¡VIVA VILLA! ¡VIVA VILLA! Here come Pancho Villa! (*One final war cry.*) ¡A ZACATE-CAAASS! (*The music is like the sound of a train pulling in.* PEDRO *runs out in the direction of the train whistle. The sounds end abruptly and all that remains is the ringing of a small bell at the distant railroad crossing. This fades into the sound of a church bell. Light and sound fade. BELARMINO is left illuminated by a single ray of light. He screams, a sorrowful cry of death. Darkness.)*

Curtain.

SCENE TWO

The front room. Morning. Church bells. A guitar plays "Siete Leguas." A procession in black enters. CRUZ in mourning, MINGO holding her. Then LUPE and CHATO, carrying BELARMINO wrapped in a sarape.

LUPE: I'll put Belarmino away, Mamá. (*Goes into bedroom.*)

CRUZ: (*Sitting on the couch.*) The Señor knows what we shall do now, my sons.

MINGO: Pa was a good guy.

JOAQUÍN: You liar!

MINGO: You insulting his memory already? (*Pause.*) I'll let that one go this time.

LUPE: (*Reentering.*) He's asleep.

CRUZ: He was tired, poor man.

MINGO: I don' think we shoulda take him.

CRUZ: It was his padre, my son.

MINGO: He sang "La Cucaracha," din't he? Pa was my Pa too, Ma. I wanted him to have a good quiet funeral. What was the name of that other "bit" you did?

JOAQUÍN: "Siete Leguas."

MINGO: What?

JOAQUÍN: Seven . . . leaguews. (HE *chokes up with grief.*)

CHATO: That's okay, ése, e'rybody like what you did.

LUPE: It was so sad to see them let mi 'apá down into his grave and all the time Belarmino singing "La Cucaracha." E'rybody think you like it like that, Mamá.

CRUZ: We should have had a wake.

MINGO: You still on that, Ma? The funeral parlor did the job.

CRUZ: They din' let me see him.

MINGO: There was nothing left to see. I mean, what you expect them

to do? That train hit him. I'm not even sure it was him when I identi
fied him. Maybe it wasn't. Maybe he went back to México like he
always wanted? That's possible.

JOAQUÍN: Why don't you shut up!

CRUZ: We should have had a wake! (SHE *breaks down crying.*)

LUPE: Chato, help me. (LUPE *and* CHATO *take* CRUZ *upstairs, crying.*)

MINGO: Everything's gonna be okay, Ma. You'll see. I ordered him a
stone with his name in Spanish, and a saying: "Here lies our Dad,
By Angels Guarded . . ." (CRUZ *has gone upstairs.*)

JOAQUÍN: Tried to feel sad but only farted. (*Laughs until he cries.*)

MINGO: (*Going over to him, whispering.*) What the hecks the matter
with you, Tomahawk? Pa's dead. Don't you appreciate that?
(*Pause.*) Heh, are you crying?

JOAQUÍN: Lemme alone, ése.

MINGO: Listen, Joaquín, things ain't been the best between us, but
maybe we ought to sit down and talk, huh? Man to man? I'm your
legal guardian now.

JOAQUÍN: What you mean?

MINGO: I'm responsible for you. For the whole family. I wanna help
you, Tomahawk.

JOAQUÍN: Help me what?

MINGO: Help you. You wanna join the Marines? I'll sign for you. Sure,
the service'll make a man outta you. Look what it did for me. How
about it?

JOAQUÍN: Nel, I awready tried. They don' like my record.

MINGO: That bad, huh? Well, how about night school? (JOAQUÍN
makes a face.) Okay then, come and work with me.

JOAQUÍN: I awready worked with you.

MINGO: You still think I cheated your friends?

JOAQUÍN: I know it!

MINGO: Boy, that's rich. You know what's wrong with you? You can't
imagine anybody making an honest buck. This is a free country,
man. There's no law against making money.

JOAQUÍN: How about being a Chicano?

MINGO: Is *that* what's eating you?

JOAQUÍN: How come we're poor? How come mi jefito die like that?

MINGO: Not because he was a Mexican!

JOAQUÍN: You ever have the placa work you over in jail, ése? Rubber hoses on the ribs? Calling you greaser! Mexican bastard!

MINGO: I've never been in jail remember?

JOAQUÍN: You're still a greaser.

MINGO: Why, you little punk, don't aim your inferiority complex at me. You're so twisted with hate you can't see straight.

JOAQUÍN: Simón, I'm cross-eyed. But you wanna be a gabacho so bad, you can't see nothing. You hated mi 'apá. You hate all of us! You and your new clothes and bowling ball and shit. Well, take a good look, ése. We're greasy and lousy, but we're your family!

MINGO: Damn right, my family! But you don't have to be greasy and lousy!

JOAQUÍN: You don't have to be a gabacho!

MINGO: Listen, man, there's only one thing I ever wanted in this life. That's not to be poor. I never got that until I become a Marine. Now I want it for the family. Is that so bad? You wanna go on this way, with that stupid head eating and stinking and farting?

JOAQUÍN: He's the general!

MINGO: Come off it, buddy. Shorty ain't Pancho Villa. He's nothing but a mouth. I know, I have to feed it.

JOAQUÍN: If you ever feed him nothing again, I'll kill you.

MINGO: Okay. But how are you going to feed it? On welfare, like the old man used to do it?

JOAQUÍN: You don' even respect mi 'apá now! When he's dead!

MINGO: That's a damn lie! I loved that old wino.

JOAQUÍN: Pinchi buey.

MINGO: What did you call me!!!

JOAQUÍN: ¡Pinchi puto desgraciado!

MINGO: You talk to me in English!

JOAQUÍN: (*Swings guitar at him.*) FUCK YOU! (*Runs out.*)

MINGO: (*Running to the door.*) You goddamned delinquent! I'd turn you in if Pa wasn' dead today.

Curtain.

ACT FOUR

*Six months later. It is winter. The walls of the house are covered
with red cockroaches of various sizes.* LUPE *is studying the walls. Carrying a flyswatter. She is pregnant, but is nevertheless knocking down
cockroaches energetically and capturing them in her apron.*
BELARMINO *is on top of an old, broken-down TV set. His eyes are
wide open, following every move that* LUPE *makes. The door to the
side bedroom is new and has "Private" painted on it in big black letters.*

LUPE: Cucarachas . . . big fat cucarachas. There's one! (SHE *knocks it
down.*) Gee man, this is a big one!

BELARMINO: NARRH!

LUPE: No, you pig! This is mine and I'm gonna eat it by myself.

BELARMINO: NAAARRRRGGGH!

LUPE: ¡Pediche! You ain't hungry. You just don' want me to have it,
huh? Well, now you going to have to eat it! And I hope you choke!
(SHE *crams it into* BELARMINO*'s mouth.*)

CRUZ: (*In the kitchen.*) Guadalupe?

LUPE: ¿Sí, Mamá? (SHE *backs away from* BELARMINO.)

CRUZ: (*Enters.*) Did Belarmino shout? (BELARMINO *spits out the
cockroach.*) ¡Una cucaracha!

LUPE: It's not my fault, man. I can't watch him all the time.

CRUZ: Ay, little woman. Go bring the tortillas.

LUPE: There's no more.

CRUZ: And the dozen there was?

LUPE: I ate 'em. (*Pause.*) Well, what you want? I was hungry! Besides,
there's plenty of food there—bread, steaks, milk, eggs, orange juice.

CRUZ: It all belonged to Mingo.

LUPE: Sure, pure American food. Well, what about us? Are we suppose
to eat cucarachas? (*Angry.*)

CRUZ: No! Now stop this foolishness and go make tortillas, ándale.

169

LUPE: Tortillas . . . I should work in a taco bar. (*Exits, angry.*)

CRUZ: (*Loud voice.*) And don' touch Mingo's food! (BELARMINO *growls.*) Sí, my son, I know. She coming with your frijolitos. You mus' be very hungry, no? You have eat nothing for days. (*Pause.*) Here. Eat one little cucaracha, eh? But don' spit out the shell. I don't want your sister to know. Here.

MINGO: (*In the kitchen.*) Aha, I caught you!

CRUZ: ¡Mingo! (SHE *turns, searching for him. Noises come from the kitchen. A chair falls, a glass breaks. We hear the voices of* MINGO *and* LUPE, *arguing.*)

MINGO: Drinking my orange juice, eh? What you eating?

LUPE: None of your business!

MINGO: What's that?

LUPE: Give 'em back!

MINGO: You crazy?

LUPE: Gimme 'em back!

MINGO: Oh no, sister, we're going to see Ma.

LUPE: No, Mingo, please, ay!

MINGO: Shut up! (MINGO *comes in from the kitchen, pushing* LUPE *in front with her arm twisted behind her back.* MINGO *is dressed in fashionable casual clothing.*) Heh, Ma, you know what this pig was eating?

CRUZ: (*Resigned.*) Cucarachas.

MINGO: How do you know?

CRUZ: What's wrong with you, woman? You want to kill that child you carry? You going to be a madre.

LUPE: I'm not either. I don' got no baby. Only a belly full of cockaroaches! And I'm still hungry. We never have any meat in this house! (*Exits.*)

MINGO: (*Shouting after her.*) Meat? Well, tell your Chatito to get a goddamn job! How d'yuh like that? What's her husband for? Just to keep her pregnant? Tell the bum to go to work.

CRUZ: It is winter, Mingo. There's no work in the fields.

MINGO: Then to the breadlines, lady. The welfare department. Anyway, that's all they know.

BELARMINO: (*With rage.*) ARRRRRGGGGGGH!

MINGO: Heh!

CRUZ: Belarmino, behave.

MINGO: (BELARMINO *stares at him with hate.*) Look at him, señora, look! He's enraged! Well, now I seen everything. This freak getting insulted. (BELARMINO *growls with rage.*)

CRUZ: My son, calm down!

MINGO: Let him blow his top. He can't do nothing, anyway. Maybe he's been eating my food, too, no Ma? You sure you ain't slip him one of my TV dinners?

CRUZ: No, Mingo, your poor brother he haven' eat nothing in four days.

MINGO: So what?

CRUZ: Look how skinny he is. He's shrinking on me, and he still don' wanna eat nothing.

MINGO: Maybe he knows something I know.

CRUZ: (*Suspiciously.*) What?

MINGO: (*Calmly, deliberately.*) That he ain't got no guts.

CRUZ: (*Alarmed.*) Don' say that!

MINGO: It's a fact.

CRUZ: No!

MINGO: Look at him!

CRUZ: He's sick.

MINGO: (*With meaning.*) He ain't got a body, señora. (CRUZ *stares at him unbelievingly.*) Let's face it, okay? He's a head. (CRUZ *turns away shaking her head.*) You gotta accept it, Ma. Shorty's a head and that's it.

CRUZ: No!

MINGO: (*Angered.*) Then, where's all the food going that he's eating? I become a contractor to make more money, but each week that I make more, he eat more. Last week it was $127. By himself! Beans and tortillas!! He blew my whole check. (BELARMINO *laughs.*) Shut up!

BELARMINO: ARRGGH!

MINGO: All these years we been poor and stinkin', working the fields, for what? To stuff his fat belly which he don't even got! What kinda stupid, useless life is that? I don't wanna end up like Dad. I wanna get outta this slum!

CRUZ: Por favor, Mingo, no more.

MINGO: Look, Ma, I wanna help you. I'll even let Lupe and Chato freeload on us for the winter, if you do one thing.

CRUZ: What?

MINGO: Stop wasting money on beans and tortillas. Admit Shorty's a head.

CRUZ: No!

MINGO: Ma, it's nothing but dumb pride. Be realistic. Be practical.

CRUZ: (*Determined.*) My son is not a head!

MINGO: (*Pause.*) Okay, suit yourself. Just don't expect me to pay the bills at the store no more. (*Adds quickly.*) But don't worry, I'm still gonna help the family—with my example. See that little red sports car in front of the house? It's mine.

CRUZ: Yours?

MINGO: I trade it in for my Chevi. I also took 200 bucks outta the bank and bought new clothes. See? Everything new. You should see how great it feels! Instead of the head, I'm spending money where it counts: on self-improvement. And with my credit, I can get anything else I want. Thirty-dollar shoes, color T.V., a Hi-Fi stereo, a new bowling ball, steak dinners, cocktails! I can even go to college. Sure, State College! The G.I. Bill will foot the bill. Heh, you get that? G.I. Bill foot the bill? I know it's below your mental intelligence to comprehend the simplicity . . . (*During his speech* MINGO*'s voice changes from a Chicano accent to the nasal tones of an Anglo; he also begins to talk down his nose at his mother.*)

CRUZ: ¡M'ijo!

MINGO: (*Coming to his senses.*) ¿Qué?

CRUZ: What about us?

MINGO: Well . . . hustle! Didn't Joaquín go to work?

CRUZ: He say he have little jobs to do.

MINGO: What little jobs?

CRUZ: I don' know.

MINGO: What about mi 'apá? He can still work. Where is he, boozing again?

CRUZ: (*With fearful surprise.*) ¡Tu padre está muerto!

MINGO: ¿Muerto? Dead? (*Laughs.*) You're kidding.

CRUZ: For six months. That train kill him. (SHE *crosses herself.*) But . . . how did you forget? Wha's happen to you, Mingo?

MINGO: Six months?

JOAQUÍN: (*Outside the house.*) ¡Viva mi jefito! (*Shouts of viva.*) ¡Viva Pancho Villa! (*More vivas.*)

BELARMINO: ¡AY, YAI, YAI, YAI, YAI! (*Outside the house we hear the music of a band. Drums and trumpets sound with revolutionary enthusiasm.*)

MINGO: What the hell's that? (*Goes to the front door.*)

CRUZ: Mariachis.

MINGO: The hell, it's a pachuco band.

CRUZ: No, ees a Charro. It's . . . Joaquín!! And ¡Chato! (*A police siren sounds in the distance. There is immediate confusion outside. "En la madre, the fuss!" "Le's go!" "No, don' run!" etc. Various voices, besides the voice of* JOAQUÍN *and* CHATO, *indicate there is a small group of young men outside, which now breaks out running in all directions.* CHATO *runs in, frightened, dressed in huarache sandals and white Mexican peasant clothing. He wears a straw hat, and carries a drum and a trumpet. He enters tripping over his feet, making noise, trying to hide.*)

CRUZ: Chato, hombre, wha's happen?

CHATO: The placa!

MINGO: The police? What did you do?

CHATO: I din' do nothing!

JOAQUÍN: (*Outside.*) Open the door, sergeant!

CRUZ: Joaquín!

JOAQUÍN: (*Still outside.*) Sergeant, the door!

MINGO: How come you're dressed like that? You look like a peon.

JOAQUÍN: (*Still outside.*) ¡CHATO!

CHATO: Yes, my general! (HE *opens the door.*)

JOAQUÍN: It's about time, *corporal!* (JOAQUÍN *enters dressed in the traditional costume of the Mexican charro, complete with a pair of cartridge belts criss-crossed on his chest. Hanging from one shoulder on a strap, he carries a 30–30 carbine. On his shoulders he carries two big sacks, one on each side.*) Here you are, jefita. (HE *lowers the sacks.*) One hundred pounds of flour . . . and a hundred pounds of beans, like I promised you.

MINGO: Where did you get this?

JOAQUÍN: I'm sorry, I don' speak gabacho.

MINGO: Don't act stupid, where did you get these sacks? You swipe 'em, huh?

JOAQUÍN: (*Ignores him.*) And this is for you, jefita. (*From his jacket he pulls out a beautiful white rebozo—a shawl.*)

CRUZ: Where did you got this, hijo?

MINGO: He swipe 'em, don' I tell you, señora? (HE *grabs* JOAQUÍN *by one arm.*) You going to have to return them!

JOAQUÍN: 'Tas lucas, gringo.

MINGO: ¿Gringo?

JOAQUÍN: Mingo el gringo.

BELARMINO: (*Joyfully.*) ¡AY, YAI, YAI, YAI!

JOAQUÍN: VIVA VILLA! (*To* BELARMINO.) And this is for you, mi general. A box of cigars. (HE *offers him one.*) You wan' one! (BELARMINO *smiles, grunts affirmatively.*) Órale, pues.

CRUZ: No, Joaquín, your brother don' smoke.

BELARMINO: (*Growling.*) ARRGH!

CRUZ: (*Backs up.*) Ay, Dios.

JOAQUÍN: At your orders, mi general. (*Gives him a cigar.*) Qué le haga buen provecho y qué . . . (Pause.) Corporal, a match! (CHATO *comes forward with a match.*) ¡Qué viva la Revolución! (BELARMINO *smokes contentedly, making a lot of smoke.*)

MINGO: I don't believe it. (*Laughs.*) So this is the general, eh? Who the hell do you think you are? The Cisco Kid and Pancho?

CHATO: No, he's Pancho. (*Points to* BELARMINO.)

MINGO: You lousy clown! I oughta call the cops right now.

CRUZ: No, Mingo.

MINGO: Don't worry, señora. The cops are already after 'em. I bet they even end up in jail tonight. For thiefs!

JOAQUÍN: And you? You're the one that oughta be in jail for cheating the jefitos, the family, La Raza! You pinchi sell-out traitor!

CRUZ: Joaquín!

MINGO: No, no señora. Let him spill the beans.

JOAQUÍN: We rob the rich to give to the poor, like Pancho Villa! But you . . .

MINGO: I worked to fill all of your stinking bellies! Especially your beloved general there. I got tired of stuffing his guts with . . .

JOAQUÍN: What guts?

MINGO: (*Pause.*) I won't argue that.

JOAQUÍN: Simón, because he don' got any. He's a head and tha's all.

CRUZ: No, head, no

JOAQUÍN: The head of Francisco Villa! ¿No, mi general?

BELARMINO: (*Triumphantly.*) ¡AY, YAI, YAI!

LUPE: (*Entering.*) ¡Ay! (*She doubles up with pain.*) ¡Ay, Mamá!

CHATO: Mi honey! (HE *goes to her side.*)

CRUZ: Lupe, wha's wrong?

MINGO: It's the cockaroaches she ate.

LUPE: ¡Ay! Ay, Mamá, help me.

CRUZ: Sí, m'ijita. Diosito santo, maybe she's going to have the baby?

CHATO: Baby?

CRUZ: Sí, hombre, your son. Help me with her.

CHATO: Heh, ése, I going to have a son.

CRUZ: Joaquín, no you . . . Mingo! Go call the doctor!

JOAQUÍN: Nel, jefita. I'll go!

MINGO: Not dressed like that! I'll go!

JOAQUÍN: Dressed like what?!

MINGO: Like a stinking Mexican!

JOAQUÍN: You dirty cabrón, I'm proud to be a stinking Mexican! You're dress like a gabacho! Through and through!

MINGO: You're the one that's through, Mex! You can't even bring a sack of beans home without stealing it!

JOAQUÍN: Simón, but I swipe from the supermarket, not the poor! It's no crime to be a thief if you steal from thiefs!

MINGO: Who told you that?

CRUZ: (*Entering.*) ¡Mingo, pronto! Go bring the doctor! Your sister . . .

JOAQUÍN: Who you think? The one and only who knows. And that ain't all! He also tell me that he wasn' hungry for food all this time. He was hungry for justice!

MINGO: (*Laughs.*) Justice?

JOAQUÍN: Social justice!

CRUZ: ¡M'ijos!

MINGO: What social, stupid? You don' even know what the word means!

JOAQUÍN: That's what you think, but we've had it wis your bones, ése! We're going to get rid of all the gabacho blood-suckers like you. The contractors, the judges, the cops, the stores!

MINGO: Bandit!

JOAQUÍN: Simón, like Pancho Villa!

MINGO: You want me to give you a judo chop?

JOAQUÍN: ¡Pos ponte, ése!

CRUZ: Hijos, por favor . . .

MINGO: Greasy, low, ignorant, lousy . . .

JOAQUÍN: ¡Viva la raza! (THEY *start to fight.*)

CRUZ: ¡HIJOS DE SU CHINGADA MADRE! (CRUZ is *holding the 30–30 carbine.*)

MINGO: Ma!

CRUZ: Shut up! Now you going to calm down and sit down like hombrecitos or I pump holes in you! (*Ferociously.*) Okay, MARCH! (SHE *pushes them toward the sofa, with the carbine.*) Caramba, if you want to fight like dogs, tha's how they going to treat you.

MINGO: But I didn't.

JOAQUÍN: Yo no hice . . .

CRUZ: ¡Silencio! (JOAQUÍN *and* MINGO *sit on the sofa.*) Now you, Mingo, you goin' for the doctor, and bring him here, understand? Don' make me beg you again. And you, Joaquín. You goin' to take off that crazy clothes and you going to return everything you steal.

JOAQUÍN: For what? So the fuzz can get me? Nel, jefita, I'm sorry. I rather go to the mountains and take the general with me. My jefito rode with Pancho Villa, now it's my turn!

CRUZ: NO!

JOAQUÍN: Simón, ¡Viva la Revolución!

CRUZ: No, I tell you! Ees time you know . . . your padre never was in the Revolución.

JOAQUÍN: Chale.

CRUZ: He was in Arizona all those years, working in the mines. For the gringos.

JOAQUÍN: Aaah, tha's a lotta chet. And the scar he have here in the neck, from the bullet?

CRUZ: Belarmino bite him there before you was born.

JOAQUÍN: (*Desperate.*) And this cartridge belts? And this 30–30? You going to tell me they're not from the Revolución?

CRUZ: No, because they are.

JOAQUÍN: Okay, then, mi 'apá use them. Who else could have use them?

CRUZ: (*Pause.*) I use them, Joaquín! (JOAQUÍN *and* MINGO *are shocked.*) Sí, mis hijos, your madre rode with Pancho Villa! And tha's how I'm certain Belarmino ees not the general. (*Someone knocks at the door rudely. Silence, another knock.*)

POLICE: (*Outside.*) Okay, I know you're in there! Open up!

JOAQUÍN: (*Runs to the window.*) ¡La jura!

MINGO: The cops! Didn't I tell you, señora? They're looking for him!

CRUZ: ¡Ay Dios! My son, pronto, hide. (SHE *puts the sombrero over* BELARMINO.)

MINGO: No, Ma! How can you tell him to hide? It's the law! (HE *peeks out the window.*) For Pete's sake, this is embarrassing. All the neighbors are watching.

POLICE: (*Knocking furiously.*) OPEN UP IN THE NAME OF THE LAW, GODDAMMIT!

CRUZ: Mingo, do something.

JOAQUÍN: Don' ask nothing from that sonavavichi, jefita. (*More knocks.*) Open the door!

CRUZ: No, Joaquín, they get you. (*More strong knocks, then the sound of glass and wood breaking.*) ¡Ay Dios!

POLICE: (*Entering with his club.*) What the hell's going on here? (*The* POLICEMAN *is dressed in a uniform that half resembles a highway patrolman's and half, a soldier's. He wears a helmet with the letters "MP" printed in black. As soon as he barges in,* JOAQUÍN *takes the carbine from* CRUZ.)

JOAQUÍN: (*Lifting the rife.*) Put your stinking gabacho hands up!

CRUZ: ¡Joaquín!

JOAQUÍN: (*The* POLICEMAN *goes for his gun.*) Ah! Don't try it, man! I fill you full of holes!

POLICE: You're gonna regret this, boy.

JOAQUÍN: Tha's what you think, man. (HE *takes the officer's gun.*) Heh, wait a minute. Wha's that on your hat . . . MP? Ain't you a city cop?

POLICE: What's the difference? You pachuco no le gusta mucho los cops, right? Maybe it's Military Police—maybe it's Mexican Patrol. We're looking for a couple of suspects. Supermarket thieves. "El Ladrón de los Supermercados."

CRUZ: ¿Ladrón? Ay no, forgive him, señor! He's a good boy. Him and Chato din' do nothing.

POLICE: Who's Chato?

CHATO: (*Entering the room.*) Heh, Doña Cruz, my wife is very (*Sees the officer.*) . . . lonely! (HE *exits.*)

POLICE: Heh!

JOAQUÍN: Ah, ah! Cool it, gringo!

POLICE: You cholos are in mucho hot water, you savvy that? When did you swipe the car outside?

JOAQUÍN: What car?

POLICE: The red sports car!

MINGO: (*Entering from his room.*) Sports car? Oh, no officer, that's my car!

POLICE: Who the hell are you?

MINGO: (*Pause.*) NOBODY! I don't have nothing to do with these people. I just room here. I'm a college student.

CRUZ: Tell him, Mingo, explain . . . you got the words.

MINGO: What my landlady here means, officer, is that the punk you want is right there. He's the Supermarket Thief.

JOAQUÍN: Simón, ees me! But so what, you can't do nothing! Maybe the Revolución break out right now. What you say, General? We go to the mountains?

BELARMINO: AY, YAI, YAI, YAI!

POLICE: Now what?

JOAQUÍN: Pancho Villa!

POLICE: What the hell's going on in this place?

JOAQUÍN: I'm going to blow you to pieces, that's what. One side, jefita!

CRUZ: Oh, Joaquín, that carabina don' shoot. It don' got bullets.

MINGO: It's not loaded.

POLICE: Not loaded?! (HE *tries to jump* JOAQUÍN.)

CRUZ: NO! (SHE *steps in front of the officer.*) Por favor, señor, don' take him.

POLICE: Get outta my way, lady!

MINGO: Get away, landlady!

JOAQUÍN: Hold 'em there, jefita! (JOAQUÍN *pulls gun.* HE *runs to* BELARMINO.)

CRUZ: Joaquín, what you doin'?

JOAQUÍN: I'm going to the mountains with my general!

CRUZ: No, hijo, you drop him! (MINGO *knocks down* JOAQUÍN's *gun.*)

JOAQUÍN: ¡VIVA LA REVOLUCIÓN!

POLICE: Why you little son of a . . .

CRUZ: ¡Joaquín!

MINGO: I'll help you get him, officer!

POLICE: (*Chasing* JOAQUÍN.) I warn you, punk! It'll go worse for you resisting arrest! (*Everyone chases* JOAQUÍN *around the room, trying to catch him and* BELARMINO. CHATO *peeks in.*)

CHATO: Heh, ése, throw it over here! Over here! (JOAQUÍN *throws* BELARMINO *like a ball.*)

MINGO: Stay out of this, Chato!

CHATO: (*To* JOAQUÍN.) Run, ése, run!

JOAQUÍN: Not wisout the general!

CRUZ: Gimme him, Chato!

JOAQUÍN: Throw it back, ése! (CHATO *throws* BELARMINO *back to* JOAQUÍN, *but* CRUZ *catches him. The police officer nabs* JOAQUÍN. CRUZ *takes* BELARMINO *back to the TV set and examines him. In a corner of the room, the officer beats* JOAQUÍN.)

CHATO: ¡Órale, watcha eso! (*The officer pulls out handcuffs.*)

CRUZ: No! Not those, señor! (SHE *goes to* JOAQUÍN, *leaving* BELARMINO *on top of the TV set.*) Por favor, he's my son, señor! ¡M'ijo!

POLICE: Sorry, lady, I'm only doing my job. (JOAQUÍN *resists and the officer beats the sadistic hell out of him.*) It's only my job.

CRUZ: (*Embracing* JOAQUÍN.) ¡Hijo, m'ijo!

POLICE: Lady, I . . . (*Tries to pull her away.*)

JOAQUÍN: Leave her alone!

POLICE: Shut your mouth, boy! (HE *pulls* CRUZ *away.*) All right, señora.

CRUZ: ¡Joaquín!

JOAQUÍN: (*Blood on his nose.*) Don' worry, jefita. I ain' scared of 'em. You'll see. I going to return with 50,000 batos on horses and Chivis! Lemme go, huh? (CRUZ *silently makes the sign of the cross on* JOAQUÍN's *forehead with her thumb.*)

POLICE: Okay, boy, let's go!

MINGO: Here's your gun, officer.

POLICE: That's okay, boy. Just put it in my holster.

JOAQUÍN: I'm coming back, jefita! I'm coming back! ¡VIVA VI-LLAAAAAA!

CRUZ: ¡Joaquín! Joaquín, my son!! (*She weeps at the front door. Silence.* MINGO *approaches* CRUZ.)

MINGO: (*Pointing to* BELARMINO.) Look, señora, there's your son.

CHATO: ¿Hijo? ¡Hijo de su! Lupe's gonna have my son! We need a doctor! Órale, brother-in-law, loan me your sports car to go fast. Ees for your carnala.

MINGO: What are you talking about?

CHATO: Tu sister, Lupe.

MINGO: I don't have a sister.

CHATO: ¡La negra!

MINGO: ¿Negra? Not my sister, boy. You trying to be funny? I just room here.

BELARMINO: ¡DESGRACIADO!

MINGO: Who said that?

CHATO: Not me.

BELARMINO: ¡TRAIDOR A TU RAZA!

CRUZ: Ees Belarmino. He's talking!

MINGO: What did he say?

BELARMINO: ¡LAMBISCÓN!

MINGO: Obscenity, obscenity.

BELARMINO: ¡CABRÓN!,

CRUZ: ¡Ay Dios! (*Crosses herself.*) Belarmino, don' say that!

BELARMINO: ¡PENDEJO!

CRUZ: ¡Ay Dios! (*Crosses herself.*)

MINGO: I'll shut him up! (HE *approaches* BELARMINO.)

BELARMINO: ¡BABOSO!

CRUZ: ¡Ay Dios, mi chorti! (SHE *approaches* BELARMINO.)

BELARMINO: ¡SINVERGÜENZA!

CRUZ: Ees the devil!

CHATO: Nel, ees the general!

MINGO: I'll fix this general!

BELARMINO: AARRRGGHH! (HE *bites* MINGO.)

CRUZ: Dios. (*Crosses herself.*)

BELARMINO: (*Getting up steam.*) AMERICANIZADO, DESECHADO, DESARRAIGADO, DESVERGONZADO, INTERESADO, TAPA-DO . . .

CHATO: Go, go, General!

BELARMINO: ¡AGARRADO, EMPAPADO, FIJADO, MAL-HABLADO, TROPEZADO, AHOGADO, CHIFLADO!

MINGO: Shut up! Shut up! Speak English! (CHATO *whistles.*)

CRUZ: Chato, don' do that, por Dios! Go bring the doctor! And a priest!

CHATO: Priest?

CRUZ: Tell him to bring Holy Water! Ándale, run! (CHATO *exits.*)
BELARMINO: ¡NI SABES QUIÉN SOY! ¡NI SABES QUIÉN SOY!
MINGO: Speak English! Speak English!
BELARMINO: ¡PANCHO VILLA!
MINGO: SPEAK ENGLISH! (*Goes on repeating.*) SPEAK ENGLISH!
SPEAK ENGLISH! SPEAK ENGLISH! SPEAK ENGLISH!
BELARMINO: (*Simultaneously with* MINGO.) ¡PANCHO VILLA,
PANCHO VILLA, PANCHO VILLA, PANCHO VILLA!
CRUZ: (*Simultaneously, kneeling, crossing herself hysterically.*)
¡¡DIOS, DIOS, DIOS, DIOS, DIOS, DIOS, DIOS, DIOS!!

Curtain.

ACT FIVE

Two years later. A Winter night. The walls of the house are still covered with cockroaches. Some of them have grown to a tremendous size. CRUZ is sitting on the sofa with BELARMINO to her side. A kerosene heater is nearby flickering with a weak, useless flame and heating absolutely nothing. Everything looks more run down than ever.

CRUZ: (*Singing sadly.*)
Adiós torres de Chihuahua
Adiós torres de Cantera
ya vino Francisco Villa
pa' quitarles la frontera
ya llegó Francisco Villa
a devolver la frontera.
(BELARMINO *is snoring.*)
Ay, my little chorti. What a good hombre you are. I would not be sorprise if some of these days the Señor he give you a big body for being so good, no? Not a little body but a great big body with arms and legs strong like a macho. Tha's how Pedro always want you to be. May God keep him in peace. (*Crosses herself. We hear a terrible cry more animal than human coming from the kitchen.* CRUZ *rises and calls.*) Guadalupe, what you doing to the niña? (*More cries.*) ¡Lupe! (*The cries stop.*) Don' you know how to feed her yet? (*Lupe enters with a small bundle. She looks like* CRUZ *in hair style and dress, having taken on the role of a mother.*)

LUPE: How can I feed him? He bit the nipple on the bottle and ate it. Look, he's all cover with bean soup.

CRUZ: What is she shewing?

LUPE: A cucaracha. (*Pause.*) Oh, don' look at me like that, man. He like 'em. At least I peel off the shell first.

CRUZ: Qué muchacha. What kind of little mother you be, eh? You want to kill her?

182

LUPE: He's not a her, Mamá!

CRUZ: How you know? He don' get mustaches. His uncle Chorti was born wis mustaches.

LUPE: I don' care. I know. I'm his madre.

BELARMINO: (*In his sleep.*) La tuya.

LUPE: There he goes again, man.

CRUZ: He's sleeping.

BELARMINO: (*Dreaming.*) Señores, I am Francisco Villa.

LUPE: See? He's dreaming just like mi 'apá used to do it.

BELARMINO: ¡Pancho Villa!

CRUZ: My son?

LUPE: Why don' you pull his leg. (*Laughs.*)

CRUZ: You chattap. You think your son gots so much?

BELARMINO: I am Pancho Villa.

CRUZ: No, my son, you're Belarmino.

BELARMINO: ¡VIVA VILLA!

LUPE: Shut him up, man! He's scaring my baby. Pull his ear!

BELARMINO: VIVA PANCHO VI . . . (CRUZ *pulls his ear.*) ¡YAH-aay jijos! Who pull my ear?

CRUZ: I do it, my son. You was having a bad dream.

LUPE: And it gets worser every day. Look like that's all you learn to talk for. I'm Pancho Villa! ¡Pancho Villa!

BELARMINO: I also talk something else, babosa jija de la . . .

LUPE: Ah ah. Speak English. Without English there's no welfare.

BELARMINO: How I'd like to keek your butt.

LUPE: Well, try it . . . Shorty! (*Laughs.*)

CRUZ: Stop it, negra. You shoulda have more respect for your older brother. Since Mingo leave and Joaquín's in jail, he's the man of the house.

LUPE: The head of the house.

BELARMINO: Chattap! Your madre's right. I'm in charge.

LUPE: Of what? Starvation?

CRUZ: (*Sighs.*) If Mingo was here, we wouldn't have to worry about nothing. He always work so hard.

BELARMINO: Chure, on us! Forget Mingo, señora. Mingo go away forever. I'm here and I take care of you now. Just wait till the Revolución.

LUPE: What Revolución? What we need is welfare so we can eat.

CRUZ: I only pray to Dios Nuestro Señor that Joaquín come back from jail serious . . . Ready to marry and settle down and support a family.

BELARMINO: Sí, like *our* family, for one ejemplo, no? ¡Huevonas! I know what you up to. You itching for Joaquín to come so he can support you! Well, what happen to all that pedo about welfare? We got a right to it. I'm disable.

CRUZ: They want to come to investigate first.

BELARMINO: To investigate? Wha's that?

LUPE: They wanna see how come you don' get a job.

BELARMINO: Huy, pos let 'em come. I don' hide nothing.

LUPE: You got nothing to hide.

BELARMINO: (*An angry burst.*) Tú ya me estás cayendo gordo, ¿sabes? ¡Vale más que te calles el hocico! ¡Yo mando en esta casa y me tienes que guardar respeto! ¡Malcriada, Pendeja, Malhablada! (*Pause.*) Chihuahua, what a relief. There's nothing like saying what you got to say in Spanish. Like chili in the beans. But I say the same thing in English if you push me, eh? You goddamit!

LUPE: Ay, okay pues. Don' bite me.

BELARMINO: Well, don' come too close. Ma? What time is Joaquín coming from the jail?

CRUZ: I don' know, my son. I'm worry already. Chato go to get him this morning and ees already night. (*There is a knock at the door.*) ¡Ay! Maybe tha's him?

LUPE: No, I bet it's the welfare man.

CRUZ: No, ees my son. I feel it's Joaquín.

LUPE: No, señora, why should Joaquín knock? He lives here.

CRUZ: But maybe he's . . .

BELARMINO: Bueno pues, don' just argue. Open the door!

CRUZ: (*Hesitant.*) Ay Dios. You open it, Lupe . . . I can't do it.

LUPE: (*Opens the door.*) There's nobody.

CRUZ: Nobody? (SHE *goes to the door.*)

BELARMINO: Look outside, maybe he's outside! Stinking viejas! If I had your legs I would have already run around the house. You don' see nobody?

CRUZ: Nothing. I wonder who it is? (LUPE *crosses the door.*)

CHATO: (*Outside.*) Órale, don' close it! I'm coming!

LUPE: It's Chato! (CHATO *enters, dressed in* PEDRO's *old clothes. He has a moustache now, and in appearance and behavior he has begun to resemble* PEDRO.) What a joke you trying to pull, hombre? Knocking at the door.

CHATO: What door? ¡Vieja sonsa! I din' knock.

BELARMINO: Where's Joaquín?

CRUZ: Yes, Chato. Where's my son? (CHATO *says nothing.*)

BELARMINO: We'll talk, hombre!

CHATO: I din' find him.

CRUZ: What?

CHATO: I went to the prison door and wait, but he din' come out.

CRUZ: Ay no, my poor son! They din' let him come out!

LUPE: Din' I tell you? He haven' change. He do something and they take away his parole.

CHATO: They din' neither! I ask 'em. They let him out today.

BELARMINO: Then where's he at? Baboso, maybe you miss him.

CHATO: Nel, I notice good all the batos that come out. Joaquín wasn't nobody of 'em. I mean . . . nobody look like Joaquín.

BELARMINO: ¡Me lleva . . . ! What you think Joaquín look like? Like Joaquín! A muchacho wis arms and legs! Did you look good by the road? Maybe he come walking?

CHATO: Nel, I look up and down. I even run outta gas and have to leave my carrucha by the road. I din' have even enough to buy a gallon of gas. (*Pause.*) Don' worry, Doña Cruz. Maybe Joaquín come in the bus or something. He'll come today. (*Pause.*) What about here? Did the welfare bato come? (*There is another knock at the door.*)

CRUZ: Ees my son! (SHE *goes to the door and opens it.*)

BELARMINO: Ees him? (*Pause.*) How do he look? ¡No la jodan pues! Tell me who is it?

CRUZ: Ees nobody. (SHE *closes the door. There is another knock at the door. Stronger this time.*)

BELARMINO: ¡Épale! They knocking over here, señora! (CHATO *opens the door to the side room, "Mingo's room." MINGO is standing in the doorway. He is dressed in a professional gray suit and is carrying a briefcase. He wears a smart hat and glasses, shoes shined, etc. His face is unusually pale: in fact, it almost looks bleached.*)

MINGO: Good evening. Is this the home of Mr. Belarmine?

LUPE: Who?

MINGO: Belarmine, I believe it is?

LUPE: Oh, you mean Belarmino!

BELARMINO: Abusada, raza, es el bato de la welfare.

LUPE: Yes, this is the home of Mr. Belarmino. Come in please.

MINGO: (*With an Anglo accent.*) Muchas gracias. (*Enters, takes off his hat.*)

CRUZ: (*Approaching* MINGO, *awed.*) Mingo? My son, my Domingo! (SHE *leaps at him and hugs him.*) You come home!

MINGO: I beg your pardon!

LUPE: (*Trying to pull* CRUZ *away.*) Mamá! Please! This gentleman isn't Mingo! Mingo's gone! (CRUZ *backs up.*) This is my mother, please excuse her. She thinks you're my brother who went away.

CRUZ: (*Touching* MINGO's *face.*) ¿Cómo te llamas?

MINGO: (*Pause.*) Mi nombre is Sunday, señora.

LUPE: You speak Spanish?

MINGO: Un poquito. It's part of my job.

LUPE: You see, Ma? He's call Sunday, not Domingo. Let him talk with Belarmino.

MINGO: Gracias, let me see . . . ¿Usted es Mr. Belarmine?

CHATO: No, him.

MINGO: Him?

BELARMINO: Quihúbole, chavo.

MINGO: Mucho gusto. I have here your application to receive county welfare aid, and oh, do you speak English?

BELARMINO: Oh yes, more better than a gringo.

LUPE: ¡Belo!

MINGO: Ha, ha. It's okay, I don't mind. It may surprise you to know that I'm Mexican American and fully aware of the sympathies of the culturally deprived. Now Mr. Belarmine, all we want and need before your case goes through is a few personal facts about your-self for our records. ¿Me entiende?

BELARMINO: (*Nods.*) Pícale a la burra.

MINGO: Well, for example. You've applied for our disability coverage, so we need to know who you sleep with.

BELARMINO: ¿Qué?

MINGO: Do you sleep alone?

BELARMINO: None of you bis'ness! Pos mira . . . sonavavichi!

LUPE: Belo!

MINGO: I'm sorry, but we need to know.

CRUZ: He sleep with me.

MINGO: Oh yeah? And where's your husband, señora?

BELARMINO: Está muerto.

MINGO: Let her answer please!

CRUZ: He is dead.

MINGO: Well, I don't mean to question your traditional moral values, but don't you think it's wrong just to shack up with this fellow? You're both old enough to know better. Why don't you get married?

CRUZ: Because he's my son!

MINGO: Oh. Oh!

BELARMINO: Cochino.

MINGO: Well, what kind of disability do you have?

BELARMINO: Pos take a good look.

MINGO: (*Pause.*) Hmm. You did have a rather serious accident, didn't you? Have you tried to find any work at all?

BELARMINO: Doing what, being a fútbol?

MINGO: Do you have any stocks or bonds or private property?

BELARMINO: Uuuy.

MINGO: Well?

BELARMINO: Nothing, nada, ni madre!

MINGO: Good. I guess that does it. We have your application with all other facts, and with this, we'll be able to push your case through. But there's just one more thing.

BELARMINO: Pues sí, there's always just one more thing.

MINGO: I would suggest you get a haircut.

BELARMINO: Haircut?

MINGO: A crewcut.

CRUZ: No! No, señor, please. Not his hair! When he was born like he is, I promise the Virgin never to cut his hair if she let him live.

MINGO: Oh, I see. An old supersti—religion, huh? Well, I was only thinking of your health. I know it's hard in these barrios to keep the city clean, but we gotta give it that old 100% try, know what I mean? I'm going to let you in on a little secret, maybe you'll feel better. Once a long time ago . . . I was poor too. That's right. I also used to live in a lousy dump with cockroaches, a lot like this one. Everything was almost exactly like this . . . but that was a lotta years back . . . in another barrio . . . another town . . . another time. (*Snapping out of it.*) Now I'm middle class! I got out of the poverty I lived in because I cared about myself. Because I did something to help myself. I went to college. So now I'm a social worker helping out the poor! Which means that I want to help you to take full advantage of what our society has to offer. There's nothing to lose and everything to gain, believe me!

BELARMINO: I believe you. When do the checks come?

MINGO: Oh, I figure in about thirty days.

BELARMINO: Thirty days!

LUPE: But we don' got nothing to eat.

MINGO: I'm sorry but that's the best we can do.

LUPE: What about Aid to Needy Children?

MINGO: What needy children?

LUPE: My baby. (SHE *shows him the baby.*)

MINGO: Cute. But what does he need?

LUPE: Look. (SHE *opens the blanket.*)

MINGO: (*Double take at* BELARMINO *then at the baby again.*) Another one! What happened?

LUPE: He's sick. Like his uncle.

MINGO: Runs in the family, huh? Well, I'll tell you. There's a good chance you might be able to get some kind of help, but nothing before 30 days at least.

BELARMINO: Okay, that do it! Señora, fry me some cucarachas! I hungry.

CHATO: Don' worry, Doña Cruz. I bet Joaquín gets some coins.

MINGO: Joaquín who? Another man in the family?

BELARMINO: Simón limón, more man than you think! Es más hombre que la ching . . .

CRUZ: ¡Mingo! Oh, Joaquín, no—Lupe, ah, tú—Chorti!

MINGO: Joaquín . . . ? Oh yeah! I forgot! Where is this Joaquín? (*No one says anything.*) Okay, let me put it different. Where was this Joaquín? In prison?

CHATO: How you know?

MINGO: And he was just released today?

CRUZ: Yes, on patrol.

BELARMINO: Parole.

MINGO: What's he like? Tall, short, light, dark?

CRUZ: Yes, tha's him! Why?

MINGO: Because tonight when I was coming across town I passed by this good-looking Mexican walking along the road. It was pretty cold, so I gave him a lift. He'd just gotten out on parole this morning.

CRUZ: Joaquín, ees my Joaquín!

CHATO: Where's he at?

MINGO: Outside in my car. I forgot he came with me. I'll go get him.

CRUZ: ¡Ay Dios! My son is outside!

MINGO: Oh, another thing. It looks like the prison term helped him a lot. He seems very reformed, rehabilitated. Lots of spunk. A clean cut American boy! Be right back. (HE *exits.*)

BELARMINO: ¡AY, YAI, YAI! Now you going to see the Revolución burst out! Joaquín is back!

CRUZ: (*Overexcited.*) ¡Viva la Revolución! (*Pause.*) I mean gracias a Dios, my son is back.

LUPE: I bet you pass up Joaquín when he was walking, huh? ¡Menso!

CHATO: ¿Cómo que menso? ¿Quieres que te meta un guamazo en el hocico? Huh, pos mira. Who's the boss around here pues? (HE *goes to door.*)

CRUZ: You hear what the social worker says, Lupe? My Joaquín is change, he's serious and reform.

BELARMINO: He don' say that. He say he got lots of spunk. He's revolutionary!!

CHATO: (*At the window.*) Here they come! (*Pause.*) ¡Qué caray! Tha's not Joaquín!

CRUZ: What?

LUPE: (*At the window.*) ¡O no, Joaquín!

BELARMINO: ¿Qué? What you see?

MINGO: (*Opening the door.*) Okay, folks, here he is! (MINGO *comes in.*) Well, Jack, come in. This is where you live.

CRUZ: (*Standing in the doorway.*) Dios mío, my son. (SHE *weeps.* JOAQUÍN *comes into the house.* HE *is well dressed, BUT HE HAS NO HEAD.*)

BELARMINO: Chingado, they got him.

MINGO: You see? Rehabilitated. He even grew a little. Congratulations, Jack, I know you'll make it. Well, I guess I better be on my way. Don't forget the crewcut and general cleanliness, okay? Buenas noches. (*Exits.*)

LUPE: I don' think he looks so bad, Mamá. He look cleaner.

CHATO: Quihúbole, ése. (*Shakes* JOAQUÍN*'s hand.*) No wonder I din' reco'nize him on the road.

LUPE: You shut up. I think Joaqu-Jack's gonna be okay, Ma. He can still find a job in the fields. Now we can all plan together for the future. Like my son, he's not going to have a poor life like us. I'm going to make sure he study so he can go to college someday like Mr. Sunday. With the help of God, my son will grow to be a decent man. Maybe someday he even find a body he can . . . (*Pause.*)

BELARMINO: (*Quickly.*) Heh, señora, bring Joaquín over here! I want to see him. Pos what you know? Look at the big arms he gots . . . and the big body! Oye, Ma, I got an idea.

LUPE: No you don't! I see him first!

BELARMINO: What firs'? I got years waiting for him! Anyway, he don' even fit that little head you got.

CRUZ: What you two arguing?

BELARMINO: Pos what? There's the body and here's the head. Le's get together! Pick me up!

CRUZ: But how, hombre? Joaquín's your brother.

BELARMINO: Pos there you are. We keep it in the family. Pick me up somebody!

CRUZ: No, Belarmino.

BELARMINO: Órale, Chato, gimme a lift!

CRUZ: No, I say!

LUPE: See? He's mine, huh, Mamá?

CRUZ: Neither his or yours or nobody but me. Joaquín is mine. Buenas noches. Come on, my son. (*Exits with* JOAQUÍN.)

BELARMINO: Heh! Wait, señora! Wait one minute!

CRUZ: ¡Cállate tú, cabezón!

LUPE: You see, stupid? We both lose! Come on, Chato. (*Exits.*)

BELARMINO: (*Shouting after* LUPE.) Both lose, eh? Bueno, we see who have more pull wis the old lady! Stinking woman! They don' understand Revolución for nothing. We men must carry on the fight. We machos! No, Chato?

CHATO: Simón, we machos!

LUPE: (*Shouting.*) Chato, come to bed!

CHATO: Oh, that vieja apestosa! Buenas noches, ése.

BELARMINO: Buenas noches. (CHATO *exits.*) Well, here I sit . . . broken hearted. But tha's okay cause I still got time to wait. Sooner or later, the jefita gots to come across wis Joaquín's body. All I need is to talk sweet when she give me my beans, eh? In other words, organize her. Those people don' even believe who I am. Tha's how I wan' it. To catch 'em by surprise. So don' worry, my people, because one of this days Pancho Villa will pass among you again. Look to your mountains, your pueblos, your barrios. He will be there. Buenas noches.

Curtain.